Alan Robson is a househ[old] and is a popular presenter programmes like *College* show, *Robson's People*. [He] listened-to phone-in for [its] audience of 52 per cent in the region. His regular page in the *Sunday Sun* helped it to become Newspaper of the Year, and his last book of legends, *Grisly Trails and Ghostly Tales* (focused on the North-East), was an overnight bestseller. Alan has also been involved for over ten years in ghost hunts and investigations into the supernatural, and took part in the first-ever Black Magic ritual to be broadcast live.

NIGHTMARE ON YOUR STREET

*More Grisly Trails and
Ghostly Tales*

Alan Robson

To those who helped me through
the most difficult year of my life:
Barry, Rosie, Sarah
and Maurice – God bless 'em!

First published in Great Britain in 1993 by
Virgin Books
an imprint of Virgin Publishing Ltd
332 Ladbroke Grove
London W10 5AH

A catalogue record for this book is available from the
British Library

ISBN 0 86369 716 X

Phototypeset by Intype, London
Printed and bound in Great Britain by
Cox & Wyman Ltd, Reading, Berks.

CONTENTS

Ghost in Waiting? – The Pilton Park Phantom, Barnstaple – Nelson and his Lady in Dawlish – The Bloody Monk of Exeter – The Woman Who Died Twice, Exeter – The Devon Highwayman – The Devil's Rolling Stone – The Pirate of the Jamaica Inn – The Helston Devils

The Longleat Murderess – The Wiltshire Body Pit – The Hampshire Devil Dog – The Highwayman Captain Jacques – The Phantom of Winchester – A Demon's Hands – The Surrey Puma – The Witches of Guildford – The Headless Ghost of Sir Walter Raleigh – The Bognor Banjax – The Real Scarlet Pimpernel – The Rye Owlers – Too Disgusting for Hell

The Ripper of Abergavenny – The Trefachan Dancer – Home or a Haunting, Conwy – The Man Who Loved the Dead – The Warning Mist of Llandeilo – The Fairy Tree of Maesteg – The Grave of the Partly Innocent – The Welsh Aliens

The Burning Soldier of Aberdeen – Aberdeen's Union Street Clencher – The Dragon of Arbroath – The Stumphand of Ayr – The Phantom Teacher of Tayside – The Crying Girl of Princes Street, Edinburgh – The 'Well-Hung' Englishman – The Glamis Secret – Galleon of Lost Souls – The Ghost of King Duncan – The Strathclyde Strangler

The Land of the Giants, Not the Leprechauns – Ireland's Dead Centre – Dublin's Phantom – The Clare Head Hunter – Cacky Collins, The Killer Leprechaun? – The Kilkenny Lovers – Prophet of Irish Doom

INTRODUCTION

I have always been amazed by the number of legends we have, yet many never get written down. So after the success of *Grisly Trails and Ghostly Tales*, which covered mainly the North Country, my next step was to go nationwide. I admit that many of these legends have different versions, but in each case I have chosen the 'juiciest' and most interesting.

The tales have been passed to me by people who have witnessed the events, or who have called late-night phone-in programmes. (The most popular of these programmes in the UK is the one which I host at Metro FM.)

I wish to thank those individuals at other independent stations across the country who have helped and guided me in my mission. All of the tales have been researched in good faith, so come with me and experience the horrors of another 'Grisly Trail'.

My sincere thanks to *Night Owls*, Metro FM, Tyne Tees Television, the *Sunday Sun* and all at Virgin Publishing.

THE NORTH

THE DIRTY BOTTLES OF ALNWICK

The Old Cross Inn on Narrowgate in Alnwick used to be a wine shop and bakery. Now it's a quality 'olde-worlde' pub.

They have an old ledger dated around 1810 telling of an incident involving a man who was creating a window display with the latest collection of sherry. As he was installing the bottles he felt a sharp pain in his chest and collapsed backwards on to the floor and died. The lady owner of the shop declared that his display must never be touched again, and had the entire window boarded up.

The window is said to be cursed, and anyone who dares to move the bottles now shrouded in dust and cobwebs, would suffer the same fate as the man.

The staff of the Old Cross are very worried indeed at present as the heavy wooden casks that the bottles stand on are rotting away. One cask has already crumbled, smashing some bottles, sherry soaking into the floorboards, and the others are going the same way. The staff don't know whether to clear up the mess, leave it as it is, or try to restore what is a legend that has lasted close to two hundred years.

THE BRIGAND OF BARDON MILL

Hardriding Farm, Bardon Mill, near Haltwhistle, was once the centre of the legend of a brigand who caused a great deal of suffering in the 1300s. The legend seems to change each time I am told it, so I will present the mainstream version of quite a gruesome tale.

From 1345 to 1371 a brigand used to prey on travellers and farmers alike covering an area between Wark in the north and Alston in the south, Brampton in the west to Hexham in the east. It was a sizeable patch and he became quite a thorn in everyone's side, with crimes attributed to him ranging from murder, arson, and wounding to rape, buggery and child molestation. A wicked

1

man with no scruples, apparently who would satisfy his perverted desires on the old and young alike.

Described as a round-shouldered man, with a pock-marked face and bloated jowls, he must certainly have been strongly built, for it is said he once physically picked up a horse with rider aboard and threw them to the ground.

The final straw from this wicked man came in August 1371 when he stopped two young lovers as they walked along the banks of the river at Hexham. It was midday and the riverside was choked with people, yet still the rogue drew his sword and demanded money. The man refused and was stabbed through the heart. As he lay there dying the brigand emptied his pockets and pushed the girl into the river. She was almost nine months' pregnant and could not swim. Despite all attempts to save her, she was swept to her death. As he made his escape he trampled two three-year-old children, leaving them both in critical condition.

Two locals out riding witnessed this and decided to follow at a discreet distance, so they could guarantee his eventual capture. The brigand not realising he was being followed, returned directly to Hardriding Farm, secreting his horse, and counting his gold. The men decided to finish him on their own, bursting into the house with swords drawn and hacking him to death. They said that even once it was severed his right hand had crawled across the table to grasp at the gold coins, so insane was his desire for money.

They swept the remnants of his butchered carcass into the front yard, where they placed scrubwood around it, and set it on fire.

The robber's ghost was regularly seen up to a dozen times a year until 1900; since then it has appeared only twice.

*In April 1927 a young woman felt a man's hand reaching for her purse as she sat in front of the range at Hardriding. She turned to see the hand disappear over the back of her chair. On looking around there was no one there.

*In 1933 the owners of the farm heard yelling and screaming from the living room, as from a violent fight. On rushing into the living room they found all was at peace.

BEADNELL: WHERE THERE'S LIFE THERE'S HOPE, WHEN THERE'S DEATH . . . ?

Beadnell Tower was built by the Forster family who also owned Adderstone Tower, both in Northumberland. When the family sold it off it became part of a public house called the Bull Inn, latterly The Craster Arms. The Craster family had owned Beadnell Tower and its coat of arms is still proudly placed in the centre of the building. The motto reads '*Dum Vivo Spero*' 'Where there's life there's hope'.

But what of when there's death? I spoke to an elderly Craster man who had come back from Australia to visit his family in Alnwick. He told me the story of Frank Charlton who used to work in the Bull Inn in the early 1820s. He was a bar/cellarman who also did odd jobs around the local villages. Frank was greatly loved, a man of immense good spirits, always with a smile or a joke.

He was also greatly loved by several of the ladies who lived thereabouts, especially when their husbands were out in their fishing cobles or tending their land. It came as no surprise when Charlton told the landlord that he was going to have to move on. He didn't give any reason but the landlord surmised that one of the husbands was on his trail. That night, in a barn not 300 yards from the pub, Frank's headless body was found. He had been lashed with whips, and was only recognised by a heavy silver ring he always wore.

As in all small villages, rumour spread like milk over cornflakes, no one would speak of the incident. Although at least eight women had been his secret lovers, none spoke out. The authorities sent in people to investigate, and eventually it was catalogued as accidental death. They didn't know how his head had been detached, nor where it was, but at least the case was tied up very neatly that way.

This was only the beginning of endless strange happenings, sightings of a headless man walking the streets crying out in pain (I wonder how he did that?). Drinks would move across the bar, women would feel hot beery breath on their neck, dogs would refuse to enter the pub.

Things seemed to be getting worse and worse, until a very odd thing happened.

One day the landlord of the inn opened his doors to find the carved stone head of Frank Charlton on his step.

There was a note with it, apparently written by one of the

3

wronged husbands. 'He took my wife, so I took his head. It seems he can't rest without it. As I cannot return the real one, here is one he can wear.'

The landlord had the carved head built into the wall of the inn, where it remains to this day.

WARNING IN BEDLINGTON

Over the centuries there have been thousands of stories about people being warned by 'a knocking on the window', 'a tapping on the wall' or being confronted by a ghost who says nothing, just stares at you.

Death usually ensues.

Such was the case at a house in Millbank, Bedlington, in the mid-1960s. A woman was lying in bed when she felt as if someone was watching her. In a cold sweat she sat up to be confronted by a World War I soldier. 'Who's that?' she asked, and the figure faded out in front of her.

Eventually she managed to get back to sleep. The following morning she learned that her elderly next-door neighbour had passed away at the exact time that she had come face to face with the apparition.

On describing him to her neighbour's family they all became convinced that it was the old woman's husband, who had travelled back from 'the other side of the curtain' to guide his wife's spirit.

THE BARBER OF BELFORD

In the 1880s there was a barber in Belford known as Watty, serving both the living and the dead. For even after someone had died, Watty was called in to shave him so that he would look decent when laid out in the parlour, as was the custom of the day. He did not have sufficient work in Belford to keep him going, so he was also well known as a travelling barber throughout the area, from Beadnell and Bamburgh, Bellshill, Chatton and Wooler.

Although Watty was getting on in years, when he suddenly quit, questions were asked – he had, after all, been a local institution for over forty years. Watty explained that the last three months of his working life involved nothing other than shaving or cutting the hair of the dead or dying. Then, during the last shave of a dying merchant, Watty claimed, the Devil appeared in a cloud of fire and brimstone and declared, 'That'll do, Watty, I'll take him as he is.'

THE BELLINGHAM PEDLAR

When the aristocracy are away the great halls and mansions are run by the servants, who do their best to keep the place neat and tidy with the minimum of effort. Such was the case in the early 1720s when the home of Colonel Ridley, Lee Hall, was visited by a pedlar carrying a huge rucksack on his back. He politely enquired if they would put him up for the night.

As the Colonel was away on business, the servants felt that they could not invite him into the house, but allowed the traveller to spend the night in one of the stables with the horses. He asked if he could leave the rucksack inside, as it contained all of his wares, and he did not want them stolen while he slept. The maid said that that would be all right, so the pedlar placed the pack up against the fireplace in the kitchen. While the maid was locking up before making her way to bed, she saw the pedlar's pack move, and heard a noise like a sigh. She tore around the corridors crying out for help, as the pack began to wriggle all the more. Members of staff hastened to her aid, one carrying a musket. As the pedlar's pack began to roll around the kitchen floor, the man fired into it, and blood splashed the wall and began to trickle into a red puddle on the floor.

When they opened the pack, out fell the lifeless body of a tiny man. It seems that the pedlar had planned to rob the house, with his accomplice hidden in the pack, ready to sneak out once the house was quiet to let in his partner. (Some say it was a gang of cut-throats ready to murder the entire household; a two-man operation seems likelier, though.)

The legends vary at this point, some say that the servants found a horn in the pack, and when they blew it the pedlar arrived. This fails to explain how, if it was a prearranged signal, the entire household wouldn't be woken by it. More likely is that one of the servants opened the door, and in the early hours the pedlar crept into the house to be surrounded by the staff and to be brought face to face with his dead companion. He was badly beaten up, his nose broken, and his right hand stamped on until it was utterly useless.

*If you visit the churchyard in Bellingham you can see the gravestone of the tiny robber, carved in the shape of the rucksack he was killed inside.

THE MURDERED MINSTREL OF BELLISTER CASTLE

The Lord of Bellister Castle, near Haltwhistle, once hired the services of a talented minstrel whose songs and parodies entertained many a guest. The old nobleman believed, however, that the young man was also wooing his young wife. So one day he decided to spend the whole day at home, to see if his suspicions had any foundation. As he turned the corner into the rose garden he heard some laughing and giggling. There in a mountain of petticoats lay his young wife, with the minstrel astride her, both totally lost in their lovemaking. The Lord bellowed out his anger, calling for his servants to come and apprehend the man who had seduced his wife. The minstrel ran for it, racing away from Bellister Castle toward the river. He was just beginning to relax when he heard the baying of hounds, and, looking back towards the castle, he saw half a dozen of the Bellister hounds. And he was their prey!

He fled along the banks of the River Tyne, but was pulled to the ground by one of the dogs, as the others tore him to pieces. The only part of his face that remained remotely recognisable was his beard.

*Things at Bellister Castle were never quite the same again. It is said that the heartbroken ghost of the old nobleman still walks the halls, and is known as 'The Grey Man'.

The spirit of the minstrel is said to inhabit the woods near the River Tyne, where he can be seen running, or standing pointing towards the Castle with blood running from his beard.

THE LORD CREWE ARMS, BLANCHLAND

Out of all of the haunted pubs and hotels in the North, the Lord Crewe Arms is by far the most famous, and yet why it should be is a complete puzzle. No one there has ever suffered a tragic death, as far as is known, no one has even hurt themselves particularly, yet the string of strange happenings over the year is hard to match.

The Lord Crewe sits in a wonderful woody hollow, surrounded by the kind of countryside that could have saved Hammer Films a fortune in sets. The weather often obliges too, enveloping the area with a thin, eerie mist, that has your knees knocking long before you enter the house. And that is the kind of chilly building that is custom-built for a haunting. It has a good restaurant, is charmingly run... but you sense that there is something not quite right somewhere.

The ghost is supposed to be that of Dorothy Forster whose brother chose the wrong side in the Jacobite Rebellion and ended up in Newgate Prison, later being sent into exile as a traitor. Although Dorothy missed her brother, she could do nothing to bring him back to England, and, it would seem, accepted this. She got married and settled elsewhere, and happily lived out the rest of her natural life, never returning to the Hall that is now the Lord Crewe Arms; in fact she was never ever seen in Blanchland again. So why she would choose to cross that great divide to haunt this pub for ever is a complete mystery. Yet it is claimed that she still does, and many people claim to have witnessed a woman in long skirts waiting at a window. Visitors have been woken up by someone in their room, knocking on their doors, doors opening even when they are locked, lights flashing on and off, pictures moving and articles being moved about.

I have put this to the test twice. The first time, I placed Mrs Kay Williams from Redcar in the Lord Crewe overnight, linked to me by telephone. Kay had this to say: 'It was a lovely modern room, nothing like what I expected, but I could not rest. When I did begin to nap I felt someone close to me, as if they were tucking in. I don't think it was my imagination, but it was as if my husband was cuddling in to me. I sat up with a start when it happened. Later that night I was reading a magazine when I felt the end of the bed go down, as if someone was sitting on it. It took me almost five minutes to gather the courage to peep over the top. There was nothing there, but I could have sworn that the bedding did have the signs that someone had sat on it! I didn't believe in ghosts, but this has made me think.'

If it isn't real, what is it? Imagination running rampant? Well, I had to test that theory too, using a simple technique. I had an assistant working for me on the late-night phone-in on Metro FM, Alice Keens-Soper, a right charlie of a lass, whom I thought the world of. She was always game for a laugh, with a sharp sense of humour and a dirty laugh. When I was seeking a volunteer for a ghost hunt, she was swift to put her name forward, and in due course was taken by taxi from her trendy Jesmond home to Blanchland. Unbeknown to me she had smuggled her current boyfriend along too. On discovering this, I asked her to assure me that he would not be in her bedroom with her. I needed her to be alone for the experiment that was to lie ahead. To tell Alice to keep a boyfriend at bay was rather like pouring sugar on the ground and telling an ant to leave it alone. Even so, she was as good as her word, and was placed in 'Dorothy Forster's room'.

I decided to play with her imagination, to see if I could plant ideas in her mind, and create a reaction. Once again linked only by a telephone, we kept in touch, live on air to over a million people dotted around the North. At first she had nothing to report, except that the window had rattled a little bit. At that I told her that it had been from that very window that Dorothy Forster had kept vigil, and every fifteen minutes it would creak, as she looked out, waiting for her brother to return to her. This had the desired effect, and the next time we spoke she was definitely getting nervous. Then she mentioned hearing footsteps, certainly nothing unknown in any hotel, but I suggested it was Dorothy Forster pacing the room as she did every night. Later Alice told of how the chair next to the bed had suddenly started squeaking a little. This gave me another excuse to fib, saying that that was Dorothy's own seat, and how she must be sitting next to Alice at that very moment. These mind games culminated in Alice being very, very frightened and quite convinced that the Lord Crewe Arms was haunted.

It proved something very different to me – that the imagination is rather like plasticine; it can be sculpted and moulded to fit what people want to believe. Alice swore that ghosts existed for some months afterwards, until she finally began questioning what had happened to her.

*Many phantoms have been witnessed over the years at the cemetery in Blanchland. Figures of women in long skirts, monks, Roman soldiers and weeping children. The most enduring ghost is a ginger-haired monk with a ragged habit, who many believe lived in a monastery that existed in Blanchland from about 1150 to 1588.

THE WHITE LADY OF BLENKINSOPP CASTLE

In the 1500s Blenkinsopp Castle was at the height of its powers, commanding a splendid situation near Haltwhistle on the River Tippalt. It was owned by Bryan de Blenkinsopp, an imposing warrior who ruled the savage countryside nearby with a kindly hand, though he was known to deal harshly with anyone who caused him problems. It was said that one day he came upon a robber assaulting a young woman near Gilsland, took his lance (he had been hunting boar) and chased the man away, cornering him in the woods and running him through. He chose to leave the body in the forest, to feed the land as his lands fed him.

His people loved him, for he kept them safe, yet they knew he was a most materialistic man, so tight he could peel an orange in his pocket. He made it commonly known that he would never marry, because then he would have to share his riches. The most common version of this tale tells of how he 'promised to marry only a woman capable of filling a chest of gold that it would take ten men to carry'. It is said that this is how rich he was, and that he would only take a bride whose wealth could equal his.

Sir Bryan went off to fight in the Holy Land and ten long years later he returned to flourishing Blenkinsopp Castle with the daughter of a sultan as his bride. Her skin was black, and you can imagine the stir that made among the locals who had never in their lives seen a living soul that colour. And to marry a 'heathen' – that was worse than if he had married a peasant. But then the Sultan had given her a dowry of treasure so huge it took twelve of Sir Bryan's entourage to carry it.

At first, the marriage seemed a happy one, his bride filled the Castle with laughter, only occasionally feeling homesick for Arabia. As time went by, however, she began to suspect that his love was more for her treasure than her company. To test her husband's affection, she sent her two personal handservants, believed to be eunuchs, to bury the treasure where her husband would never be able to find it. In a fury Sir Bryan stormed out of Blenkinsopp Castle with four of his soldiers, never to return. Many stories circulate, some that he went back to the Holy Land, others that he travelled to Scotland where he was killed by Border reivers.

His wife tried many times to return to her home, but never managed. After five years of waiting for her husband to return she died of a broken heart, in the dungeon where she had dug up her treasure.

It is said that Sir Bryan's wife walks the castle walls late at night, and can be seen sobbing in the dungeons. Wearing a wispy white robe, she glides across the floor, her dark features often invisible

9

in the darkness so that what is seen is the white gown floating by apparently of its own volition.

BUCKTON'S GRIZEL

At Buckton in Northumberland walks an interesting ghost known as Grizel, short for Grizelda, the daughter of Sir John Cochrane who lay rotting in a dungeon in Edinburgh Castle for the part he played in Argyll's rebellion against James II.

When he succeeded his brother, the rather randy Charles II, the King declared that the role of the monarchy would never be tainted by debauchery again. His new order was far from popular, particularly when he ordered his soldiers to arrange that the Whigs were defeated, assuring that the more manageable Tories were elected. At 'the Bloody Assizes' Judge Jeffreys sentenced 320 of the Duke of Monmouth's supporters to hang, 840 to be sold into slavery and many others to be lashed with the whip or the cat-o'-nine-tails. The Duke of Argyll's supporters met with a similar fate, and the Judge sent out execution warrants throughout Britain to mete out what was loosely termed justice.

Knowing her father's death warrant was to be delivered to Edinburgh by coach, Cochrane's shapely daughter Grizel dressed herself as a highwayman and held up the coach. She took all of the mail including the death warrant.

It was her timely intervention that gave Cochrane's followers sufficient time to half-plead with and half-bribe officials into getting Sir John a pardon. Near Buckton there is a copse of trees known as Grizzy's Clump, the cluster of bushes where she lay in wait for the coach.

The ghost of that girl on horseback, dressed as a highwayman is said to appear at the end of every month.

*Mrs Marjorie Burke said: 'I was one of the sceptics who had heard of Grizel but refused to believe it. Yet one night in 1987 I was driving home in my Ford Fiesta when I heard a horse. I turned to see someone riding a black horse, wearing a black cape and tricorn hat. It was almost eleven o'clock at night and I can't imagine anyone riding about in fancy dress at that time. You don't think I'm stupid, do you? And I hadn't been drinking!'

THE DIVELSTONS OF DILSTON

Dilston Castle was one of the many castles seized by the Crown when its owner the Earl of Derwentwater chose the wrong side during the Jacobite Rebellion in 1715.

However, there is another legend that goes back many more hundreds of years. The Divelstons owned the Castle, and it became accursed not long after John Divelston's marriage to a woman called Elizabeth, who was born in York. He did not know, when he fell under her spell, that she was a witch. Their marriage soon soured when he discovered his wife bathing in the blood of a slaughtered cow. He was appalled by this, and from that day they lived separate lives.

Elizabeth contented herself by 'romancing' practically every other man in the Castle, and many from local villages. It was obvious to Divelston that he was becoming a laughing stock; he had to get rid of this woman.

One evening he crept into her bedchamber, and found her in bed with a servant. He killed the boy with a sword blow to the head. To his utter horror the woman began bathing in his fresh blood. 'Try and kill me and this Castle will be cursed!' said Elizabeth, reaching into the boy's open skull and eating his brains.

As Divelston vomited at this vile sight, Elizabeth stood up, her naked body covered in gore, and walked to him saying 'You and I must become husband and wife again. I shall take no more lovers, but you must return me to your bed.' He looked at her, a beautiful creature with long black hair, the blood dripping off her every curve. She smiled, and a trickle of blood dribbled from the side of her mouth, as she reached out to caress his cheek, smearing it with the servant's blood.

Divelston forced an answering smile, and turned away; and then in a flash he swished his sword around and severed the witch's head. The body remained standing; the head fell upright on the bed, and to his horror it spoke. 'Now you've done it, John Divelston. Within a hundred years your family will be gone, and all of the occupants of this castle will live in misery!' At that the eyes closed, and the tongue hissed between the lips like a snake, until eventually the vibrations ceased.

John Divelston had the body carried over the border into Scotland and cast into a ravine.

THE FEATHERSTONE PHANTOM

Strange bumping and banging can often be heard at Featherstone Castle, near Haltwhistle, by visitors and staff alike, and they know exactly what it is.

Sir Reginald FitzUrse used to rule the area with an iron fist, swift to clamp down on anyone who stood in his way. There are stories of how in the castle grounds he would take pleasure in whipping stable boys with a cat-o'-nine-tails just because they hadn't polished the saddle of his horse sufficiently. He and his cronies had once ripped the clothes off the back of a young girl and were on the verge of committing rape when her father intervened to stop them. Later the father's body was found with a knife in his back.

FitzUrse was eventually stopped, and he was locked up in the tower of Featherstone Castle. No one really knew what to do with him, so they did nothing; they didn't feed him, they didn't give him water. They just ignored the fact that he was there. It took him almost three months to die of starvation.

He ate his leather boots and anything else he could find, and drank what little rainwater he could catch and his own urine. All the while he would scream out in torment, begging anyone to open the door. He would hammer on the thick oak doors until his hands were bruised, he would claw at the wood with his fingernails until they bled.

Now the ghost of the knight can still be heard most nights at Featherstone Castle, walking across the floor, emitting deathly groans, and hammering on doors and walls.

MURDER AT KNARSDALE HALL

Four miles from Haltwhistle stand the proud portals of Knarsdale Hall, rugged stones which hide a most terrible secret.

Legend tells of a selfish and arrogant lord of Knarsdale Hall, who by the time he was in his middle forties had still not found a wife. This really was no great surprise for he had a face like a ripe tomato, jowls like a bulldog, and the form of a sack of horsemanure tied with string.

They say that money talks, and it spoke most clearly to the parents of the most beautiful girl in the Tyne Valley.

On meeting him she thought him a loathsome creature, and told her father how disagreeable she found him. However, he was the richest man in the area and the parents thought it a great honour that their lovely daughter would become the Lady of Knarsdale Hall. So the bands were read, the marriage arranged and the sweet beautiful blonde became the wife of the jelly-bellied Lord.

Honeymoon nights are remembered as a time of passion and joy, of the fulfilment of mutual desire: their honeymoon was equally memorable. Not for passion, however, but rather for temper. The servants heard voices raised in anger, china being thrown and windows broken as the battle ensued. The arguments continued throughout their unsatisfactory marriage. The people watched, describing her 'as a most perfect beauty trapped in a cage of gold'. She seemed to become accustomed to her lifestyle, and just got on with life, but never showed the least glimpse of affection towards her portly and dribbling husband.

After some months, however, everyone began to comment on how happy the Lady of the Hall had become. You would hear her laughing, she was wearing new dresses, and she always made sure she was wearing the latest scents from abroad. Many believed that she was beginning to love her husband, and that things would be happier for everyone now.

The truth was that she had taken a lover, a young man – some say he was her husband's nephew, others his cousin – who also resided at Knarsdale Hall with his sister.

As often as they could they would meet under the light of a single candle, kissing, exchanging chit-chat and being young and in love. They always made sure that her husband was out hunting, visiting town or away on business. Some servants were sworn to secrecy, and bribed to ensure their discretion.

It was a chilly November evening, the wind was howling up the valley, and the young wife shivered with anticipation; her lover would be coming to her on that stormy night. He padded along the cold wooden corridor, sneaked into her bed chamber. There she was in the candlelight, her long blonde hair hanging in ringlets, a long, white satin nightgown hanging off her shoulder. Surely there had never been a more beautiful woman. They kissed, a long lingering kiss, and then they made love.

It was at the very height of their union, as two voices moaned in unison that the bedroom door opened, and there in the shadow stood a figure. It was the young man's sister; shocked at what she had seen, she scurried back to her room. The lovers held each other tightly, sick to their stomachs at the thought that they had been found out. They reassured themselves that surely she would

13

not tell the husband, if only to protect her brother and their tenancy of the Hall.

Worry nagged the lovers like a sore tooth. Whenever in her presence they felt on a knife edge. What if they were to quarrel with her? What if she were to talk in her sleep? What if she made a deal with the nobleman? It was all irrational, for she had sworn to her brother that she would not breathe a word to a living soul. But the young wife had already decided that the only sure way of the girl keeping their secret, was if she took it to her grave with her.

It was another wet and windy night, thunder crashed in the darkness, lightning flashed and the errant wife lay in bed with her foul husband. The darkened room exploded with light as the electricity charged atmosphere turned night into day. The wife complained that a banging door was keeping her awake, and that she would only be able to sleep if it were closed. Her husband sat up and reached for a dressing gown, but she stopped him, suggesting that he should send his young niece to close it. So he called to the girl, and off she went to the other side of the house in her flimsy white nightgown to undertake the task.

She reached the door that was swinging wildly back and forth with the wind, and as the rain gusted in upon her soaking through her nightgown, she shivered with the chill. Then a strong hand grasped her across the mouth, another round the waist and she was carried out into the storm.

She struggled, bit the hand, and screamed, but with the storm at its height her cries were lost. Eventually, she wrenched free from her attacker and turned to see it was her own brother.

He told her to follow him, grabbing her arm roughly and dragging her. She lost her footing but he refused to stop, towing her through the mud, scraping the flesh from her feet on the gravel paths and dumping her unceremoniously next to the Hall's small lake.

Although the lake was only small and not terribly deep it had overflowed with the torrents of water falling from the sky. He held her in his arms tenderly, looked into her eyes, and she began to feel a little more reassured. Yet as his hand cradled the back of her neck, his grasp began to tighten and he forced her face towards the water. She clawed at him, she wriggled and writhed but all to no avail. He held her face under the murky water until all life had drained out of her.

He then picked up a huge stone, knotted it into her nightdress,

14

and waded out with her into the lake until the weight took her body down.

The Lord and his Lady snuggled into their blankets, content that the banging had stopped, and sleep soon took them over.

Nearing four in the morning the Lord was awoken by a particularly loud crack of thunder, and the noise of his hounds baying in his stable. He walked out of his bedroom to a window overlooking the stable and all seemed well – but why were they making that racket?

As he turned back towards his bedroom he saw his young niece standing in the firelight; she was soaked to the skin, and her face was ashen pale. Her hair hung like rats' tails, and her nightgown was ripped and muddy. 'What's wrong, child? Why aren't you in your bed?' he asked, and then in a blink of an eye she was gone.

When morning came they searched the grounds but she was never found. The nobleman always blamed himself for not having secured the door himself, and often chastised himself for his selfishness. He may have been an ugly old cuss, but he had more humanity in him than his callous wife. The relationship between the lovers was never as fiery again, the passion had died on that stormy night. Soon the lover disappeared too. There were many stories. Some claimed that she had murdered him whilst in a rage, because he was said to have made pregnant a girl in Haltwhistle. Others that he rode into Scotland to escape from her clutches. The most commonly related story tells of how his lordship discovered his wife's infidelity and strangled the young man. Whatever the truth, he was never found, dead or alive.

Ten years later the Lady of Knarsdale Hall was a psychotic paranoid, and believed that everyone was against her. She would cry for no reason, often for hours, and would rant at anyone who would take it. She was burdened with guilt, knowing she was responsible for one, maybe two deaths.

One night she was shouting at her husband and said, 'Don't you ever treat me like that again, or you'll end up on the bottom of the lake, just like that little witch did!' He wondered what she had meant by this, and had the servants drag the lake, and there to his horror he found the body of his niece!

He thundered back into the house and accused his wife of her murder, and drove her even further over the edge of sanity. Her remaining days were spent locked in one of the bedrooms, stark raving mad. She was completely incapable of doing anything for herself and had to be looked after like a baby. But she often lashed out and injured her helpers and had to be tied down even to be fed. She was possessed with a huge unhappiness of spirit, and it was a mercy for everyone when she died.

*Every year visitors see the ghost of the young girl travelling from the Hall to what is left of the lake, her silken gown gliding over the grass. It is said that she is only seen on the anniversary of her death, yet many people have seen her in different parts of the Hall.

One guest also complained of hearing mad laughter echoing around the upstairs rooms; others hear a slamming door whenever there is a thunderstorm. Maybe houses remember what has gone on within them, and require no excuse to share the experience.

HAUGHTON CASTLE'S MAN WHO ATE HIMSELF

Out in the wilds of sixteenth-century Northumberland stood Haughton Castle owned at that time by Sir Thomas Swinburne who was Lord of the Manor. Those that lived on his land would have been happy were it not for the gangs of robbers and Border reivers that plagued the entire area. Many of these Scots had been forced out of their own country by the various religious altercations that were becoming commonplace. The most troublesome clans were the Robsons, the Dodds, The Elliotts, the Charltons and, arguably the worst, the Armstrongs.

On a dark November night Sir Thomas Swinburne led an assault on a reiver encampment, killing dozens of men and capturing Archie Armstrong, their chief. After they had locked Armstrong up in a dungeon, they passed the night in feasting and celebration, before Sir Thomas sped off to York early in the morning.

At this point there are variations in the story. Some believe that Swinburne walled Armstrong up in the dungeon to be left to starve to death. Others declare that on nearing York he remembered that he had left no instructions for the prisoner to be fed, so either sent back one of his representatives, or returned to Haughton Castle himself.

The timescale, too, varies; some say that the representative arrived back a week later, some say it was only days later, others say it was a month later. What they discovered was quite disgusting. The dungeon lay in silence, and on pushing the door open they found Archie's lifeless body in the corner. He had been so desperate to survive that he had attempted to eat his own arms and legs, and had drunk his own urine and blood. He sat there covered with human bite marks; he had even chewed away half of his cheek. What Archie had started both rats and weevils had continued. His eyes hung down his cheeks, vermin having eaten away his eyelids; and as Swinburne stood at the dungeon door, they stared horribly at him.

It was said that Sir Thomas was so horrified by the way his prisoner had died that he refused ever to sentence anyone to those cells again. The door was sealed, and often his private staff would claim to hear strange moanings and screams.

The Castle was exorcised but ghostly happenings occasionally still occur.

THE BLACK BITCH OF BLACK HEDDON

In the 1700s a woman visited Black Heddon, claiming that she was collecting for the poor. People gathered up their old clothing, shoes, food and whatever pennies they could afford, and sent her happily on her way. She always dressed in black, and tried to squeeze as much kindness as she could out of people. It was believed that this woman may well have been the first charity collector in the North of England. The sadness is that she never gave any of the goods or money to the poor. She kept it all for herself and lived quite a fine life. Much of the stuff was sold, once again to 'raise funds for the poor', who would of course never receive a penny.

She was finally run out of Black Heddon by a landowner who had spotted her drinking in a tavern in Newcastle and boasting of how she was 'conning those country bumpkins out of their shekels'. So when next she appeared he tipped all her collected sundries on to the ground and chased her out of the village with his horsewhip, threatening to 'hang the bitch if she ever returned'.

The story goes on to tell how this woman was killed in the vicinity, trampled to death by two horsemen who had heard how she had fooled them. They had meant to frighten her but had gone further than planned, when one of the horse's hooves crushed her throat.

Since then, many people riding horses have been surprised by a woman in black wearing a long rustling gown. The horses shy and try to throw their riders. Then suddenly she just disappears.

Many riders find their way barred by the ghost, and have to turn back or find another, longer route to avoid the spirit.

Some say the only way to force the 'bitch' to get out of the way is to wave a hangman's noose or a riding whip, others recommend some witchwood from a rowan tree. Yet, while she may be deterred, she cannot be got rid of, as, it is said, she still walks the country lanes of Black Heddon in search of a horseman or woman.

THE HEXHAM EXTRATERRESTRIALS

During the winter of 1904/5 some very strange things happened all over Britain. What I am about to describe happened not only at Hexham, but also, at precisely the same time, in Gravesend, Norwich, Badminton, Aberdeen, Abingdon and Hull.

Twenty days running, from Christmas Day well into the new year, local farmers discovered that their animals were being butchered as they stood. Bodies torn open, literally wrenched into pieces, were found on both sides of the River Tyne. Many had their internal organs missing; in others the hide and innards were there and undamaged, but not a bone was to be seen. To remove an entire skeleton and leave the internal organs apparently untouched is an impossibility, yet that is what had been done, and without even disturbing the fleece. Despite keeping them closely guarded, animals continued to be butchered – cattle, pigs, chickens, goats and eight horses from a nearby riding school. It was almost as if someone or something were shopping for parts, taking certain items from different creatures.

It is alleged that three locals disappeared during that period. Some said that they had merely moved further south; others believed that they had been taken by whoever was conducting this strange, almost scientific dismembering of animals.

Local newspapers of course ran stories about these killings; they also ran a story about 'swarms of strange aeriel lights in the sky, reminiscent of airships'. Was there a connection? As always, the authorities played down these stories as 'fanciful in the extreme', but they could not explain the animal rippings.

Was Hexham visited by people from outer space? Were they responsible for the dissections? We will never know, but it is an interesting coincidence.

THE GHOST BATTLE OF LANGLEY

Langley Castle is one of the most magnificent of buildings set in idyllic countryside in Tynedale, Northumberland. Yet in the course of the past 250 years several passers-by have claimed to see it burning.

*In 1799 one of the Duke of Northumberland's servants went to deliver a message to the Castle, but returned home to report 'seeing it being sacked by rebels'.

On going back to the Castle he discovered it was in perfect condition.

*In 1885 John Douglas Hope of London was visiting Langley Castle with a variety of haberdashery items and draperies. As he was looking at the Castle he witnessed hundreds of soldiers burning and looting it.

*In 1979 Robert Fulton did research into 'ghost battles' and was told by Mrs Rose Robertson from Leeds that she had witnessed a ghost battle at Langley Castle.

An incumbent at the Castle when telephoned said, however, that 'It's the first I've heard of it. The Castle does have several ghosts, but I've not heard of a battle.'

*Research into the Castle's history shows that it was actually destroyed in 1405 when Henry IV brought his forces north to destroy the joint forces of Archbishop Scrope and the Earl of Northumberland. Could it be another case of the videotape of history being replayed?

NAFFERTON CASTLE AND WELTON HALL, CURSED FOR EVER

It is written that a 'twisty-faced man' known as Lang or Lanky Lonkin built Nafferton Castle with his construction gang for Lord Wearie. Wearie was a cunning swine and managed to use some fine print on their agreement as an excuse not to pay them. They had laboured for years to create the magnificent hall, and had only received their basic living expenses, Lonkin decided to wreak his revenge on those he felt had done him down.

There are about nine different versions of this story; I have chosen the one that is most entertaining.

Lonkin heard that Lord Wearie's family were staying at Welton Hall, barely a stone's throw away. He bought the co-operation of Lord Wearie's grandchild's nurse, and she left a downstairs window open, through which he crept in. First, he and his accomplice stabbed Wearie's baby grandson dead. When she heard her baby's cries subside so swiftly the child's mother ran into the room to find her baby dead in his crib. She saw the murderers but was so distraught that all she could do was collapse on to the cot, hugging her murdered child to her breast. Her other child, Betsy, aged about fifteen, rushed in while Lonkin and the wet nurse were poised to stab her mother, and she begged them to spare her mother, offering her own life in exchange. Lonkin said, 'Nay, lass, Lord Wearie must get his deserts, for Nafferton Castle and Welton Hall are cursed for evermore!'

He ordered the girl to watch as they stabbed her mother, forcing young Betsy to catch the blood in a golden washbasin as it oozed out of her.

When the rest of the household came running, attracted by all the screaming, Lonkin and the wet nurse managed to escape. Three days later, however, they were cornered. Rather than be captured, Lonkin hanged himself from an oak tree near Whittle Dene. First, though, so that no one else should have the money and jewels he had stolen, he wrapped them in a leather pouch and threw it into the swirling water. It is said to remain there to this day.

The nurse wasn't courageous enough to follow his lead, not after witnessing his agonies of dancing in midair until his neck snapped. She was to meet an even more painful death, burnt at the stake by Lord Wearie's men on his return from London.

*The lady's ghost is said to walk Welton Hall, looking in anguish at the death of her child. She is often heard crying, or seen in the downstairs rooms, seated in one of the chairs, wringing her hands.

*The oak tree near Whittle Dene is said to carry the outline of the hanged man, and whenever anyone sees it a deep pool known as 'the whirl dub' begins to swirl and bubble.

THE NORMAN OF PRUDHOE CASTLE

After the Norman conquest William the Conqueror rewarded his knights by giving them huge areas of land, and much of Northumbria came to belong to the French. One lucky knight was Robert de Umfraville, known locally as 'The Bearded One' or 'Robert of the Beard', who inherited the entire area of Redesdale, including Prudhoe Castle.

Many who have told of seeing a strange bearded figure there, knew nothing whatsoever at the time about the knight or the history of Redesdale and Prudoe.

*Louise Cuthbert from Battle Hill in Wallsend stopped off at Prudhoe one day on her way home from Hexham. Not knowing that Prudhoe had a castle, she spotted it, she decided to take a look. On getting close she caught sight of a Norman soldier wearing a bright green tunic over chainmail. His helmet, which had a nose-guard, did not completely cover a big black bushy beard.

*Colin Ryder, a canny lad I worked with many moons ago, told me that he knew of several people having witnessed 'things'. He, himself, lived a street away and had no run-ins with phantoms.

*One of the most dramatic sightings was by two American tourists, Roy and Irma Mankowietz from Boston. They were visiting the Castle, and after they had finished taking photographs Irma asked where they would go next; they took out a map, spread it on the ground and pored over it. While they were crouched down they caught sight of a pair of chainmail-clad feet behind them. They glanced around to see a Norman soldier with sword in hand, mad staring eyes and a long black beard. They left the map and ran into the village where no one took them seriously.

They wrote their story in an American magazine called *Phenomena*.

*The Umfraville seat passed to the Percy family when Gilbert de Umfraville's widow married Henry de Percy in the 1380s. There had been no ghostly occurrences until Prudhoe Castle lost the Umfraville name.

THE SALTSKIN OF SEGHILL

In the early 1400s Seghill Tower was one of the largest in the entire country, standing three storeys tall, with battlements, and a bell to give warning of unwanted guests.

The legend I have been told came from a Scottish gentleman called Roy McIntosh from Glasgow, whose relatives came from Seghill.

The country had been at war with France and King Henry V was just about to snatch their crown too. He had married Catherine, the daughter of the imbecile French monarch Charles VI. Henry would have become King of England and France on the death of Charles, but fate intervened. Henry became seriously ill and died aged only 35. One day England had a strong soldier and military genius as her king, the next the entire nation was fearful of a total collapse of their international authority.

Groups of armed soldiers decided to use Henry's death as an excuse to loot and pillage, and although the North Country seemed more peaceful than the south, the residents of Seghill were fearful that all their foodstuffs would be stolen by marauders. So they asked the keeper of Seghill Tower to protect their stores, by locking them, with him, in the tower. The building was believed to be unassailable, so high was it, with walls three feet thick. A single man, an ex-soldier, Allen, maintained the tower, living in the vault, and keeping vigil by day. He readily agreed to help his friends protect their stock. Within a week, Seghill Tower was full of corn, wheat, oilseed rape, flour, salt, vegetables and fruit of every kind.

Then one day from his vantage point he saw horsemen approaching at speed, and rang his warning bell. The villagers were ready for that sort of emergency, and ran out into the fields and countryside. Not one of the fifty or so locals remained in Seghill, except for Allen safe in his tower. In ransacking the village, the looters came away with only a handful of chickens and nothing of value at all. They pounded on the thick wooden door of the tower, but Allen wasn't even going to reply. Instead he was on the top of the battlements heating some pitch to pour down on them should they try to batter the door down. The battlements had huge stockpiles of rocks and missiles to hurl at potential enemies, and Allen was the man to use them.

The marauders spent the night sleeping in the beds of the locals. At three o'clock in the morning, believing them all to be drunk, Allen crept out to do vengeance to them as they slept. He took a dagger and a sword, and slit the throats of several of them. But he was overheard by one who roused the camp. As Allen ran back to the tower, they were only yards behind him. He slammed the door shut behind him, and fastened bolt after bolt in a cold sweat. Then he raced up to the battlements to hurl rocks down at the villains. He had taken a risk, but it had paid off, surely, he thought; they would never come back to Seghill.

Yet it was at that very moment that he felt a blow to the back of his head. He tried to turn but blackness swallowed him up. One of the marauders had crept in while he had been out paying them his murderous visit. He awoke to find himself tied to a post in the storage yard, and all around him cavorted the marauders, drunk and wild with rage at how he had despatched their comrades. They took turns to peel the skin from his body. Each time he passed out with the pain, they would wait until he regained consciousness before beginning again. Then when he stood there naked, completely peeled, they gouged out his eyes and hurled him into the huge mounds of salt he had agreed to store. The extremes of agony he went through are unimaginable; suffice to say that he died within minutes. Minutes that must certainly have appeared like years.

*It is said that Allen, 'the Saltskin of Seghill', still occupies that vault today, protecting everything inside. Strange noises and cries have been heard, but more commonly just a very white apparition gliding along from wall to wall.

The vault has been used as the storage cellar for the Blake Arms Hotel.

TRICKY DICKY OF STAWARD

An ex-lead miner turned poacher, known as Dicky of Kingswood, is said to haunt Staward Pele, the ruins of a tower some ten miles from Hexham. It is wedged between two rivers and was the perfect place for catching fish and trapping game. This wasn't his only occupation: he also stole cattle and horses. He was a cunning man; once confronted by a farmer whose sheep he had stolen and who was threatening to kill him, he swore that if his life was spared he would reward the farmer with a gift worth more than the sheep. The farmer let him go. He visited another farmer, stole a string of goats and presented them to the first farmer.

On another occasion he had stolen two prize oxen from a home-

23

stead at Denton Burn village, and sold them for gold to a Cumbrian farmer. During the transaction he noticed that this farmer owned a beautiful black horse. So, late that night, he crept back and stole it. As he was fleeing from the Cumbrian he ran smack-bang into the man from Denton Burn whose cattle he'd half-inched. He didn't panic, however; he coolly sold the Newcastle man his newly acquired horse so that he could chase the man who stole his oxen. He then pointed him towards the Cumbrian so hot on his tail. The two victims cut each other down, and Dicky was there to take both of their horses, as they lay battered and bleeding.

Dicky is known to play practical jokes on anyone who goes to see ruins of Staward Pele. He takes things from people's bags, putting them into other people's pockets.

WHO WALKS AT WARKWORTH

One of Northumberland's fiercest strongholds for centuries was Werceworde, named after a witchy woman with magical powers called Werce who first settled on the spot now called Warkworth.

The history of the Castle is amazing. It was given by King Ceolwulf of Northumbria to monks to use as a safe refuge against the Picts, Scots and Norsemen. This is how it stayed for hundreds of years until the Percy family took it over in the early 1330s.

The 1st Earl of Northumberland and his son Harry Hotspur lived there. Hotspur made his name as the hero of the battle of Otterburn Hill, where he saved hundreds of lives, and claimed at least that many from the Scots.

So powerful were the Percys, particularly the gallant Harry Hotspur, that it was merely by putting the name behind Henry of Lancaster Hotspur was instrumental in the deposition of Richard II.

All went well for the Percy family until they began to disagree with the actions of the man they had helped place on the English throne, and conspired to overthrow him. Henry IV knew full well of the romantic hero-worship felt for Hotspur by everyone in the north, so brought armies to face him. Harry Hotspur was hacked to death during the bloody battle of Shrewsbury, as the King marched on towards the north to destroy the seat of Percy power – Warkworth.

Warkworth Castle would never ever be quite the same again; the glory days were over.

Although much of the Castle is in ruins there tales have been told by visitors and staff alike of the ghost of a young and vigorous man, running along the walls, loping up the stairs two at a time, or keeping vigil at the Great Gate Tower. You rarely get a chance to ask a ghost his name, but wouldn't it be grand if this was Harry Hotspur, arguably one of the North's greatest ever heroes.

*In 1972 on a school trip outing to Warkworth Castle, school-teacher Mrs Gibson met a man wearing tights and a chainmail shirt. She takes up the story: 'I told him how pleased I was that someone had taken the trouble to dress up for the children. The man just looked puzzled and walked up the stairs ahead of me. On reaching the tower I found no way out, but the man had disappeared. Believe me, he was no ghost; he looked like solid flesh and blood, but I can't explain where he went. I said nothing at the time, not with thirty-two youngsters in my charge!'

*In 1991 Jean Coles from Cullercoats phoned Metro FM's *Night Owls* programme to tell of how she was once knocked off her feet by 'something' at Warkworth. It was a bright sunny day, she had been walking across the grass inside Warkworth Castle, when she felt 'a force hitting her tummy' that knocked her down. She had not been drinking, she wasn't within twenty feet of another person and is still puzzled as to what it was.

THE GATESHEAD GRUNT

In the early 1700s when Gateshead was very much Newcastle's poor relation, times were hard and only those with money ever prevailed. One such man was Charles Henderson who used to buy and sell goods from both Scotland and the south, selling them at a huge profit to anyone he could. He created an early form of 'car boot sale', taking his goods on a horse and cart to homes and villages as far afield as Durham, Stanley, South Shields and Hexham. Within a year he was wealthy, within five years he was rich. Henderson's 'gallowa's' (horses) were renowned, people believing that they were getting bargains. Admittedly the things he sold were only available in the big cities, so to find fine fabrics, delicate ornaments, luxury food items, etc. in a back lane in a small village was bound to create interest. The richer Henderson became, the more he delegated the work to younger men, all quite poor and keen to earn any kind of living. By 1755 Henderson was in his late thirties, rich, yet still unfulfilled, so he took himself a bride. Her name was never known; some say he bought the young girl from her father for a sum of five shillings.

Henderson's close friends were introduced to a staggeringly attractive brunette whom he called 'Sophie'. She never left his house on Windmill Hill, just out of the centre of Gateshead, over-looking the River Tyne. Her only visitor was the old tinker who had 'provided' her, who claimed to be keeping check on his daughter's progress.

Within a year she was pregnant and Charles Henderson was thrilled; he would have an heir and all of his hard work could become a 'family concern'. Everything was going for him, he had started providing coal carts and coach services, his 'gallowa's' were still pouring profit in his direction, and overtures were made to him to go into politics. When in November 1756 the Duke of Newcastle resigned as Prime Minister, the groundswell of northern opinion was that Charles Henderson would put himself forward. This he refused to do, claiming 'This war with France will ruin many men but not Charles Henderson'. William Pitt became Sec-retary of State and gathered other northern ministers to face the French threat.

Charles Henderson was very much his own man, and despite it being totally against tradition, he attended the birth of his son. The delivery had been difficult, and on seeing the child, Henderson reeled back in horror. The infant's face was horrifically deformed. Storming out of the house, he ran along the street crying out, 'God has cursed me with a devil for a son!' He was found by friends sitting in a inn on the corner of what is now Charles Street, where he was trying to drown his sorrow; he then sobbed uncontrollably into the arms of an old woman. Some say he refused to return home for almost a month, but when he did his demeanour was very different from that of the loving man he once was. He became an ill-tempered brute of a man, hurling abuse at servants, and behaved contemptuously towards his wife. His son was named George after the composer Handel, but Henderson refused to call him that, preferring to call him 'Grunt'.

Young George had one eye higher than the other, his nose was totally flat and a cleft palate had viciously twisted his mouth, causing him to talk in a low 'grunt'. Henderson consulted phys-icians but none had the expertise to do anything for the youngster. As the boy entered his teens his problems increased; it seemed the taller he grew, the more stooped he became. On his sixteenth birthday the terrifying truth emerged. During a vicious argument

Sophie told Henderson that George was not his son. She had been carrying such a great burden, and it all spilled out like a leak in the Atlantic. First, Henderson learned that Sophie's mother was also her sister, who had been the victim of incest since she was twelve years old. And once Sophie reached that age, their father turned his attentions upon her. Even after her marriage he had been visiting her, and having sex as he had done throughout her childhood. Sophie had been too frightened and ashamed to tell her husband. The child was deformed because of inbreeding.

It was as if someone had wrenched out his heart. Henderson grabbed his silver-topped cane and went straight to the slums that existed on what is now Gateshead bus station. He entered the home of the tinker and beat him to death. He then set fire to the hovel and left.

The authorities interviewed Henderson who admitted to beating the old man, but claimed to have left before the fire started. Such was his influence that charges were never brought against him.

From that day young George was never allowed out of the old mansion on the Windmill Hills, and remained confined to his twelve-foot room. He died of influenza at the age of only 39 in 1795 having been hidden away for almost 24 years. Henderson never slept with Sophie ever again, and she ran off three months after her son died. It was believed that she set up home with a butcher in Saltmeadows Road.

Henderson's financial empire crashed around his ears; he had no appetite for it any more, and he allowed various parts to be taken from him by his own employees, who struck out on their own. In 1789 there was a mysterious fire that burned down the business-man's mansion, and despite a thorough raking through the ashes no one ever found the body of Charles Henderson. Some say that his spirit will not rest until it is found.

Two ghosts are said to walk Windmill Hills – one, the grief-stricken old man with a silver-topped cane, who can be heard weeping or seen holding his head in his hands in doorways. The other desperate ghost is said to be that of George Henderson, who hammers on doors begging to be released, clawing with bloody fingernails at heavy wooden doors.

*One of the buildings built on the site of the Henderson home later became an unemployment benefit office, and an ex-employee who wishes only to be known as Tom said, 'I worked there for a good few years and often heard, late in the afternoon, doors slamming, and hammering coming from upstairs. If you followed the sound it came from one of the rooms on the very top floor. Despite our radiators it was always bitter cold. Occasionally people claim to have seen glimpses of a man with a hunched back hobbling around. Once one of my colleagues, a woman in her fifties, actually fainted while sitting in the ladies loo because she heard a man grunting behind her in a sexual manner. We had to burst the lock on the door to get in, dress her, then take her to the Queen Elizabeth Hospital outpatients. She had such a shock she was off work for almost a month. She came back for a fortnight, then found a job with the local Electricity Board.'

*Whilst walking her dog past Windmill Hills one cold Sunday morning in 1982 Mrs Kathleen O'Connor experienced something very strange. She claims that she heard a woman screaming, and flagged down a police car. She pointed police towards the old house, telling them she had heard shouts of 'Father, no! Don't do this to me!' followed by screams of agony and torment. The police checked the scene yet found no evidence of wrongdoing. Had that been the horrified pleadings of young Sophie, raped yet again by her incestuous father?

THE TERRIFYING TRIO OF HOUGHTON LE SPRING

Many pubs believe that a ghost is good for business, a talking point for punters, and a bit of living (or dying) history. The Robbie Burns pub in Houghton le Spring has not one, but three ghosts on the premises.

The hauntings – as recounted in my first *Grisly Trails* – began back in 1984 when the manageress was down in the cellar collecting a crate of soft drinks when she felt a tremendous crack to the back of her head. She spun round, but there was no one else to be seen in the cellar. She had a lump on the back of her head as big as a goose's egg to show for it. Every evening from then, strange music could be heard, a banging and crashing too, yet whenever you investigated there wasn't anything out of place.

*In 1984 the figure of an old woman wearing black was seen; she melted into a wall.

*In 1985 one of the one-armed bandits in the bar went beserk. No one had put any money into it yet it started playing itself, the handle going down, the wheels spinning, and often pumping out a fortune in ten-pence pieces.

*In 1985 two customers and one of the staff saw the silhouette of a man, yet within the shadow there was nothing at all. They watched it as it walked through the pub.

*The third phantom was that of a young child with fair hair, wearing baggy, Victorian-style shorts.

*Since then countless other things have happened: various electrical appliances have caused trouble, notably the bar pumps, the television and the radio. Things have moved of their own accord, including a clock which threw itself from a wall and smashed in the middle of the floor.

THE BLACK MAGIC WOMAN AND THE GEORDIE

Newcastle lad Barry Hunt was on holiday in Jamaica in 1972 when all hell let loose in a small village on the outskirts of Montego Bay. He was sunbathing when newspaper men began following a portly black woman who was approaching the beach. She removed a wrap-around skirt and went in for a swim. The newsmen snapped away until a group of Jamaicans arrived to push them away.

The woman was called Mamma Yepo, a native Jamaican who had recently visited New York to find a young man who had made a Jamaican girl pregnant. She did manage to track him down using a map given her by reading chicken entrails. On finding him she ripped his face twice with a chicken's claw, and within two days the boy was dead.

No cause of death could be found other than fright. His hair had turned white and his face was contorted in panic.

Mamma Yepo returned to Jamaica where she was already renowned as a witch queen, a voodoo lady, schooled in the dark sciences.

Mamma Yepo had conducted surgery on people without using any medical instruments, and had successfully cured people suffering from cancer, tuberculosis, growths and had even conquered a gangrenous limb. One of Mamma Yepo's protégés had once attended actor Peter Sellers, helping him with a back problem.

29

Barry visited the same beach during his stay in Jamaica, Doctors Cave Beach, and each day Mamma Yepo would appear with her entourage for a swim. One day she dropped a small black pouch and Barry spotted it and picked it up. He grabbed his towel and chased after her. He was stopped by two tall Jamaicans who would not allow him within ten feet of the large voodoo queen. When he explained that she had dropped her pouch she thanked him, and offered to help him with his knee.

Barry was gobsmacked, no one knew he had a cartilage problem; he didn't limp or show any other visible signs. She gave him an address and told him to be there at nine that night.

He arrived in a very seedy part of Montego Bay by taxi, and entered a blackened room apparently covered in spiders' webs. In the light of flaming torches, her eyes shining like polished ivory, her skin like ebony, he saw Mamma Yepo. He was aware of dozens of pairs of eyes watching his every move, but couldn't go back now.

She told him to sit, and hold up his knee. He was wearing shorts so there was no need to undress, to his relief. She began to chant, and threw things on to a small fire that crackled and spat as it consumed them. Barry felt no pain at all but almost fainted when Mamma Yepo seemed to open up his knee clear to the bone with her bare hands. He watched as skin and sinew peeled back in the same way you would remove a banana skin. He saw her scrape the bone with what looked to be a small potato knife; she then removed what looked to be gristle, and placed both of her hands over the open wound. When she moved her hands away the wound was closed. The knee was swollen and a little stiff, but not painful.

Mamma Yepo told him to rest that night, and in the following morning all would be fully recovered. He did and it was.

On returning to Britain he visited his hospital who X-rayed it and told him he did not need the operation that only three weeks earlier they had said was absolutely essential if he wanted to remain walking normally.

That was Barry's last contact with Mamma Yepo. Not long after that incident the Jamaican government became frightened of her immense power and made arrangements to have her arrested. However, she had supporters in the police force who warned her of the plot and she fled to Cuba. Before she left she phoned the police chief and cursed him. The most successful young police officer ever to serve in Jamaica, at 38 he was their youngest ever police chief.

He committed suicide four days after receiving that telephone call.

THE DISCO-DANCING MONK OF NEWCASTLE

A Middle Eastern monk is said to walk the streets of Newcastle to this day, most upset that they closed his favourite disco!

The 'monk' is believed to have travelled to Britain after having been converted to Christianity in the Holy Land. His name was Yusef, a dark-skinned six foot five, and only capable of broken English. He journeyed to the monastery in Blackfriars in Newcastle City Centre having arrived aboard a trading ship at Hull. On reaching the monastery he was banned from entry, as the Christian monks believed he was still a heathen, despite his conversion to their faith. This giant had journeyed for almost eight months to reach 'a house of God' and had been shunned by it.

His faith was so strong that he decided not to be put off, and took a job on the Newcastle Quayside to be able to afford a dirty upstairs room near the monastery. The room was situated in the building that later would become La Dolce Vita.

Yusef was never allowed to join the order of monks that he so desperately wanted, and his demise was said to be at the hands of one of the monks. He had become a thorn in the monks' side, many locals having realised that his faith was far stronger than any of the monks. They used to take money from the poor to feed themselves, while the Moor Yusef would give his last penny to any beggar that would ask for it. He was truly a Christian man, and was showing the monks up for the greedy egocentrics that they were.

Some tales tell us that Yusef choked on some food and died, but the most common explanation is of a rather more murderous end.

The monks visited Yusef saying that they were to allow him to join their order. They had brought food and wine to celebrate. Yusef was in joyous spirits, at last his dream was about to come true. The monks shared a drink, but the food was eaten by the Moorish giant. He unsuspectingly ate two half-chickens and some fruit. Such were his stature and constitution that the poison in the food only made him groggy, and was far from being fatal. Realising their plot was about to fail, one of the monks wrapped a knotted rope around Yusef's neck and began to pull and twist for all he was worth. In his doped condition, Yusef could not fight back and the life was squeezed out of him.

The following morning one of the monks told people that Yusef had returned home, having been rebuffed by their order. No one would question the powerful monks, and nothing else was ever said about it. Yusef's body was taken away in the night, and buried on the land that now houses Blyths Keel Row shopping complex.

*Patricia Brown used to visit La Dolce Vita in Newcastle twice a week for almost ten years and claims to have seen 'a swarthy-skinned man' with a long robe, on several occasions. 'Everybody saw it,' says Patricia, he was common knowledge to all the regular customers, and some of the staff told me his name was Joseph.'

*Bill Hardy was a temporary barman at La Dolce Vita. 'Everyone said I was pissed at the time, but I did see Joseph, a ghost in a long monk's habit, dancing amongst the crowds at the disco. He didn't have the modern steps, he moved more like one of those African tribal dancers, but he was dancing! . . . I know what I saw. I've not made money out of this, and everyone thinks I'm either stupid or a liar. I did see it, and I don't care what anyone says!'

*Viv, a regular caller to the *Night Owls* programme on Metro FM claims to have seen Joseph/Yusef in Blyth.

THE HOPPINGS' HEAD BOY

Europe's largest fair, 'The Hoppings', comes to Newcastle's Town Moor every year, but in the early 1900s a smaller version came into the city. One of the most popular stalls belonged to a young traveller called Mo. It was called 'The Emporium of Freaks' and featured sheep with five legs, dogs with two heads, and other rarities. After having handed over your money, you discovered that all of these animals were either stuffed or pickled in jars. The stuffed creatures were more often than not composites made to order by a taxidermist. Putting two dead sheep together to create an apparent bizarre freak of nature.

More gruesome were the human heads Mo displayed in jars. The cards told the public that they were the heads of mass murderers stolen from their graves. The police had been called several times to the fair as it travelled the country, yet each time they left satisfied that the heads were just models.

However, while the fair was at Newcastle, one visitor to the Emporium recognised the face of one of the heads – it was *her father!* He had died the previous year when the fair was in town. Mo must have spotted a fresh grave and taken the opportunity to add to his exhibits, servering the head roughly with a spade.

She screamed and caused a huge rumpus, demanding that the police investigate. Mo tried to quieten her down, claiming that the heads were only clay, but this didn't placate her.

The following morning the police arrived, but Mo and his emporium had gone. On locating him three days later at Alnwick, they searched the tent for the heads but they were nowhere to be seen; neither were the specimens – which included babies – in glass jars. Nothing could be proven.

*The descendants of Mo still have a regular plot at travelling fairs.

NEWCASTLE'S PHANTOM OF THE THEATRE

Newcastle's Tyne Theatre is a beautiful building now restored to its former glory having been a soft-porn cinema for many years. It may have been built for people without any legs, but it is a tremendous building.

The ghost that resides in that building is rather like the Phantom of the Opera, often seen, but never witnessed. It is the ghost of a theatre-goer who was less than fortunate in his inadvertent 'audience participation'.

Many years ago during a performance of a play an old-fashioned gadget was used to create the sound of thunder. It was a metal track that swung around the top of the set over the heads of the upper gallery, 'the gods', and back behind the stage again. How it worked was very simple, you merely placed a heavy bowling ball on the top of the slide, and as it ran over the metallic channel it 'thundered'. One night, however, the track was very slightly buckled, and as the bowling ball built up speed it hit the buckle, and flew off hitting an unfortunate man in the audience and killing him.

The apparatus was taken apart so no similar accident could occur, and an alabaster figure was placed in the seat of the dead man, as for years people refused to sit in that spot.

*The spirit that resides in the theatre has been seen by thousands, including the theatre's cleaners, one of whom told me in 1984:

'Once I was cleaning the stairs when he walked past me. I thought it was one of the staff, I turned to tell him to watch his feet on the slippy floor, when he just disappeared!'

*It is said that the ghost is a bit of a pesky poltergeist too, stealing props, hiding items of clothing and making things move of their own accord.

One year impersonator Jessica Martin couldn't find her woollen jumper and suspected an unkind joke. No one had the guts to tell her it may not have been something earthly that had half-inched her pully.

*Young actress Sharon Percy, who starred in the title role of the very successful stageplay *Annie*, said, 'I was very young, and felt a lot of strange things. As if someone was pushing past you, yet when you look there is no one there. You'd put a brush down on the table, next time you look it's on the chair. Stuff like that is common at the Tyne.'

*The Tyne Theatre were kind enough to allow me to place two listeners to *Night Owls*, my late-night chat show, in the theatre overnight.

So two total sceptics, Sandra and Marjorie, both bundles of fun, were locked in, and told to keep by the phone and awake.

The telephone in the theatre went berserk, lights flashed on and off and their own radio began to suffer the most dreadful interference. This made them begin to get the wind up, but things were to get much worse. Sandra tried to take a photograph of Marjorie sitting next to the alabaster figure, but the camera wouldn't work, even though it had worked perfectly an hour before. They took the camera outside and it worked perfectly there.

WHEREVER YOU GO YOU'RE SURE TO FIND A GEORDIE

Three days before Harry Fallon died he sent me an old wrinkled document about his great-great-great-grandfather.

Robert Fallon had travelled to America and had earned a basic living as a carpenter in and around San Francisco in the 1850s. To supplement his earnings he would go into saloons and play poker. The West was still wild and woolly in those days, and selecting your opposition was impossible. So you took a chance, some nights you could win a fortune from cattlemen or merchants, on other evenings you would be fleeced by cardsharps and gunmen. Over an average week he was well ahead.

But while he was playing a game at the Bella Union saloon one of the other men in the game, known as 'Wildeyes', pulled back the table to see an extra card on Fallon's lap. He stood up, drew his Colt, and slowly pulling back the hammer, he fired four shots into Fallon's head and chest. Cheating at cards was almost as heinous a sin as stealing a man's horse or hitting a woman. Shootings were fairly common in San Francisco, so the body was covered up and put in a backroom until the undertaker and the Sheriff could arrive.

Rather than let it spoil the night, the blood was wiped off his chair, and they shouted along the bar to see if anyone else wanted to play cards.

Most people were reluctant to take a dead man's place, but one young man stepped forward, sat down and began to deal.

By the end of the evening he was quite a rich man, having cleaned out his opposition. The amazing coincidence was that he was Joe Fallon, the son of the man who had been shot hours before. He had not seen his father for years, and was not aware he was even in San Francisco.

Joe Fallon returned to England after spending ten more years in America as a professional gambler. Fate certainly played a hand on that bloody night, when a son filled his father's shoes.

NEWCASTLE'S WILLIE WATCHER

At the end of Nelson Street in Newcastle there is a pub that used to be called the Cordwainers that had a most peculiar and playful phantom. It waited until you were in the gentleman's toilet then it would begin playing games. Sometimes it would turn the light out on you. Other times it would push you into the urinal stall, soaking your trousers and making you piddle down your legs.

The scariest of its tricks would be to wait until your yellow river had begun and then tap you on the shoulder, breathing a foul beery stench into your face as you turn around.

Other customers had had pennies thrown at them while seated in the cubicle, yet they knew they were the only ones in the toilet.

Customers regularly complained that whilst in the toilet they felt as if there was someone watching them. Occasionally they even chose to use the toilets in nearby Eldon Square rather than spend a penny in the Cordwainers.

One Saturday morning they were hosing the toilet walls down, after a particularly messy Friday evening and something turned off the hose half-way through.

Once the bar manager found a red sludgy substance on the banisters, which he couldn't remove. It took four people a week to get it all scraped off and destroyed. Having seen the film *Ghostbusters*, they thought it similar to ectoplasm.

The Cordwainers was known for having long lights hanging down about eight feet from the ceiling. One night an entire pubful of people were terrified when every single light began to swing from side to side, without anyone having touched them!

It has been renamed, since when there have been no episodes reported . . . yet.

THE PHANTOM OF WINDOWS ARCADE, NEWCASTLE

A girl called Carol who had worked in a shop in Newcastle upon Tyne's Royal Arcade (often known as 'Windows Arcade' from the music store J. & G. Windows that takes up much of the space) for years and told me how she had often seen something rather eerie. Each evening after six, when she had completed her paperwork, she would walk through the building and let herself out of the huge metal gates that were secured each evening. She was usually the last to leave, and witnessed on at least thirty occasions an odd and terrifying apparition. I asked her to jot down her story back in 1982. 'Each time I've seen him he has been bleeding from the head and mouth, and he's wandering about as if he was blind, walking with his arms held out. The people in the Arcade say that someone was murdered in here, but I don't know anything about that.'

Carol once dared to challenge whatever it was: 'It was in September 1977. I saw the man coming towards me so I shouted out, "What do you want? Can you not just leave me alone!" As soon as I raised my voice the figure just vanished. I didn't see him again for almost a year.'

I made a few enquiries as to whether there had been a murder or a death in the Arcade and apparently there had been. A clerk for the Trustees Savings Bank had been beaten to death. The man,

Joe Millie from North Shields, was found in his office in the bank, his skull shattered to pieces and his face battered to a pulp, the carpets soaked with his blood. He had been murdered with a poker that lay at the scene covered with his blood, hair and sinew.

Whether this is Millie's ghost or not remains uncertain, but it sounds pretty close.

THE VIKING OF ROWLANDS GILL

There is a romantic tale about a Viking family who had fallen out with their warlord Hagga, and had escaped to the north of England, setting up home at Gibside. They erected a small lean-to, and with the tiny stream nearby they could survive, hunting in the woods and growing some basic foodcrops.

The locals were at first very worried about having a full-blown Norseman living beside them. A fearsome-looking mountain of a man, Bidor stood well over six foot tall, and had muscles in his spit! His beard was so bushy it was if he was looking over a hedge.

After almost a year had passed the people began to accept him and his family into the fold, and often went with him on his hunting trips. Legend says that he could hurl an axe almost 200 feet, and struck down many a stag or wild boar.

One autumn day a Viking longboat sailed up the Tyne, docking at Swalwell (where the Marina is currently sited) and the wild men from Scandinavia poured off to steal, rape and ravage. By chance one of the Vikings spotted and recognised Bidor's son, and began chasing him, as the youngster tore off into bushes. The boy was barely fourteen and they trailed him to Gibside, bursting in on Bidor's wife as she prepared a meal. Treating the entire family as traitors they disembowelled the boy in front of his mother, slaughtering the other two children in their cots. They tied Breda, Bidor's wife, to a tree outside the hut, and lay in wait for the Viking refugee to return.

Bidor and his fellow hunters had been told of the Viking landing, and were rushing back to their homes, none more keenly than the Norseman. What made him stop no one will ever know, but instead of returning home he made his way down to the Tyne where the longship lay at anchor, guarded by three burly Vikings. Bidor approached them cheerily, they reciprocated, but once he got aboard he swung his axe taking off the heads of two of the men with a single stroke. The third drew his sword, but had no time to use it before he too was downed.

As, one by one, the Vikings drifted back towards the boat and stepped aboard, Bidor would kill them, rescuing dozens of young girls taken as slaves or bedwarmers.

Finally, one of the Viking leaders rolled up to the ship, drunk and swearing, laughing at the times he had had ashore. Bidor grasped him by the throat and told him never to return to the Tyne again. The Viking spat in his face, so Bidor brought his body down on his knee, breaking his back. The Norseman wasn't dead, but his spine had snapped, and he couldn't move anything but his eyes, which darted to and fro in a panic.

Bidor had killed most of the crew, and there certainly wouldn't be enough men left to guide the ship home, so he returned to Gibside.

Nearing his hut, he heard talking in one of the bushes, and he crept stealthily through the greenery, to see a carefully laid trap. Four men on one side, two across the other side of the clearing, directly behind a tree where Breda was tied.

He saw a huge red stain on the ground, and there in the middle of it was his eldest son, his eyes looking up to the skies but seeing nothing. He knew that they would have killed his babies too, and a volcano of emotion welled up inside him. Although he was barely ten yards from the four Vikings Bidor stood up and roared his pain and torment to the world. With an axe in one hand and a sword in the other he was with one bound amongst them, swinging and swinging until the four Vikings lay in pieces before him.

The other two ran towards Breda shouting, 'Kill her, kill her!' As the first neared the petrified woman, he raised his sword to hack her to death when Bidor's arm swept down in a flash sending his axe spinning through the air, deep into the Viking's chest. The other Viking turned to run, yet tumbled into three of Bidor's friends who lived in the Gill, and they were swift to club him to death.

It is said that Bidor's heroism saved the people of the valley from further Viking attacks, and they all saw out the rest of their lives in peace.

*I sent a friend, Father Flanagan, to visit the site, and he claimed to hear strange voices, not speaking any language he could identify. He doesn't believe for a second in ghosts, but that language could have been Scandinavian.

*It is believed that my family line began in that part of the world: many people think that I still have a face like a Norse!

THE RUDCHESTER ROMAN

A bizarre event took place in 1971 when the Dobson family from Filey decided to spend a week camping along Hadrian's Wall.

They had no particular knowledge of the history of the area, although they knew that several forts along the wall, which stretches from the east coast across to the west coast, had been inhabited by Roman soldiers. They were far more interested in the breathtaking scenery of Northumberland and the Border Country than in the various piles of stones.

They spent their first night parked on the sea front outside South Shields and started moving inland along the northern bank of the Tyne. As Newcastle's West End peters out into suburbia they had a meal at a local pub, then set up camp near what used to be called Vindobala or the Rudchester Fort. They had first parked down a dark road near a quarry but had decided to move.

The two children were bedded down early in the cramped caravan, and Frances and Bill Dobson brewed a pot of tea on their Calor gas stove. It was a warm, balmy evening and reinforced against the wind by a drink or two, Bill decided to take a walk out into the darkness. The moon was full, and the sky was illuminated by the reflections of the streelights of Fenham, Benwell and Slatyford, a few miles down the road.

Frances had a cup of tea and a fig roll, and impatiently waited for her husband to return. She couldn't stray far from the caravan because of the sleeping children. So instead she walked towards a rough, dry-stone wall and lit a cigarette. As she did so she put her hand behind her to rest on the wall, and felt something cold and steely. Startled, she jumped up and turned around to see a man covered with dirt. She asked him what the hell he thought he was doing, and received an answer that was unintelligible, obviously in a foreign language.

She tried to look him up and down, but with the moon constantly dimming as the clouds relentlessly rolled by, she was unable to see much. She did however, catch sight of a glimmer of metal, and of a dark ruddy-coloured robe that had the most obnoxious smell.

She walked slowly back towards the caravan, and the man walked behind her; her sand shoes made no sound, but he flip-flopped along in what seemed to be sandals. When Frances got to

39

the caravan she reached inside the door for a torch, but when she turned around the man was gone. All that remained was a horrendous stench that filled her chest. The smell was similar to that of a boneyard.

Slowly but surely Bill ambled back, and refused point-blank to believe his wife's story. She, however, had been so alarmed that the following day she stopped at a tourist information centre and asked about the fort. She was neither the first nor the last visitor over the years to claim to have seen a Roman soldier, or soldiers, along Hadrian's Wall.

*The most famous sighting was when a coach party of over forty men, women and children saw four fully-armed Roman soldiers running along the top of the wall. The truth was less than dynamic: it was a group of four clerks from the DHSS Longbenton raising money for charity by running the length of the Wall in fancy dress.

Frances Dobson even phoned a lecturer at Newcastle University, who confirmed that the Romans at Rudchester Fort would indeed wear a ruddy-coloured tunic, as they were the First Cohort of Frisiavones.

On discussing what this stranger said, the lecturer spoke in a strange tongue and asked if that resembled the man's words. It may well have been Roman but it wasn't close to the original. Then the lecturer tried again, and at once Frances said, 'Yes that's it, that's definitely it!' The lecturer was speaking Dutch.

That particular Roman cohort was made up of 'honorary Romans', containing an entire tribe from Holland.

There was no way Frances Dobson could have known about the Dutch connection, and to this day she swears that she saw a Roman soldier, still guarding Hadrian's Wall.

It explains the smell too, if you're over 1,900 years old I think you can allow yourself a hygiene problem.

THE JACKHAMMER MAN OF SOUTH SHIELDS

If you lived in or around South Shields in the 1840s you would know Jack the Hammer, a traveller who picked up manual labour as he found it. He would carry out any jobs such as carpentry or repairing pots and pans. Although everyone felt comfortable to have him around he never managed to gather any friends around him. He lived in a part of South Shields that is now known as 'The Nook' and remained almost a hermit in his own home.

He never answered a knock at his front door, merely stared down from his tatty net curtains, a tall blond man with sagging shoulders and a huge beak-like nose, grimacing at anyone that dared bother him. People were so often rebuffed that they simply stopped calling on him. Neighbours never heard a sound from him, even when he was at home for long periods. When, in his fifties, he suffered a bout of flu he remained in bed and tried to sleep it out of him. All that happened was that he became weaker and weaker, eventually dying from lack of nourishment.

His neighbours were not aware that he had died, and the body began to decay in the rocking chair that he died in. Eventually, though, a pungent stream of mixed bodily fluids began to seep down on the couple that lived below him. They were eating lunch when a dripping began, dropping into their soup. At first they thought it to be condensation, but it built up to be a fair old stream, stinking out the lower flat.

On investigating they discovered the man almost mummified. He was covered in cobwebs and sat there palely as they shrieked in horror.

He was carried out of the house in the chair, covered with a sheet, and taken away for burial on the back of a cart. In due course the house was sold and nothing untoward was reported. However, many of the South Shields people claim regularly to see the shape of a stooping man at around six in the evening, walking along 'The Nook'. Some said that he appeared on the riverside during times of thunderstorms and gales as a sign that someone is about to be lost at sea.

Other tales tell of how he hammers out a warning of impending doom on the wall of any house occupied by a man who goes out to sea.

*In 1941 Mrs Margaret Brown heard tremendous hammering sounds on the side of her home in South Shields. Two days later she received a letter saying that her son had lost his life aboard the HMS *Hood* sunk by the *Bismarck* when only a handful of the 1,421 crew managed to survive.

*In 1982 Mr Roger Douglas of Tynemouth was staying with his friend Paul Somerville in South Shields. He was woken by a loud hammering on the wall of the house, and immediately looked out of the window as the hammering continued. There was no one there.

The following Saturday Paul received a letter from an aged persons' home to say that his mother had died.

THE EBCHESTER INCINERATION

They say 'Where there's a will, there's a relative' and such was the story of Robert Johnson, a rich landowner who lived on the outskirts of Ebchester in the 1760s. A hardworking and frugal man who didn't believe in wasting money, he spent the last twenty years of his life trying to instil this into his son, to no avail. The son, a spoiled brat, paid no heed to his father, buying drinks for anyone and everyone, spending a fortune on prostitutes, and gambling at every opportunity.

During a blazing row over huge sums paid to a local farm girl whom his son had made pregnant, Robert Johnson changed his will to disinherit his son. This, he thought, would oblige the young man to work for a living, and perhaps give him some real character.

Legend has it that one Sunday, Johnson declared to the entire church congregation: 'May my right arm burn away before I give my son sixpence.'

Five years later his son had become a changed man, holding down a steady job, with a wife and young children. Robert Johnson decided to change his will again, reinstating his son.

In ther course of time, Johnson died, leaving his fortune to his son. Friends and relatives came to pay their last respects to the body lying in the library of his Ebchester home. As one of his cousins leaned over to give him a last kiss, she smelt burning. The undertaker rushed in to pull back the sheet, and saw that Johnson's right arm had burned away to nothing!

THE HAWK OF HIGH FORCE

In the twelfth century a violent murder took place on the cliffs overlooking England's highest waterfall, near Middleton in Teesdale. It involved a brute of a man called Bob Milburn who had long had a blood feud with the Robson family from Barnard Castle. Big Bob was a cutthroat of a rogue, who thieved, bullied and intimidated his way through life. He had no one to tame him or bring him to heel, so ended up totally out of control. Big Bob fought Tommy Robson on the rocks above the falls and eventually battered his head to pulp with a rock. To cover up the murder he dragged the body across to the torrents of clay-brown water that feed the falls, and pushed the body into the stream, and watched as it rocketed over the edge. It seemed to be the perfect killing. Bob Milburn looked around to see if there were any witnesses and there were none, save one hawk that seemed to hover directly over him.

The Milburns used to drink at the local inn nearby, and now, every time Bob looked up he saw the bird, bright eyes homing in on him.

But soon he was planning another murder. He invited Frank Robson, the leader of the Robson clan, to High Force for 'a chat'. However, for some unexplained reason, Frank's young daughter Elsie came instead. Milburn was disappointed as he'd planned a major coup against his most despised foe, now all he had was this child. She asked what he wanted, but he said he would only talk at the top of the falls. So slowly and delicately the young lady ascended the crudely built steps to the very top of High Force. Milburn's mind was working overtime – if he negotiated with a child his reputation would be destroyed. But, he thought, he could rape her – then send her back to the Robsons as the ultimate insult. On getting to the top of the falls, Elsie Robson removed her shawl to show a wimple. She was a nun.

This shook Milburn, but soon he had decided that to rape a nun would be an even greater show of disrespect to the adversary. Instead of talking he walked menacingly towards her, pushing her back off the rocks on to the grassy knoll. She screamed and ran towards the edge of the falls shouting, 'If you come near to me I'll jump!'

'Then jump, you stupid cow,' barked Milburn. 'Why did you come instead of your father?'

'You would have killed him, like you did his brother.'

'Aye,' said Big Bob, 'and like I'd have killed you!'

He began walking towards the girl, and was just about to grab her when suddenly a hawk swooped down and clawed at his eyes. It flew back into the skies carrying the eyeball and some gory sinew. Milburn screamed in anguish and ran at the Robson girl, pushing her over the edge. The hawk swooped down again and seized the girl's dress in its talons, fluttering frantically to ease her safely on to the rocks nearby. Then the bird spotted its prey, the one-eyed monster on the cliff, and without a pause, flew at him.

Milburn tried to run, yet every which way he ran the hawk was there before him. Eventually he was shepherded back to the edge and found himself falling, not over the falls, but on to a small shelf some twelve feet from the top. His relief lasted only until he discovered that there was no way off, except to jump about a hundred feet on to the rocks below. There was no way he could climb back up the cliffs.

'Save me, please save me!' he shouted to the Robson girl.

She turned away, saying 'You are now in the hands of God.'

Milburn eventually starved to death, as no one who saw his plight thought he was worth saving. He was such a villain, everyone was glad to see him out of circulation. His body lay on the rock for almost ten years before a strong wind tore what was left of the corpse from the cliff face and sent it careering into the foam.

*Legend claims that the hawk watches over High Force to make sure that justice is done. Many hawks are seen there every day.

MAN EATER OF SEAHAM

One of the toughest 'grisly trails' to follow was the story of a merchant seaman from Seaham Harbour on the north-east coast. A man known locally as 'Slavvery Jack' had started visiting a girl called Beatrice Robinson, much to the disapproval of her puritanical father, who ran a grocer's shop. Jack's nickname 'Slavvery' had come about because he always flirted with the local women, calling them 'my dear lady', 'you sweet poppet', 'princess' and his favourite phrase, 'precious buttercup'. This did nothing to endear him to Mr Robinson. Fortunately, Jack was at sea for most of the year and would appear for no more than six weeks a year. During Jack's time aboard ship Mr Robinson tried to matchmake his daughter with any suitable young man in the vicinity, all to no avail.

In January 1909 Beatrice was thrilled and Mr Robinson horrified when Jack announced he was giving up the sea and settling in Seaham for good. He even had the audacity to enquire if Mr Robinson would employ him in his grocer's shop; the reply he received was far from polite. Finally, Mr Robinson told Jack that he could never marry his daughter, and swore that he would see to it that she never saw him again.

Within days Jack was off to sea again, his last trip before seeking work on land. Beatrice knew that his ship was leaving the Wear to travel to Africa, and decided that she would smuggle herself aboard ship. This she did, and made herself known to the ship's captain only when they were three days out at sea, and couldn't turn back.

Her father knew what she had done, and each evening around six he would walk along Seaham Harbour wall waiting for his daughter to return.

Jack and Beatrice were married at sea on 21 April 1909, little knowing that they would be married for less than 48 hours. Beatrice fell ill with food poisoning, and the ship had to land on the Gold Coast, where during a fever fit she choked on her own vomit and died. She was buried close to the beach, and Jack was allowed to stay there until the ship returned to collect him on the way back. Jack was inconsolable; his only ambition had been to settle down with the woman he loved, and now she was planted in a strange land hundreds of miles away from the home that she loved.

At that time Africa was firmly under the thumb of the white money men who ruled with the lash and the gun. So Jack was treated well, and a local tribe gave him shelter and food. What Jack didn't realise was that he was being fed with human flesh. Lost in his grief he would sit out in the sun at temperatures of up to 115° Fahrenheit, his hardened skin flaking from his body. He seemed impervious to pain; he once stood on some sharp coral which sliced off his smallest toe, yet all he did was bind the wound then continued his walk.

Almost three months passed, and the ship returned to find a stranger waiting for them. Jack had grown a long white beard, his face was blistered and burned, and his eyes were mad and staring. At first the Captain refused to believe this was the man he had sailed with for almost fifteen years, and had it not been for a distinctive anchor tattoo on Jack's shoulder he might have left him there.

When the ship got back to the Wear, Jack ran off into the town centre, without his pay or belongings and was never seen again. Or was he?

This is where the stories differ, the first version of the tale tells of how Jack returned to Seaham and told Mr Robinson of his daughter's fate, whereupon the old man suffered a heart attack and died. It is said that on foggy nights you can see the shape of a rotund old man waving a lantern towards the sea, in a desperate attempt to beckon his child home.

The juicier finale to the story came from Captain R. McNulty, a merchant seaman who retired in the 1940s.

Jack, the captain reported, slipped away from his ship in a raging madness, kicking and punching harmless passers-by. He was totally demented and even assaulted a policeman near a local shipyard. Although he knew Sunderland well, it took him three days of meandering around Wearside before he found his way to Seaham, where he stayed hidden until he tracked down Beatrice's father making his evening trek to the harbour to wait for sign of a ship carrying his beloved daughter.

At this time David Lloyd George had presented 'the People's Budget' that involved a new 'supertax' of sixpence in the pound for all those earning over £5,000. This had broken many businesses and had added to the numbers of beggars on Wearside. When Mr Robinson came upon this mad, bearded shape he presumed it to be another broken soul with his hand out. He raked around his pockets for a couple of farthings, hurling them into Jack's face as he strode past him. Jack, mad beyond any hopes of recovery, picked up a wooden stake and crashed it into the skull of the grocer with such force it cracked like a coconut. Blood exploded across the harbour wall, as Jack hammered blow after blow into the lifeless man's corpse, mashing his face beyond recognition. In his insanity, Jack believed that Beatrice had died because her father would not let her live her own life, so his own life had been forfeit.

Jack picked up the old man's body, placed it in some sacking and heaved it across his shoulders and marched it through Seaham. It was dusk and no one took any notice of what they presumed to be a tramp. He walked for miles until he set up a camp on the outskirts of Cold Hesledon. There, having lit a fire to cook his supper, he took out his knife and skinned the old man's body, placing his innards on the fire and feasted upon them.

The locals believed that Mr Robinson the grocer had fallen into the sea that night, as a storm had risen; others claim he travelled to Africa in search of his lost child. What actually seems to have happened is rather more vile – he was completely eaten up by his son-in-law.

A rhyme aboard merchant ships at the time went:

'Auld Slavvery Jack took a bride
She took a fit and sadly died.
Her father waited and he cried
Until our Jack took him inside.

46

He soon cured the auld man's pains,
He ate his liver and stewed his brains.
You can hear him screaming down leafy lanes
As Slavvery Jack scrapes down the stains!'

Jack died two years later in a fight with a man in a public bar in Murton. He was never charged with any crime, and not a trace of the old man's body was ever uncovered.

*One letter, sent in by Mrs L. Knighton from Sunderland, told of a man who had lived in the early 1900s who used to go around all of the local hospitals asking for the amputated limbs of patients. He claimed they were for his own medical research – but some say he wanted them for cannibalistic purposes. At first I thought this story was of no consequence, then I wondered . . . could this have been 'Slavvery Jack' looking for food after he'd consumed the carcass of Mr Robinson?

NONE SHALL SLEEP AT WILLINGTON MILL

Willington Mill used to be an old Quaker House owned by a most puritanical man who ruled his family with a rod of iron.

In the late 1970s it was taken over by a man who was determined to make it into his home. Yet after twelve years of abject misery he was driven out by what he claimed was 'a madman in white'. The room on the second floor was always freezing cold; it had been the Quaker's private study, where he would beat his children until blood ran down their backs. It was said that he had sexually abused his daughters too, but in those days such things never came out in the open. That room felt evil; it had a strange eerie atmosphere that even the uninitiated could sense.

The white 'madman' infested the rest of the house too, leaving the fridge open to damage the food and soak the kitchen floor; turning the fire up full until there was a risk of burning the house down; making washing in the machine dirty; creating a mixture of vile smells in various parts of the house. And the noise – almost every day there was banging, the crashing of doors, the smashing of ornaments. It got too much to bear and at last the man moved out, only too glad to leave. As he made his way down the path to his car, he looked back, and there at the window on the second floor, stood the Quaker, in white, roaring with laughter.

47

NORTHERN ENGLAND
TO THE MIDLANDS

THE BLOODY FOOTPRINT OF OAKWELL HALL, BIRSTALL

The winter of 1684 was an extremely cold one: the River Thames had frozen so completely that a 'Frost Fayre' was held, with stall holders setting up shop on the ice, for people to slip and slide their way around this amazing market. Eventually sawdust was placed on the ice so the older people could also peruse the variety of displays. So thick was the ice that they even roasted meat on spits, played football, quoits, throwing the cock, ninepins and various other games. The most extraordinary sight was thirty horses and their riders galloping over the ice in a mock fox hunt. Music was playing and children all enjoyed themselves on their primitive 'skeetes' (ice skates).

The rest of England was gripped by one of the fiercest cold snaps in history. Snowdrifts of up to forty feet had been seen in Scotland, no roads in Northumberland were passable and the Yorkshire moors were a death trap. Thousands of cows, sheep, horses and goats froze to death where they stood.

In spite of the deathly cold weather young William Batt of Oakwell Hall, Birstall, in West Yorkshire, had been called to London on business. He set off, promising to be back on Christmas Eve to share an old-fashioned family celebration. Two days before Christmas Eve his family watched him walk into the house, not saying a word despite his lengthy absence. His face was pale and gaunt and his eyes deeply sunk into his head as he sombrely climbed the stairs to his room.

The family knew something was troubling him so allowed him some peace, but prepared his supper and set his place. Then they called for him to come down. When he didn't they went to look for him. He was not in his room and they scoured the house. No sign of him was found. But there, on the varnished staircase, was

49

a bloody footprint. They tried to clean it but it would not go away, remaining there until the New Year.

After Christmas, word reached Oakwell Hall that William had been set upon and murdered on the night of the 22nd, the very evening they all had witnessed his return.

It is said that every year on 22 December the bloody footprint returns and is so wet you can touch it and it will mark your hand.

THE BRADFORD GROPER

Poltergeist activity can often be particularly violent, but short-lived, ending as swiftly as it began. It is rare that you can identify the troubled soul that is in such violent torment that it wishes to make as many lives as miserable as possible. One case that springs to mind is of a particular pesky poltergeist from Bradford in the late seventies.

Douglas Smith was a very confused young man, having spent several months in mental hospitals, and getting very little help. His parents knew he was disturbed, but loved and cared for him as best they could. They owned a small terraced house in Stott Hill, and tried to give Douglas whatever he wanted. His passion was going to the theatre or the cinema, and there was a glut of such places in Bradford in 1979. The only problem was that Douglas enjoyed visiting these places not to watch the show or the movie, but to annoy and disturb the audience. He was thrown out of the Majestic Cinema eighteen times for grabbing the legs of young girls or swearing at people who complained that he was singing.

The Alhambra Theatre had barred Douglas after he had pulled down a lady's low-cut boob tube during a pantomime. He was a well-known pest to the Odeons 1 and 2 on Princes Way, and the ABC had finally closed their door to him after he had excreted on a seat in the front row in full view of the audience.

Finally the only place for Douglas to go was the Cine Centa Cinema on Cheapside. Surprisingly he was learning to behave himself; he would still try to disturb people, but he tried to do it in ways that he couldn't be barred for. He'd rustle his bag of popcorn, he'd make a loud slurping noise, sucking at a drink carton for over an hour long after it was empty. At least he still had one cinema to visit. Then fate played a tragic card, he had just been to watch *The Maltese Falcon* at a special season of Bogart films, and was walking home when he stepped out to cross Forster Square without looking and was hit by a furniture van that crushed him against the crash barrier. He was hospitalised for months; on getting home his condition just seemed to worsen and he died within six months of the accident.

It was then that for a month there were 38 separate incidents at cinemas across the city.

Marion Ross, an usherette, was interviewed by an American phenomena magazine in 1980. 'I have worked for three of the cinemas and know a lot of the staff, and things have really gone crazy. Women are screaming out loud in the middle of films, saying someone is groping them. You know, putting their hands up their skirts or grabbing their boobs. I was goosed once. I saw someone coming into the cinema after the picture had started so I got up and walked up the stairs to guide them into a seat, and I felt a hand slide up my thigh and squeeze my bum. I spun round to give them a slap but there was no one there. I know the other cinemas are having things like this happen too; I don't know if they're all haunted, but I'm sure that something's going on!'

Although at that time people hadn't linked the late Douglas Smith with these incidents, something was to happen that was so incredibly weird that it brings us to no other conclusion.

It was one month to the day that Douglas had died, and his parents Rose and Peter Smith decided that they would visit the ABC Cinema on Charles Street. During the film a girl four seats away from the Smiths screamed, and her flared skirt could clearly be seen being lifted by some unseen force.

At that moment Rose Smith yelled, 'Douglas, no more, damn you!' The cinema was suddenly plunged into darkness as the lights fused; all that was left was the dim green glow of the exit signs. Members of staff begged for calm, and within minutes the film resumed.

Across Bradford, cinema audiences could relax for the poltergeist that was once Douglas Smith has never appeared again.

Did his mother really damn him? Is he frightened she'll tell him off again? Or has he just not found a film to interest him? Only time will tell. Whatever the truth really is, it is reassuring that even beyond the grave you still pay heed to your mam!

LEATHERY COIT OF ELLAND

Out of all of the names to spring from Yorkshire surely Leathery Coit must be one of the strangest. Leathery was a well-known travelling salesman, selling a variety of wares ranging from cloth to wines. His well-established path covered all of Yorkshire and parts of Lancashire. At the end of each day he would return to his base, the Fleece Inn at Elland, where he would stable his horse then enjoy a few bevys with his pals. His routine never changed, and as usual Leathery was upstairs late one evening drinking copious amounts of gin when something went sadly wrong. Something, no one knows what, sparked off an argument; then there came a loud crashing sound. The innkeeper set off to investigate, shouting through the closed door, and a voice called back that Leathery was drunk again and had fallen from a chair.

The innkeeper knew that Leathery often overindulged his love for the loopy juice, so he returned to his bed. It was true that Leathery had fallen from his chair, but only when he had been smashed in the face with a wooden club so hard that the bones of his nose were found in the back of his brain. He was killed instantly, his head a disgusting mulch of blood and brains.

The murderer acted quickly and dragged the body as quietly as possible down the stairs into the courtyard. Then he dumped it and fled into the darkness.

He had hoped that people would think that Leathery had left the inn, and was attacked and killed outside. In the darkness the murderer was not aware of the bloodsoaked trail he had left trickling down the stairs and staining the well-trodden floor.

The murderer was never caught, however, and it was said that 'So long as the murderer walks free, the blood shall lie as ye can see.'

The bloodstains can still be clearly seen, and not even the strongest industrial cleaning agents can shift them.

THE GODLESS IN GOATHLAND

In November 1534 King Henry VIII finally broke away from Rome to become head of the English Church, thus taking on the responsibility to deal with heretics. Many said that this was good, as the Roman Catholic Church had a great deal of power, and at a stroke King Henry took total control.

What had started as Henry merely seeking a divorce to allow him to find a wife to give him a son and heir, ended up in a political revolution. The whole of the north of England and the Border Country was a political backwater, and people carried on believing what they chose, until one Catholic decided to use the pulpit to voice his view. Word of this filtered down to the King, and, rather like 'Chinese whispers', by the time the story reached London it sounded like an armed Catholic insurrection. The King contacted his military commanders based at York, telling them to clamp down on all northern Catholics. This they did even when they were not on duty, leading to what was called at the time 'The Massacre of the Innocents'. A family of staunch Catholics lived in a small village called Goathland, south-west of Whitby, and they were known to be the leading lights of the North Yorkshire Catholic community. On learning about them twelve soldiers decided to visit the family and have some 'fun'. They had often laughed at how the Catholics were being forced to knuckle down to the new Church of England. Many priests and Catholics had been put to the sword, hanged or whipped if they dissented.

So, full of drink, the soldiers approached the farmhouse belonging to the family. They saw lights at the window and the spiralling wisp of smoke from the chimney soaking into the black sky. They tied their horses to an old farm cart, spilling its hayload on to the ground, as they drunkenly staggered towards the house. A heavy leather-gloved hand hammered on the stiff oak door until it opened with a creak.

A tiny female face peered into the blackness, staring at the unshaven faces of the soldiers. 'Can I be of service to you gentlemen?' enquired a timid voice. 'Oh, you'll serve us all right,' bellowed the soldier, pushing the door open and barging into the room. A man wearing a nightshirt rose from a wooden chair close to a roaring open fire, and stepped towards the trooper, who drew a sword and speared the man just below the heart. He hung there rather like a marshmallow ready for a toasting, his face knowing what had happened, yet not understanding why. He never would, for the soldier tilted his cavalry sword, allowing the man's weight to slide from the blade, crumbling on to the wooden floor. An older woman ran in from another room screaming loudly, and hurled a pan of boiling water at the soldiers who were surprised, and reacted savagely. They grabbed her, pushed her to the ground and kicked her to death.

The young girl had been held firmly by two of the soldiers, and as she screamed, two younger girls in their very early teens appeared in their nightclothes from an upstairs room.

'Well,' said one of the soldiers, 'it seems we have the night's entertainment to hand!'

The girls were taken upstairs and raped over and over again.

After the brutish men had finished their perverted 'sport', they left the house, hurling fiery torches inside, burning it to the ground.

No one survived the inferno, and the soldiers made their way back to their encampment at Egton.

Justice, however, has a way of catching up with wrongdoers of whatever kind. The troop left Egton to journey up-country towards what is now Darlington to impress upon them the need to belong to the Church of England. As they reached Great Ayton they stopped by the river to take a drink, water their horses and rest a while. The water was contaminated and almost thirty soldiers perished along with seventeen horses. It is said that if you visit Great Ayton, and watch the waters tumbling down the shallow river that cuts right through the town, the frothing waters echo the cries of agony from those poisoned horses.

*Colin McFaddon from Middlesbrough once looked into the river on a bright sunny day in 1990 and swears that he saw an unshaven man staring back at him. he got such a fright he refused to look a second time, in case he saw it again.

*There is a saying 'red sky at night, shepherds' delight' yet around Goathland right up until the middle 1700s whenever there was a beautiful red sky at dusk the people would say 'Tomorrow will be fine, for they're roasting Catholics again.'

THE YORK ROMANS

There are several dozen different ghostly tours you can take when visiting historic York, said to be one of Britain's most haunted cities. Among the most remarkable of the York hauntings are the three separate sightings of an entire Roman legion marching through cellars.

At a shop in The Shambles a haberdasher called Arkwright was shifting boxes around in his cellar when suddenly he heard marching feet from behind the wall. To his astonishment a troop of Roman soldiers then came marching past him. The Romans looked as though they had no feet, their legs appearing to be cut off at the knee by the floor as they walked below its surface. When he reported this incident, he was scoffed at by most, but some said that the original Roman road was almost a foot lower than the cellar floor, which would give some weight to the hapless shop-keeper's story.

Two more identical incidents have occurred in cellars within a hundred yards of the old haberdashery shop, and many York residents swear they have witnessed many 'silkies' and Roman soldiers around the City.

*In 1742 a Roman soldier's armour was found buried in a pit near Baile Hill. The man who found it claimed that the body of the soldier within it was totally preserved, as if he had just died. He gathered his friends around to see the soldier; he looked barely 25 years old, and indeed did look freshly dead. Then, right in front of their eyes, the soldier began to decompose, skin drying and flaking from the bones, the bones then turning to dust, until there was only the armour left. The finder declared that Baile Hill was cursed, and refused to ever visit it again.

*Two middle-aged ladies, Mrs Taylor and Mrs Harding, were walking along Davygate early one Monday morning in 1958 when they heard a metal clattering. On swinging around and looking towards Church Street, they saw about a hundred men fighting with swords. Some were dressed as Romans, the others like tramps wearing animal skins. They couldn't believe their eyes, and didn't know whether to run or to stand perfectly still. The battle came so close to them they could have touched the participants. At that moment a delivery van honked its horn, making both ladies run back to the kerb to let is past. After it had trundled past there was no sign of the vision they had experienced.

Many others claim to have witnessed almost a 'video replay' of battles in the sky around York. It is almost as if history has been captured and re-enacts the entire story from time to time.

*Ray Giles from York was walking across Lendal Bridge early one Sunday morning in 1962, and saw two Roman soldiers guarding the crossing. He took it to be a student prank, perhaps connected with their rag week. On passing he barely glanced at them, until he noticed a small Yorkshire terrier barking ferociously. It ran past him, snapping at the costumed troops, and then went straight through the shin of one of them. They disappeared into a grey mist.

*In November 1992 war veteran Harry Gregg from Leeds was walking through the City War Memorial Gardens on Leeman Road, when he saw a man, wearing very little, lying on one of the graves. He was about to shout for him to show some respect when he noticed that the man was badly wounded, with blood oozing from a deep stomach wound. Harry tried to talk to the man, who spoke in a strange foreign language. Harry then took out his handkerchief, and tried to press it into the wound to stem the bleeding. He looked around for assistance; when he turned back to the bleeding man, he had vanished. Only Harry's handkerchief remained, and it was covered with blood.

THE COTTINGHAM WOLF MAN

Cottingham is now a well-respected suburb of Kingston upon Hull in Humberside, but in the early 1600s it was merely one of dozens of tiny villages that looked to the estuary for work.

In 1603, when Queen Elizabeth died at Richmond, suddenly the thrones of Scotland and England were united under the Scottish king, James VI, who became King James I of Great Britain. This gave many Scots the incentive to come down to England to find work, and such a man was Stewart Scullion. He had no money, no job and no accommodation, and having tried his hand in Doncaster, he turned northwards and set up home on a tiny island on the Humber now known as Read's Island; in the 1600s it was known as the Island of the Wolf. There Scullion built himself an underground shelter, carved out of a bankside. It was warm and safe, and, like any fisherman, he could provide food for his plate.

One day while he was casting his net off the island shore, a rowing boat appeared, carrying a fat, bearded man with a rosy complexion and a cheery grin. It wasn't long before they were sitting by a roaring campfire, sharing stories and eating his newly caught trout.

The man was Francis Clayton, a Cottingham man who worked on the river as a foyboatman, using his small rowing boat to carry the tall ships' mooring cables to the shore where he would then tie them up. His hands were huge and calloused, testifying to the rigours of his occupation. When Scullion fell into a deep, contented sleep, Clayton picked up a rock and smashed it down upon his skull. The Scotsman's head broke open like a coconut, and Clayton leaned down over him, pushed his face into the open brain cavity and began to eat.

Clayton was impressed by the accommodation on the island, and proceeded to use it as his secret retreat. By day he worked on the river, as the jolly boatman; in the evening this woolly-faced man killed and ate men, women and children. Between 1600 and 1622 over eighty people had disappeared in mysterious circumstances, and this takes no account of the many travellers who passed through.

It was in October 1622 that Clayton made his first mistake; he told his foy partner Jack Smith that he liked the taste of human flesh. Smith thought his jocular friend was having him on – until Clayton reached into his bag and pulled out a small human head, cleft open at the top.

Smith ran off and told two soldiers, who thought him either mad or drunk. Clayton roared with laughter.

The experience of seeing a child's head in his friend's bag had driven Smith into a panic, and he managed to convince a local magistrate to act. That evening, six soldiers were despatched to arrest Francis Clayton. His belongings were collected together and he was taken to the magistrate's house in Hessle. On going through the pack they found various strange types of salted meat, and in his satchel they found the half-eaten head of an eight-year-old child.

Within two days Clayton was held for trial by a judge in Beverley, at which point there are differing stories. Some say that Clayton was declared mad and put in a York prison for the rest of his life. The other tale is far more sinister.

During the trial, the jolly and rotund form of Clayton made the jury totally disbelieving of the evidence. In fact, Clayton pointed the finger at Jack Smith, saying that Smith had wanted to take over his job as leading foyboatman and had planted the head in his sack. He was very convincing. But before the trial was over something began to happen to him. Suddenly his back became stooped, the curly beard and hair on his face began to bristle and straighten, and his teeth appeared to be elongating.

Women in the court screamed in disbelief as Clayton went down on all fours and began to howl like a wolf. Two courtroom guards ran to secure their prisoner, and as they wrestled with him, one was badly bitten on the face, and needed a surgeon. The other held him tightly by the neck. It took almost twenty minutes to restrain him, but at last they got him down on the floor. As he lay there he vomited, and there, in the contents of his stomach, was the hand of a small child.

He was taken into the countryside and hanged, his body was buried in unconsecrated ground near the village of Swine.

In 1625 that Clayton's hideaway was discovered on the Island of the Wolf (Read's Island), where they uncovered human bones, pickled flesh and wolf tracks. Was he a werewolf, a cannibal or just a madman? Perhaps we will never know.

Clayton is a fairly common name in the Kingston area – perhaps there are descendants of his among them, and if there are, the question we need to ask is: is his wickedness hereditary?

THE BLACKPOOL WITCHES

When we talk of witches we think of the gnarly wrinkled old hags in Shakespeare's *Macbeth*, yet the good people of Blackpool tell a very different story from World War I.

Three sisters lived in an old house where Forest Gate became North Park Drive, near Stanley Park in Blackpool. They were three of the most charming people anyone could hope to meet, always polite, always well dressed and willing to help anyone. These were dark days for Britain, every news bulletin seemed to spell out more bad news – the Turks attacking Suez, German U-boats sinking supply ships, Zeppelins raining death on our cities and thousands killed in the new offensive in Ypres. It was a time when, with the majority of men fighting overseas, women were urged to leave their homes to keep the factories running. It was May 1915 when the sisters Flaherty, – Emmeline, Flora and Ruth – let it be known that they were trained nurses and were willing to give assistance to anyone who needed it. Medical staff were thin on the ground, many having joined the forces, and those left having to cope with impossible workloads. The Flaherty sisters began taking in orphans and those children who were left at home while the mothers kept the wheels of industry turning.

In these troubled times records were rarely kept, and the sisters used this to full advantage, for they were not nurses, they were witches of the blackest kind.

To everyone living around them they were the caring old ladies who would do anyone a favour, yet behind closed doors they were a very different proposition. Those children who would be returned to their mothers each day were treated well, and kept amused, but others, who had no one to watch over them, were preyed upon by the evil sisters. It was an amazing double life, and the legend that follows is fascinating, yet has been told to me on three separate occasions, so is likely to have some truth to it.

The discovery of their dark deeds didn't happen until long after the Great War was long over. In fact, had there not been the Great

Strike of 1926, they may never have been found out. It was the first General Strike in British history, and was called in support of the miners following a breakdown in their negotiations with the government. Workers downed tools across the country to march, and such was the case in Blackpool. Almost four thousand men, women and children walked up the Golden Mile, up to Church Street, then along Forest Gate and past the Flaherty sisters' house. As they marched they were knocking on people's doors asking them to join the march. One young man, Charles Kennedy, near the back of the procession, knocked at the sisters' house, then looked into the window to see the three women physically abusing a tiny blonde-haired girl who was screaming. He called to his friend, Christopher Herd, who left the march to join his chum on the path of the big old house. Without further ado they broke down the sturdy wooden door, and snatched the child from the three women, who were shocked by the sudden entry. 'She was being naughty and we were disciplining her. This is none of your business!' shouted Flora Flaherty. Emmeline walked up to the two men saying, 'If you do not put that child down, I'll have the police to you!'

Kennedy was beginning to have second thoughts, and Herd was looking very anxious. Perhaps what they had seen was merely a child being smacked. They were about to leave when they heard crying coming from a room at the back of the house. On walking into the back room they discoverde almost a dozen young children aged between three and ten, all chained up and naked. Their young bodies had been cut with razors and one child was unconscious, his eyes cut out of his head.

The two men ran from the house, racing along the road to catch up with the procession as it was being supported by several of Blackpool's police. They all hurried to the house, where only two of the sisters could be found.

A search was carried out, and although a lot of children's clothing was found, and an upstairs bedroom literally ankle-deep in human excrement, there was no sign of the youngsters.

The police began an investigation and the authorities paid the sisters a visit and demanded to know what had been going on. Their only reply was 'What we do in our own home is our business!' The neighbours were questioned; all spoke of the sisters in glowing terms, so eventually the police called off their investigation. Emmeline Flaherty even tried to have Kennedy and Herd prosecuted for breaking and entering.

Yet one day, in January 1927, Ruth Flaherty was out walking along South Park Drive to the south of Stanley Park, when her bag was snatched by a fifteen-year-old boy. He ran off and hid himself in trees near where the Zoo Park is now situated, and looked inside the bag for some money. To his horror he found a small human hand, pickled and partially eaten.

He told his father, who gave him a good hiding for thieving and then reported the matter to the police. The young lad told the police where he had left it, and together they set off to find the bag. It was found exactly where he claimed it would be; however, the hand was gone, possibly carried off by a dog or a fox. The bag was found to belong to one of the Flaherty sisters. Once again the police searched the house, but found no sign of anything untoward. Several meat items were taken away to be analysed, and were duly returned when found to be pork mince and some rather rancid veal.

The sisters placed their house on the market, and moved to Eire, where they soon were well liked by everyone as the kindly ladies they were.

In the late 1930s the sewage pipes of the old Flaherty house were due to be replaced and were dug up. As they dug, the workmen came across a mass of charred bones and decaying flesh. Much of it had been pulverised as if to disguise what it was. There were dozens of teeth, patches of matted hair, all buried beneath the house, and various chemicals had been poured over the remains.

It was at this time that the country once again went to war, so the Flaherty sisters were never traced.

The entire story would have remained a mystery, yet purely by coincidence I came across an American magazine called *Phenomenon* in which I read of an old manuscript sent to them by William McGill from County Cork. He had found it in an old outhouse when he bought his home. It had been written by Emmeline Flaherty in 1948 whilst she was in hospital. It read: 'My sisters and I were born to Satan, and died to join him. I have no fear that we will be reunited. For over sixty years we sacrificed the children to him, hundreds of tributes to his glorious name. We ate of their flesh, and it gave us the power to do the lord's work. In Morecambe for five years, in Blackpool for twenty, in Ireland, we took the weak to make way for the strong. We ask no forgiveness for we were nought but the tools of nature, and lived as nature intended us.'

The house belonging to the sisters in Blackpool became renowned for being haunted. The voices of children crying could be heard, and calls of 'Mummy', and the sound of tiny footsteps running around the attic rooms. In the early 1950s the house was gutted by fire, and it was practically entirely rebuilt. The new tenants knew nothing of its history, and suffered no disturbances of any kind.

A DIRECT LINE TO THE OTHER SIDE

How many times have you heard people say 'I won't believe in ghosts until I've actually seen one myself'? Well, Diane Whittaker from Burnley was one of those. Her mother was a spiritualist medium, and professed to converse with the dead most nights. She claimed to be capable of contacting any relative who had 'passed over', and she had many paying customers convinced that she had a special gift. Literally thousands of folk from Burnley and surrounding villages knew Cecilia, who was quite a character.

Diane, however, thought her mam was 'cuckoo', and had claimed that it was all an act. Many an evening was spent arguing about whether it was or it wasn't, which eventually led to Diane leaving home. When she married and had a family she even kept her children away from their grandmother. Cis, though, continued to insist that she was sincere all the way through. Once she told Diane in front of her friends, 'I can't help being able to do this – they just come to me, and tell me things. I can't ignore them. They're in my head!'

Diane believed they were indeed 'in her head' and that, now in her sixties, she'd started suffering from dementia or some such complaint. Cis's friends had no doubt that she was completely sane.

The arguments continued for almost twenty years between mother and daughter; finally, as her mum's birthday neared, Diane decided to patch things up. At long last they agreed to disagree, and it seemed as if a decent family relationship could be possible. The following day Cis arrived at Diane's house and said, 'Darling I don't want to frighten you, but I'm going away. I don't want you to worry. I'm going to be among a lot of friends.'

Diane was not too concerned, replying, 'Well, wrap up because it's cold . . . but where are you going?'

Her mum merely turned to the door saying, 'You'd not understand, but I'm leaving tonight.'

Not wanting to strain the recently renewed friendship, Diane didn't push it, but did say, 'Well, promise to ring me when you get there.'

Cis shook her hed. 'Promise me,' insisted Diane, 'or I won't let you go!'

Finally her mum agreed and left with a smile on her face.

Two days later Diane's lie-in was interrupted by the hall telephone; grabbing her dressing gown, she plodded downstairs to answer it.

'Yes?' she mumbled sleepily.

'It's me', came the voice. 'I've arrived and I'm all right.'

'Oh good', said Diane, still not completely awake. 'So where are you then?'

Cis hesitated and then said, 'On the other side.'

Diane laughed out loud. 'Come on, be serious, where are you, you silly old bugger?'

'Now, I don't want you to be frightened but I died two nights ago, just after I left you. I'm now here with so many friends I've made over the years. So don't be scared.' Cis's voice was calm and firm.

Diane had really woken up with a bump. 'Mother, you're going stupid again, I thought we'd agreed.'

Cis continued in a warm but businesslike fashion. 'I won't be able to talk with you again, because I will only be able to converse with others like me. When you get to my house you'll find all of the insurance policies in an envelope sellotaped under the bottom drawer of my chest of drawers.'

'But, Mum . . .' interrupted Diane, 'don't be so stupid, it's not funny any more.'

'For once in your life, listen to what I say, Diane,' barked Cis, rapidly running out of time and patience. 'My personal jewellery and what little money I've got I want you and the children to have. It's there with my will underneath my pillow. I prepared everything before I left. Don't worry about me, and, remember, no matter how we behaved over the years I always loved you, and always will. I love you, Diane; kiss the children for me.'

'I will', answered a totally puzzled Diane, 'but . . . ' At that the phone went dead.

'What a silly cow,' muttered Diane and chuckled to herself, then went off to prepare breakfast. Curiosity got the better of her, however, and with barely one mouthful of toast, she got dressed and sorted through her desk drawer for her mother's house key.

She stopped next door to pick up a friend for moral support, and they set off to her mother's home, a terraced house two streets away.

On turning the key in the lock, Diane knew at once that something was wrong; there was an unpleasant sweetish smell hanging in the air. Cagily they climbed the stairs, passing Cis's handbag at the top of the stairs. She had taken that bag with her everywhere; Diane's late father used to joke how she even took it to bed with her on her honeymoon night. Yet there it was – surely she wouldn't go anywhere without it?

As they gently pushed the bedroom door open they saw Cis lying in bed; she looked so peaceful, snuggled into the blankets like a dormouse in a nest of fluff. There was a dreamy smile on her face, but she was too still and quiet. As they stood by the side of the bed their horror at finding her dead seemed to float from them, and they became touched by the look of absolute satisfaction on her face.

They must have stood there for almost five full minutes totally lost in the wonder of it all, when the telephone fired a shrill ring behind them. 'God, I nearly shit myself!' said Diane, as she lifted the receiver. There was no one there.

The insurance policy, jewellery and will were all exactly where Cis had told her on the telephone that morning. The police, ambulance and doctor were all called, confirming that she had been dead for almost two and a half days. So Cis had called her daughter well over 36 hours after she had died.

GHOST RIDER IN THE SKY

If you seek a peaceful night's sleep one place to avoid is Wycoller Hall, near Colne in Lancashire, the hall used as a basis for Ferndean Manor in Charlotte Brontë's classic novel *Jane Eyre*. This fine Lancastrian building is now sadly in wreck and ruin.

The legend I heard told of a man who hated the owner of the hall, and wanted him dead. One summer night he mounted his horse and rode to do the man to death. On arriving at Wycoller Hall he shouted for the owner to face him, and to duel with pistols. The owner refused, choosing to instruct a servant to kill him dead with a crossbow. A single bolt flashed through the darkness, striking the aggressor in the throat. Instead of falling from his horse he managed to stay in the saddle and rode off into the countryside. He almost certainly died, but no body was ever found.

Now the ruin is haunted by the phantom rider who gallops into the courtyard screaming in agony, then rides off into the mist.

*In 1978 Anthony Garbutt, a student at York University, visited the Hall because he was doing a literature project on Charlotte Brontë. He decided to camp in the grounds overnight, travelling home the next morning. He set up his pup tent and had just settled down to sleep when he heard a thundering of hooves and an unearthly moaning. On sticking his head out of the tent he found himself looking straight up at a black charger only a matter of feet away. There, sitting atop the horse, was a figure dressed in black waving a pistol. He seemed to be bleeding from the throat and screaming inaudibly. Seconds later, the horse had galloped off and silence returned. Garbutt snatched up his things and hitchhiked home.

BLAZING BETTY OF MANCHESTER

It is hard to imagine how it must feel to know that you're burning to death, and harder still to stifle a cry of pain or panic, yet amazingly that is what Betty Byrne is said to have done. Betty used to work in a hotel-cum-lodging house in Fountain Street, Manchester, and was greatly loved by all who knew her. She would take considerable care with each guest, and was always ready to babysit any young children whose parents wanted a night out in Manchester.

One night Betty was looking after an 18-month-old baby girl for the Prescott family visiting from Yorkshire, when something incredible happened. Betty was walking along an upstairs corridor when she caught a glimpse of a guest who appeared lost. She pointed him towards his room, recognising that he was rather the worse for drink. Having seen him on his way she entered the child's room to continue her watch over the child. The guest, a Mr Michael Robertson, had taken quite a fancy to the young chambermaid, watched her as she walked away. To his amazement, the centre of her body seemed to be aglow. A swirling, twirling shape appeared to be flowing from the middle of her back, and as he lost sight of her behind the door she seemed to be catching fire. Robertson could see a bright light shining under the door followed by strong smoke. At this he ran for help, and he and the manager forced open the door. There within a yard of the door were the remains of Betty, burned beyond recognition. Yet her modest uniform was barely touched by the flames. The only part of her body that had not been totally incinerated was her head. Not one hair was singed nor out of place, and although the neck was melted away, supremely cauterised, there on her face was the most contented of smiles. This was not a woman who had died in agony, more someone who had lost her life in exquisite fashion. The baby in the cot was only woken by the intruders who had hammered the door down. Even in death Betty had made sure the child in her charge remained undisturbed.

Spontaneous human combustion was not generally known about, so the management believed that somehow the girl had set herself on fire. The authorities put it down as an accidental death, claiming that Robertson's account was 'fanciful' – an opinion confirmed, they felt, by his admission to having been drunk.

The Shakespeare Hotel, which stands on the site of the old lodging house, has suffered a variety of strange phenomena, believed to have been caused by 'Blazing Betty'. She is often seen at the very top of the stairs, keeping watch over the hotel to make sure everything is running smoothly.

Despite Betty burning in such an intense fashion, some parts of the building have 'cold spots' and sudden chills can fall over a room. This is said to signify that Betty is passing by, and it is often followed by a wave of warmth as the coldness begins to dissipate.

*In 1989 Michelle McIlroy from Stockport phoned a late-night radio show with a story of how she had been drinking with friends at the Shakespeare Hotel in the middle 1970s. It was barely eight o'clock in the evening, no one had yet had much to drink, when four of them saw a young girl dressed in a long flowing cape, and her head was on fire!

One of the party screamed, then the others saw the girl; then, as other customers spun around to see what the panic was, the figure disappeared.

Whether this really was Betty's ghost or not we can't say, as Betty's head was the only part of her not to burn.

OLDHAM'S UNWELL WELL WOMAN

Squalor, filth, disease, discontent, only a few of the words that go towards describing the early 1900s in the tatty suburbs of Oldham. The industrial revolution had drawn thousands of simple country folk into towns and cities. Oldham's thriving factories were quite an attraction to those people who had tried without success to make a living from the land. The Mackays had journeyed from Scotland with their daughter Eliza Jane to take up work at a local mill. They tried to make a home out of a hovel, and so hard was the work that both mother and father turned to drink to escape the deprivation of their domestic circumstances. So little Eliza had two less than perfect role models, finding it difficult to sleep with the drunken squabbling of her parents going on often until the early hours. To keep the child quiet they would give the three-year-old rum in increasing amounts to send her off to sleep. By the time Eliza had reached fifteen she was an alcoholic, unable to last a morning unless she had taken almost half a bottle. At sixteen she was working at an inn at Scouthead, where she was able to get sufficient drink to feed her habit.

She was well liked by staff and public alike, but by late evening she would always be totally paralytic with drink and usually belligerent. If ever there was a girl destined to have an untimely death it was Eliza Jane Mackay, and she lived up to all expectations. Like most legends, accounts differ: did she commit suicide? Was she killed by a lover because she had fallen pregnant? Or had she got so drunk that she slipped and fell? Most agree as to how she met her fate – she drowned in the inn's freshwater well.

It is most commonly believed that the drink had brought on the teenager a major depression, and she decided to take her own life, hurling herself down the well. The well, now owned by a local farmer, can still be seen.

*The ghost of Eliza Jane is regularly seen at the Old Original Inn in Scouthead, Oldham, as a busy spirit floating around the building at high speed.

*In 1922 a local newspaper ran a story about a Scouthead inn (believed to be the Old Original Inn) about a young couple who were canoodling in a field across from the inn when they heard a strange noise. On sitting up they saw a bright light coming from an old well. A strange shape glowing orange and white appeared and floated about two feet above ground level and zoomed at high speed towards the inn. The terrified couple ran off, telling a policeman who chose not to believe them. They were so convinced of what they had seen that they contacted a reporter the following day.

THE SKULL OF WARDLEY HALL

If you journey about six miles out of Manchester you come upon the imposing building known as Wardley Hall. The legend takes us back to the early 1600s when this fine old building was owned by the Downes family. The last male representative of this rather ordinary family was a flash young man called Roger, disliked by everyone who met him. An obnoxious fellow, he was very much wrapped up in himself, dressed like a dandy and was keen to impress everybody with the pitter-patter of his little feats. The truth was that he was bone-idle, spent the family's money on trifles, squandering a fortune on horses, wine and women of ill repute.

He did have a job of sorts, as a courtier to King Charles II. His role was to entertain visitors and provide for their every need. This involved horses, wine and women of ill repute so he could manage very nicely in such a world of vice and corruption.

The rest of the Downes family kept themselves to themselves, rarely ever seeing Roger as he was usually in London whooping it up.

One stormy autumn night Roger's sister Maria was in the drawing room with cousin Eleanor when a tree was blown down outside the hall, the branches scraping past the old wood-framed window. The girls screamed in terror as they looked out upon the gnarled wood which seemed to come to demonic life in its contortions. As they looked out into the swirling rainstorm, their imaginations ran riot, every branch became a monster's arm reaching towards them, every curled leaf turned into a devil's eye winking at them. Their peaceful home seemed transformed into a house of horrors. There was no sign of the storm abating so the girls made their way up to their bedchambers, the draughty old manor making the flames of their candles dance all the way, casting eerie shadows on the bare white walls. The girls, frightened by the storm's ferocity, were discussing the possibility of sleeping in the same bed for a bit of moral support when a loud cry was heard.

At first Eleanor thought it was merely the wind howling along the eaves of the old building. Yet it sounded like a human cry. Surely no one would be calling at the house so late in the evening? Maria drew back the heavy velvet curtains and peered through the rain-streaked windows out into the courtyard. There seemed to be no one there, yet still this cry could be heard. Maria woke one of the servants, a doddery old chap called Dobson, and sent him out into the torrential rain to investigate.

He grumbled his way to the front door and continued cursing as he tried to avoid the deep puddles that were appearing everywhere. Soon the dark figure of the old fellow was lost in the night. The girls strained to hear the cry but it was gone.

They had returned to the drawing room where they sat in front of the dying fire; it hadn't been built up as the girls had been heading to bed. They were just calming themselves when they turned suddenly and there right beside them was a horrific face. The girls both screamed.

'Oh Dobson, it's you?' screeched a trembling Eleanor.

At this Maria collapsed into fits of near-hysterical laughter.

Dobson was soaked to the skin, the little hair he had left on his head stuck to his face like rats' tails. 'I found this parcel, m'lady,' he croaked. 'May I retire to bed now or will you be needing me?'

'No, off you go, Dobson, and thank you,' said Maria as she looked at this curious box.

They left it on a small table and looked at it for what seemed to be ages, too frightened to tear it open. It was difficult to explain, but there was something wrong, something very wrong with this package. It wasn't anything obvious, it just seemed to be evil.

They decided to leave the opening of the box until morning, when common sense seems to pour into the darkest corners of night, transforming a threat into something far less ominous. They retired to their rooms at either end of the same corridor; the box was brought to Maria's room by one of the maids.

Relentlessly the storm crashed on into the early hours, as Maria stared and stared at this menacing package, sitting on a side table directly opposite her four-poster bed. A gap in the curtains allowed brief glimpses of moonlight between the black clouds that slid across the top of the treeline like fingers through a young girl's hair. The rain still tapped on every window as if trying to keep everyone awake. A glint of light seemed to pinpoint the old box, still tied with twine, old twisted nails securing the lid in haphazard fashion, as if placed there by a drunkard.

Maria couldn't sleep, her eyes returning time and time again to the box. It was then the terror really began. Suddenly one of the bent nails fell from the top of the box; then another and another, as if being moved by some invisible hand. The twine so tightly fastened slipped down the sides of the package and the lid began to rise. Maria tried to scream but the cry seemed trapped in her throat as she gazed upon the horrific contents. There, captured in the moonlight, was a human head, severed from the neck, the face all bruised, battered and bloody. So savagely had the man died that the hair was matted and stuck to the head in a huge red-black clot of old blood. Maria never recognised the head as that of her brother Roger, for she had fainted long before any identification was possible.

The following morning Maria was awoken by one of her attendants. As white as a sheet, she glanced towards the box. To her amazement it was sealed, the battered old nails in place once again, the twine securing it as it had arrived. Rather than open the box that had taken years off her life the night before, she instructed a servant to carry the package into the stables.

No sooner had he done so than he raced into the servants' quarters and proclaimed that the Devil was present, lurking in that strange box. No one dared to enter the stable while that box was there. The horses, so used to the warmth and security of the building, chose to remain out in the cold wet fields.

Perhaps the box would have remained there for all time had Rosie not appeared. Rosie was the mistress of the head of the household staff, and would visit him for purely carnal reasons about twice a week. The only time they could spend together was a few hours in the very early morning. Rosie worked at a merchant's house two miles down the road. She was a real Northern beauty, full-figured, curvacious and with a wicked sense of fun. Her curly hair and wide-mouthed smile could illuminate the darkest room. Edwards, her lover, spotted her from the window of his apartment and to his horror saw her walk towards the stables, where they had made love many times. No one had told her about the danger waiting in there in the form of the 'Devil's box' as it had become known. Hurriedly, he pulled on his trousers and was on the verge of rushing down when he saw Rosie coming out of the stable; beneath her cloak she seemed to be carrying something.

Edwards tore down the corridors of Wardley Hall, crashing out of the back door and sprinting towards the courtyard in front of the stables. It was a quiet night, the only noise seemed to come from the garden where it sounded as if someone was digging. As he arrived in the garden he saw a huge hole had been excavated by Rosie, and he was just about to yell when she kicked the box into it.

Without a word being exchanged they both began shovelling earth on top of the accursed box, and then scurried back to the barn. They made love well into the morning, finally falling asleep in each other's arms.

The other servants were relieved and Maria Downes was told that the package had been stolen.

The following month was a happy one for Wardley Hall until one morning the box was found back inside the house next to the window – the very spot that Roger Downes had declared to be his favourite part of the house.

To this day no one can be quite certain how Roger Downes lost his head. Some say he was given the chop by the King for trying to seduce a Royal ward; others that he was sacrificed to the Devil by diabolists he had met in London.

There is a legend that runs parallel with this story, that Downes, on a drunken binge, had sworn to kill the first man that he saw on leaving an inn. This he did, stabbing to death a harmless tailor called Catchpole who was returning home from work. Roger Downes had become an arrogant public nuisance and three months later started a riot near London Bridge. Two people were thrown to their deaths off the bridge and the watchman nearly made a third. However, in his panic to defend himself, the old chap lashed out at Downes with his billhook and severed his neck. Some say the watchman was so desperate to cover up the killing that he sent the box to the sister at Wardley Hall.

When the Downes tomb was opened in 1779 the coffin of Rober Downes was opened to reveal the head still attached. The top of the skull was missing as if sliced open like the top of a coconut. This would appear to confirm the story about his death at London Bridge. A billhook could remove part of the skull, but it would take more than an old man's strength to remove someone's head completely.

This creates a problem as to whose head it is that is still on display at Wardley Hall in a locked case on the staircase wall. It is said that if it is moved, it always finds its way back to the same spot, often punishing the mover by bringing personal misfortune to them.

*Mr Douglas Crawford From Oxford wrote in the American magazine, *Phenomenon*, 'I believe the head to belong to Alexander Barlow, a devout Catholic who was arrested and taken to Lancaster Castle. He had been a friend of the Downes family and when he was beheaded his head was placed on a spike outside the Castle as a warning to other Catholics. It is thought that later that night one of the family's servants was ordered to rescue the head and bring it back to Wardley Hall where they would embalm it.'

*Old London Town was left with a vivid reminder of the skull Of Wardley Hall, for if you visit London Bridge on Midsummer's Eve strange visions will meet your eye. If you stare down at the water you'll see the shapes of the two murdered men hurled off by Downes and his fellow rioters all those years ago.

This sight is so convincing that in 1962 Mrs Dorothy Martin from Shepherd's Bush called the police saying that two men were drowning in the Thames near the bridge. The two floundering phantoms flap at the foamy water in desperation, their hands reaching upwards, begging for help. After a few minutes they disappear beneath the water until the following year when they'll rise again.

THE LIME STREET BEETLE-EATER

Visit any main street in Liverpool after closing time you'll hear strangled strains of 'Dirty Maggie Mae'. There's one line of the song that goes ' . . . and we'll never walk down Lime Street any more', and many people refuse to in case they bump into a strange phantom with the most disgusting of eating habits.

The story goes back to the 1400s when England had chilled to stories of the exiled Prince Vlad V of Wallachia. He was nicknamed Vlad the Impaler or Dracula (*dracul* being Romanian for devil). Vlad had been deposed and put in prison by the Hungarians for thousands of horrendous and sickening crimes against men, women and children. This bloodthirsty individual was said to have killed over 25,000 people by impaling them on stakes; he particularly liked to watch blood dripping, and often at feasts would place a man in a barbed cage so that he would bleed to death while the Prince enjoyed his meal. He terrorised villages and towns, arresting anyone who gave the impression that they disapproved of him. Once he ordered that an entire village be impaled on spikes around his castle walls. He forced young children to eat their own mothers, who were roasted on a spit in front of them. Some stories told of how Vlad had a taste for human flesh and was actually a vampire. With every telling, the tales became more grisly and increasingly vile.

A visiting storyteller arrived from Europe and earned a modest income touring Britain's inns telling of the Prince's atrocities. Most people enjoyed the stories as such, and left the matter there, but not George Edwards, who couldn't get enough of these horrible stories. He particularly liked the story of how a visiting Turkish diplomat had been brought before the wicked Prince, and had refused to remove his turban, so Vlad had it nailed to his head. Edwards, totally engrossed in Vlad Dracul, once nailed an innkeeper's hand to the counter after he refused to give him another drink.

Edwards moved around the countryside, picking up labouring jobs wherever he could, and scaring anyone who met him with his 'strangeness'. It was his ambition to eat human flesh, and he had enquired of a Liverpool doctor what he did with the parts of the body he was called upon to amputate from time to time. The doctor enquired as to what interest Edwards had in anatomy, and was given a complex explanation as to how he worked for a medical student and wanted the parts to learn more about them. During the next twelve years Edwards regularly collected arms, legs, fingers and other body parts that he would take away, cook and eat. He eventually moved from the country into Liverpool where he got himself a job removing the rubbish from the market stalls that had sprung up on almost every street in the centre and along the riverside. It was a time when people would barter their goods, exchanging what they had for whatever they needed. Huge amounts of refuse were left behind and some of the rich landowners paid labourers to collect the rubbish and dump it on the outskirts of town. Edwards was in his middle fifties when the doctor moved from Liverpool to Manchester, ending his supply of body parts, and completely changing Edward's eating habit. To the horror of his workmates, he began eating the seemingly endless number of beetles that thrived among the waste, particularly enjoying the huge cockroaches, crunching their shells as they struggled to escape from his mouth.

He still loved to keep up with the more depraved of current affairs, and was enthralled by the stories coming from Spain of the Inquisition where over 5,000 were 'relaxed' by the church. The term was acceptable in diplomatic circles yet it actually meant that they were burned alive.

In 1503 George Edwards collapsed on Lime Street, Liverpool, and was taken into a large house where they made him comfortable on the kitchen floor. They tried to find out what his name was by going through his pockets. As they plunged their hands into the ragged blackness of his robe they found all manner of dead insects and half-rotting sparrows. There was a pouch bound to his belt, its drawstring pulled tight; when they eased it open, all manner of creatures scurried across the polished kitchen floor – cockroaches, millipedes, a rat, several mice and a grass snake. Edwards seemed to have stopped breathing, yet his throat was still moving as if he was choking. So one of the kitchen staff pulled his mouth open and looked inside. She screamed in utmost terror, for there in the man's throat was a huge cockroach with wings out, blocking the throat, legs wriggling in desperation as it tried to free itself. As the cook dropped Edward's head on to the floor with a mighty crack, the cockroach broke free, flying from his mouth and buzzing around the heads of the kitchen staff who ran in all directions to get out of its way.

Edwards was buried in a small cemetery near Duke Street. Legend has it that now George Edwards was dead and not feasting on the insect population of Liverpool, there was a plague of cockroaches that infested almost every household.

Some said that Edward's body was cursed and should not have been buried on sacred ground, and until it was exhumed the plague would continue. So late one night, after it had been almost two months in the ground, a group of Liverpudlians dug up the body. As they opened the cheap wooden crate he had for a coffin they stared down on the face of the dead man. It looked as if he was talking, his lips were actually moving. Then, one by one, huge orange centipedes began crawling from his lips. One of the men slammed a rough shovel down on Edward's face, shattering the skull and turning the rotting flesh into a ghastly gruel.

They placed the body on a hand cart and wheeled it, covered in sack cloth, across Liverpool in the early hours. Each man could see insects crawling over his hand, climbing his arms, flying into his face and even up his nostrils. It was a hard push on uneven streets that brought them to a patch of wasteland that is close to where Byron Street meets Scotland Road, and there they dug down almost ten feet before dumping Edwards's body unceremoniously into the hole. They collected rocks from all over the countryside to make sure that he would cause no trouble again. Amazingly, from that day on the insects disappeared and life in Liverpool returned to normal.

*Up until the middle 1930s the Lime Street Ghost was often mentioned in discussions about the afterlife, then strangely went out of fashion. Even so, sightings have been recorded in the 1960s,

73

70s, 80s and most recently in 1990. The most vivid came from a retired docker called Alf Price who wrote to a local paper in 1968 that he had seen a ghost on Lime Street. 'I never believed in the things until I saw it. A man standing about six foot tall, and he had no legs, just a torso floating towards me, and he had something alive in his mouth. I don't know what it was but it was certainly alive. My wife is a spiritualist and I've given her some stick over the years, because I'm a strict Methodist. Now I don't know what to think.'

*While researching this story Carol Clayton, a television researcher, said 'It wouldn't surprise me if this story was linked to the pop group The Beatles. The outbreak of beetles in Liverpool that all those years ago caused such a sensation may have subconsciously suggested itself to John, Paul, George and Ringo.' I think not.

*The Adelphi Hotel on Lime Street has a friendly ghost coincidentally called George. The staff all know of him and know him to be no threat, only appearing on occasion to frighten new guests. They talk of him in a very informal way, because he is part of the building and commonly sighted. Surely had this been the beetle-eating cannibal of Lime Street they would not be quite so accommodating.

THE SCHOOL TERROR

There seem to be two main reasons for parents to send their children to boarding school; first, for the children to obtain as fine an education as possible, and secondly to get the youngsters out of their hair. Reasons not to do so, and not advertised in any brochure, include intimidation, bullying, torture, rape and murder. I was told a story that would turn any caring parent's hair white by a Mr Ernie Comerford from Billinge whose great-grandfather had been one of the caretakers at an exclusive boarding school for ladies at Rainford in Merseyside. As always, the accounts vary so I'll relate the horrifying tale as it came to me.

On 25 October 1854 Isobella Smallwood left her home in Manchester full of trepidation. Not only was she going to stay away from her family for the very first time, but she really was heading into the unknown: a girls' boarding school. No comfortable bedroom, no privacy, no freedom – all these exchanged for a dormitory and strict rules, so as to transform this impressionable fifteen-year-old into the sophisticated young lady her father so wanted her to be.

The school had a good reputation and its results had always been quite admirable; yet Isobella had 'a feeling' that something was not right. The school's initiation was, by today's standards, a fairly mild affair – she was made to run the length of the school perimeter in her frilly cotton underwear in a fierce rainstorm. As she ran around her clothes became increasingly see-through but as it was an all-girls school she thought nothing of it. However, the teachers were all looking on from their study, and such matters seemed of particular interest to one lecturer, a Mr R. V. Sinclair.

Sinclair was a quiet man in his middle forties, with a balding pate and a sympathetic manner. Many girls over the years became very attached to him, and would often ask his help in solving problems of a very intimate nature.

It was not long before Isobella's initial reservations faded and she relaxed. A raven-haired beauty, she excelled at most things and became as popular as any girl in the school. Izzy was made captain of the school sports team and eventually became head girl, with the added responsibility of representing any of the girls who had any difficulties. This she relished, attacking every problem with such enthusiastic gusto that it was soon overcome. Every problem but one.

One of the younger girls, a tiny little thing called Eve Mortimer, from Carlisle, had broken down in tears, claiming that she had been attacked by Mr Sinclair. Izzy couldn't believe that such a gentle man would assault one of the children in his care. Eve described how he had given her a potion to help with a severe headache. The medicine had certainly eased her pain to the degree of making her dizzy and Sinclair had put her on a chaise-longue and loosened the buttons at the top of her blouse. It was around this time that she drifted off to sleep. During her slumbers she was aware of a heavy weight pressing down on her, but couldn't remember anything about it. When she awoke Mr Sinclair was sitting beside her, looking very flushed and stroking her face. Eve felt very sore 'down below' and as she eased her legs from the couch her legs almost buckled. She thanked Mr Sinclair and made her way back to the dormitory to carry out his suggestion that she take a hot bath. She felt most queer, Eve told Izzy, and she felt damp in her pants and the more she walked the damper she became. She was embarrassed about this, believing that she had wet herself, not realising for one moment that something far more sinister had taken place.

The day after this happened Sinclair ordered Eve to meet him in his office; he had spoken to a doctor in town on her behalf, he told her. Once again he instructed her to take a potion and once again the world became black and she lapsed into unconsciousness. Then one Wednesday afternoon Sinclair called Eve to him and said, 'Well, Eve, I have to tell you that what you have been doing is very wrong, and I must punish you.' The young Cumbrian had no idea what he was talking about, for she was certainly one of the school's most dedicated pupils. Sinclair continued, 'You egged me on to have sex with you time and time again, and for that I must discipline you.' The girl almost collapsed with shock, and suddenly it all fell into place. She knew that she had not initiated anything, that he had abused her. Yet here he was with a cane about to assault her further. She tried to run from his study, but he restrained her, forcing her over his desk, and swished a stiff bamboo cane across her rear. He swore her to secrecy, threatening harsher punishments should she spread any 'lies' around the school.

Sinclair was frightened, and constantly intimidated Eve by turning up to watch her take part in sport, walking into her dormitory late at night, and occasionally giving her a thrashing for 'giving a staff member a dirty look', 'failing to shine her shoes' or 'depressive behaviour'. She had good reason to be depressed: she was being tortured and raped and seemed powerless to do anything about it.

Eve's last desperate chance was Izzy, and she felt better for having shared her burden. Izzy demanded a meeting with the Principal. This came to the ears of the staff, who were all agog to hear what was so important. Except Sinclair, who was taken ill and returned to his lodgings in town.

Eve also disappeared. So when the meeting went ahead Izzy's allegations were not taken as seriously as they should have been. The school board agreed to talk to both Eve and Mr Sinclair when they were available.

Sinclair dismissed the charges out of hand; his record was spotless and the school board had no proof whatsoever. Eve never returned to the school. The Principal wrote to her parents saying that Eve had run away from the school after circulating lies about one of the teaching staff, and was clearly now too embarrassed to return and was probably making her way home. She never got home.

The police were called, searches carried out, yet no sign of the girl was ever found. Izzy knew in her heart that she was dead.

At the time of her disappearance workmen had been adapting some of the rooms, putting in new fireplaces. It is thought that the strangled body of little Eve was walled up there so the body would cook in the heat and any smell of decay from the corpse would simply go up and out the chimney.

The school no longer exists, it has long since been replaced by a pub called the Golden Lion. Little Eve has been spotted by several customers, and usually around the fireplace, as if beckoning people to come and discover her final resting place.

THE HEADLESS WOMAN OF DUDDON, CHESHIRE

If you drive along the A51 Chester-to-Nantwich road you come upon the small village of Duddon, but try not to do so during the hours of darkness lest you should meet a most unhappy soul.

The legend takes us back to the days of the Cavaliers and Round-heads when, towards the end of the English Civil War, many soldiers were sick of the fighting and formed breakaway groups pillaging for possessions of any kind to make their war a profitable one. On 30 January 1649 Charles I was executed, the King placing his head on the block in front of a crowd estimated at some two thousand. The executioner swung the axe, its blade glinting in the sun. The crowd gave an almighty groan, some cheered, others cried. The soldiers loyal to Cromwell yelled 'Traitors!' while the people shouted 'God save the King!'

In Cheshire, a group of twelve or so Roundheads from Cromwell's New Model Army decided to go into Duddon and get drunk in celebration. The war had lasted years and the locals were glad it was finally all over. Their pleasure was short-lived as these loutish Roundheads proceeded to attack any young men they came across, and abuse the young women. Soon the locals skedaddled back to their homes, locked their doors and hoped that these brutes would leave their peaceful village alone.

It was well after midnight when Dorothy Vaughan walked through Duddon towards the home she shared with her parents. (Some legends claim she was related to the mystic poet Henry Vaughan who published a volume of religious poems, *Silex Scin-*

tillans, in 1650.) She was hurrying along the dark country lane when she was espied by one of the Roundheads. He began to chase after her, but being somewhat inebriated he ended up falling headfirst into a muddy puddle.

'You bitch!' he shouted after her. Soon they were all joking and laughing and in hot pursuit. They caught up with her literally yards from her parents' house, and threw her into a field, behind a tall gorse hedge. There they ripped off her clothing, and raped her one after the other.

Her ordeal lasted over an hour, but when, bruised and beaten, she tried to stand up, one of the Roundheads said, 'Where are you going, my beauty? I think we'll be all having you again!' At this she screamed in terror and her father heard the noise, and ran to the door. When he recognised the voice of his beloved daughter calling out for help, he grabbed his axe and ran to help her. On seeing her father running towards them, Dorothy shouted, 'Get back, Father. They'll kill you!' In a panic the soldiers drew their swords and kept the old man at bay. One of them pushed Dorothy to the ground and began raping her, all the while taunting the old man. 'Do you want to watch me riding your daughter, old man? Maybe you want to do her next?' At this her father exploded in rage, and despite being cut by their swords burst through the group, swinging the axe at the head of the soldier raping his daughter. In terror the soldier rolled the girl over and her head swept up at the very moment the axe fell and rolled across the grass. The soldier saw this and ran off into the dark. One soldier remained as he was still inside Dorothy's headless body, rivers of blood pouring from the open wound all over him. He pushed the corpse away from him, and fled into the field away from the horrified father. In his hurry to get away the soldier tripped, and fell over something; it was Dorothy's head staring at him.

He screamed and raced away as fast as his legs could carry him.

At this point legends differ, some say the soldiers were hunted down and killed by Dorothy's father, who buried them in secret to avoid retaliation from Cromwell's army. Others say that the villagers caught the soldiers in a drunken stupor the next morning and slit their throats.

Dorothy's body was collected the next day, but her head was never found. Some think it was carried off by the soldiers as some sick trophy; but it is more likely to have been taken by a fox or wild dog.

It is said that until her head is reunited with Dorothy's body, her ghost will always walk the lanes of Duddon.

*Over fifty sightings have been reported between 1900 and 1980, but the only witness I could track down was Martin Davidson, who at the time lived in Knutsford but delivered groceries to shops throughout Cheshire. He had this to say on his local radio station: 'I was just finishing my rounds, and it was about 6p.m. on a freezing cold October night. I was just leaving Duddon village to the north when I caught a glimpse of someone in my car headlights. I saw a long purple dress, and slowed down to see if the woman needed a lift. As I wound down the window I looked at the woman's face and she didn't have one. There was no head there at all, but there was blood all over the dress. The figure's hands reached out to me, and I just stood on the accelerator and I was down that road in a flash. I even looked in my rear-view mirror and I could see her clearly!'

THE GHOSTS OF HARDWICK HALL

Most haunted houses love to boast about the apparitions that glide from room to room, yet Hardwick Hall in Nottinghamshire, not far from Mansfield, is at pains to announce that its stately rooms are phantom-free. However, the same cannot be said about its gardens.

*In 1933 a young boy, Craig Cox, witnessed a strange light that seemed to float cross the courtyard, then turning towards him. As it approached he saw it had a brilliant white face that glowed. He turned to run and found he was surrounded by other glowing figures. When he got home he found he had soiled himself and his light brown hair had turned completely white. Craig Cox died in 1987, having sworn all his life that he had really seen 'ghosts'.

*Hardwick Hall was the centre of controversy once again in 1972, according to Darryl Berkovitz, an American accountant. He took his wife there on a holiday photographing places of interest. On a wonderfully sunny July afternoon, they were sitting there on the grass, tucking into a picnic, when they were almost run down by a ghostly carriage with four white horses. In the American phenomenon magazine *The Occult* the Berkovitzes are quoted as saying: 'We were eating a piece of chicken, when out of nowhere this coach appeared, being pulled by four white horses. There was no one driving them, and they started coming right at us! I pushed my wife to the ground and she was scalded by coffee, and I dived the other way and cut both my hands on the gravel. When we looked up we could see that there was no one driving the horses, and the coach rode straight through a wall and vanished!'

Whether this was true, or just an ego trip for a couple of Americans in search of stories to tell at dinner parties we'll never know.

*In January 1976 a local newspaper reported the story of Mark Gresswell and his fiancée Carol who whilst driving through the grounds of Hardwick Hall suffered a string of incidents. First he had to swerve around a fallen tree, then almost crashed head-on with another car. It was then that his fiancée spotted what she described as 'a white-faced monk'. Mark didn't really believe that she'd seen anything, but to placate her he turned the car round and drove back; the ghost had waited for them. He was tall and broad, dressed in a monk's habit, and his face was luminous. Within three months eleven other witnesses had seen this figure – including two police officers and a vicar.

THE OLDEST INN IN ALL ENGLAND

The full story of Robin Hood can be found in *Grisly Trails and Ghostly Tales*, but other stories of his adventures abound around Nottingham. The oldest inn in England, established in 1199, was, it is said, built on the site of the Boar's Head tavern, the meeting place used by Robert Hood (Robin) and his merry men. Amazingly it was directly overlooked by a castle full of the men who were searching relentlessly to bring the outlaws to justice.

Legend tells of how when Hood finally died in the 1300s at Kirklees Priory, the innkeeper and his family were put to the sword, and the inn burned down for harbouring outlaws. Some say one of Mutch the Miller's sons exchanged information for his freedom and this led to many of the outlaws being apprehended, imprisoned or killed. A new inn was built there and as the sizeable numbers of soldiers stationed at the Castle were waiting to leave England for the Crusades, the name chosen for the new inn was Ye Olde Trip to Jerusalem. By this time the chivalrous Saladin was long dead but the English still believed that the Holy War had to continue and between 1198 and 1202 they were planning the fourth Crusade, a direct attack on Egypt. (This was later considered too risky, and they diverted their attentions to Constantinople instead.)

So Ye Olde Trip to Jerusalem was an instant success, the troops guaranteeing it a profitable existence. Yet no sooner had it opened than disaster struck the nation – King Richard I, the Lionheart, was killed. The tavern, however, continued giving solace to those troops who travelled abroad, being the last party before the Crusades. These alleged soldiers of the Holy War drank themselves into a stupor and ravished the countless prostitutes who sold their services there. The soldiers were certainly far from devout, and this was borne out in 1204 when the Crusaders looted, raped and pillaged Constantinople.

*The very first ghostly experiences began to occur as far back as 1214, when King John's men began collecting names for the Magna Carta, and were in a bedchamber when they heard strange noises of festivity. On rousing the innkeeper, they were told that ghosts of the dead Crusaders returned home to England and chose the last place they recalled, the last great revelling they did on this earth.

*Oliver Cromwell was said to have visited Nottingham in May 1645, arriving in secret to check on how well prepared his men were. He was less than pleased with what he saw, as he had demanded that they abstain from drinking and adverse sexual behaviour until after the campaign. However, men being men, soldiers being soldiers, most of the inns were full of drinking and bonking. Several captains were demoted, and guards placed upon all of the inns to stop any of his men disobeying orders.

*During the French Revolution Nottingham became home to many members of the aristocracy who had fled from Paris. Many of the locals disliked their French visitors, as they had always had an uneasy relationship. One French diplomat, known as Charles De Tourney, was murdered beneath the Castle walls, set upon by local thugs jealous of his wealth, and very much anti-French. The Frenchman managed to stagger to what was described as 'a common inn' and collapsed over the bar, blood pouring from him to cover the length of it, forming a pool on the floor. As Ye Olde Trip to Jerusalem is the only inn known to have been there at the time, we are safe to presume that it was that 'common inn'. Visitors to the inn often spoke of the 'Ghostly Gaul', often in jest, but the story stuck, only going out of fashion in the mid-1800s.

*More recently, ghosts have been harder to come by, but the building is well worth seeing, particularly a hole in the cellar wall that can still be seen today. Many suggestions have been made as to what it was for; the commonest include: the medieval equivalent of a wall safe; a hidey-hole for lawbreakers, as it was originally covered by a tapestry; a stash for armaments, for a planned rebellion.

The most gruesome story around it involves a lady called Margaret, a prostitute who lived at the inn in the 1780s. She apparently had an affair with a visiting naval man called Arthur Phillip, who commanded ships transporting some of the first convicts to Australia. On one voyage Phillip took 570 men and 160 women, his cargo of convicts including a nine-year-old boy who had stolen an apple. Of them 48 died of smallpox, venereal disease or influenza during the trip. On Phillip's return in 1789 he discovered that Margaret had borne a son she claimed was his. He furiously denied this and instructed a group of his roughest sailors to go and see to her and the child. Whether this meant to pay her off, or something rather more menacing we may never know. The landlord hid Margaret and her child in the cellar, but she was found by the sailors and taken away. Margaret was never seen again.

Eight months later the landlord drew back the tapestry to find Margaret's baby, gagged to keep it quiet, lying dead in the hole. The innkeeper had presumed that the baby was taken away with Margaret.

Some say Phillip put the prostitute on another boat to Australia, to hide his shame.

THE LINCOLN EAGLE

In 1580 thousands gathered at Plymouth to welcome home one of Britain's great heroes, Francis Drake, who was still considered by many as little more than a pirate. The Spanish certainly wanted him put on trial for piracy, as he had been preying on their ships, plundering them of treasure for his Queen. Drake had proved himself to be a great captain, taking his three ships around the world by way of Cape Horn and the Cape of Good Hope. His expedition had only been marred by an attempted mutiny when they were becalmed north of the Magellan Straits at Port Julian.

Francis Drake refused to be namby-pamby and executed his friend Thomas Doughty, one of the mutiny's leaders. Doughty's co-conspirators were placed in chains and returned to England in disgrace. The grand reception given to Drake led to most people missing the sad sight of seven broken men being dragged off the ship, bundled into a hay cart and driven away towards prison. Barely a mile from Plymouth one of the more cunning mutineers buried himself in the hay, wriggling right down to the bottom, and ordering his friends to sit on him. The guards thought he had escaped and, chaining the others up sent out search parties.

As night fell Charles Murray, from Lincolnshire, crept out of the straw and ran off into the night. For almost eight weeks he scavenged a living from the bleak hills of Dartmoor, setting up camp on Ryder's Hill. He had a diet of birds, hedgehogs, and the rats that lived in huge colonies in those dark days. He was building up to returning home to Lincoln.

Murray was an unpleasant man with a bald head and ebony eyes; he hated women, having once been arrested for tearing a woman's dress hours before he had set off on his travels with Drake. As he made his way across the country towards home he stole to survive. On the outskirts of Nottingham a woman was raped and murdered; a man answering Murray's description was seen.

Before entering Lincoln he visited an old drinking pal, Ernest Pottle, who had a cottage near Doddington Hall, as he worked on the land nearby. Pottle warned Murray that there was a warrant for his arrest and he would have to lie low.

This angered the surly mutineer who swore: 'I'll make them all sorry for the day that they took on Charlie Murray!'

After finishing a flagon of ale Murray bid his friend goodbye, borrowed a change of clothing, armed himself with some knives and a cutlass and walked out into the mist.

The area then began to suffer a spate of murders and children going missing, while rapes and sexual assaults were becoming commonplace. The authorities were pressured to take action, and a troop of soldiers began searching for what was believed to be a gang of cut-throats, yet they never found any sign.

It was in 1587 that Charles Murray was discovered living in an underground shelter near Thorpe on the Hill on the outskirts of Lincoln by a farm worker called Shiney Thomas. The young man befriended the old pirate and would bring him food and ale for a share of the profits that Murray was making as a rustler. However, it was their relationship that would lead to the mutineer's undoing. One day Thomas brought his girlfriend Ruth to visit Murray, who

83

became angry because Thomas had forgotten his ale. The young farm lad told Ruth to wait there while he ran home to collect the drink for his aggressive partner.

On his way back he heard screams coming from Murray's underground home, dropped the ale, and raced to see what was happening. He burst into Murray's shelter to find the bloodied body of Ruth lying on the straw covered floor. Murray was stamping on her head and neck over and over again until the bone was smashed into a bloody mass.

Thomas tried to scream but no sound would come out. Murray reached down, and grasped the tragic woman's hair, all matted with gore and brain matter. Keeping his foot wedged on her neck, he heaved and part of her head pulled away, a bit of her cheek visible, an eye hanging down on a sinewy thread, as Murray held it up, shouting, 'She's not so pretty now, is she?'

Thomas began backing out of the shelter as Murray walked towards him, waving his horrid 'trophy' at the terrified farm worker. Fearing for his own life the lad ran back home and alerted the local magistrate that his girl had been murdered. Without delay, 25 soldiers were sent out from Lincoln to apprehend this madman, but on reaching Murray's home all they found was the girl's body. It had been stamped almost completely flat.

They searched for almost two days but there was no sign of the pirate. When the authorities learned that it was Charles Murray who was the missing mutineer, almost 200 troops were instructed to join the hunt. They were hot on his trail when he kidnapped a young woman who was playing in a field with her two-year-old son. He hid with his hostages behind a stone wall, until night fell, and the troops had passed him by. The sun slowly rose, and Murray felt the woman trying to struggle away so he picked up a stone and pulled his hand back and swung it hard into the nape of her neck. He had only wanted to stun her but she fell lifeless into the ditch, blood oozing like warm treacle from her shattered skull. The child began to cry, screaming his panic into the still morning air. Two soldiers heard the cries and set off to investigate, and soon saw the crouched shape of Charles Murray.

They drew their swords and walked towards him, as he began climbing up a tree, clutching the tiny child to his chest. He had got up as far as he could and shouted down to the soldiers, now about fifteen of them, threatening to throw the child to his death if they came anywhere near him. So they stood their ground until their commanding officer, a down-to-earth Londoner called Captain Joyce, appeared.

He ordered his men to spread out in readiness to catch the boy if he should be cast from the tree. Then he ordered two of his biggest and most aggressive soldiers to climb up after him. They were barely six feet up when Murray pulled out a curved dagger and held it to the child's throat. Captain Joyce pulled his men back at once, and Murray roared with laughter. 'You'll not catch Charlie Murray, the king of the pirates. If Francis Drake can't kill me, then you'll not stand a chance!'

He stood up nearly level with the top of the tree, and began shouting down his orders, telling the soldiers to walk until they were out of sight, then he would come down and disappear into the fields and away.

At that moment there was a tremendous flapping of wings and a huge bird flew straight into Murray's face, causing him to drop the child. A soldier dived to catch the tiny child at the expense of a fractured wrist. Murray was off balance but managed to right himself and he turned to see what creature had attacked him. There in the distance swooping to make another attack was a gigantic golden eagle. It began its descent, its talons shining in the sunlight as they raced towards Murray at such speed the bird became a blur. The eagle hit Murray in the throat, tearing into his neck, twisting and tearing out his windpipe. The mighty wings seemed to cartwheel as it spun back in flight again. Murray screamed with all his might, blood pumping into his tattered windpipe, his mind swimming in pain and confusion. He began to fall and crashed through branches and leaves until he thudded on to the grass. His back broken, he lay there looking up at the soldiers, unable to talk, unable to move as the blood soaked into the ground. He stared and stared until his stare was trapped in eyes that could no longer see.

The eagle circled overhead and seemed to be crying in celebration of his destruction of this vile excuse for a human being. The child survived to become a farmer in his own right near Newton on Trent. The site of this episode is now known as 'Eagle', though eagles, let alone golden ones, are few and far between.

*In September 1969 Mrs Kathleen Dutton of Grantham was driving towards Lincoln to meet a friend when she was forced to do an emergency stop when a huge bird flew straight at her car. She shut her eyes tight as she felt a crash as though the bird had gone straight through her Mini. When she was able to look round she saw that the windscreen wipers were both ripped off, and feathers inside the car. The feathers were brown, and were later identified as those of an eagle! How did they get *inside* the car?

*The ghost of Charles Murray has been sighted on more than thirty occasions. The American ghost-hunter Paul Jones writes: 'There is no doubt that Murray's spirit still walks the land to the south of Lincoln, England. Usually he carries part of a woman's head, with the eyeball hanging out, in front of him.' Sightings have been made as far afield as along the banks of the River Witham.

*The most recent report involved Mr and Mrs Marshall from Arnold in Nottingham. They were driving around the Lincolnshire lanes in search of a nice place to have their salmon-sandwich picnic in August 1992. They had been to Lincoln, and had turned off just past South Clifton, passing North Scarle and heading towards Eagle, when they saw a man crouched over something at the side of the road. John Marshall pulled his Astra over and shouted from his window, asking if the man was all right. He appeared to be stamping on something white, and as he turned he screamed at the car. At this the Marshalls drove off. Mrs Marshall watched through the back window as the bald man kept stamping, and later said on a local radio station, 'I was sure he was stamping on someone!' They eventually turned the car and drove back at speed but no one was there.

LINCOLN'S GHOST HOTEL

The White Hart Hotel on Bailgate in Lincoln must be one of the busiest places to stay, for even if there are no customers, it would still be full of ghosts. Practically every floor has something incredible that has happened there. A German professor, Ernst Heidegger, once said 'There are a few places on this planet that seem to act as a magnet for all kinds of strange phenomena.' The White Hart Hotel seems to be such a place. Legends of all kinds abound there.

It is believed that the original inn was constructed around 1290, and has housed all manner of men and women over the years.

The legends are so diverse I can only hope to guide you through the most well-known one at a time.

The Faceless Highwayman

In the 1600s the Hotel was a rowdy inn, used by many rogues and vagabonds, including highwaymen. It gained such a bad reputation that soldiers were sent by the local Duke to 'clean out that nest of rebellion and thievery'. This they did, arresting over seventy people in the process. In the darkness the soldiers entered one room to find a highwayman in a drunken stupor. They shook him awake and in his panic at seeing soldiers, he grabbed at his sword. One of the troopers reached to stop him swing it and his hand slid along its full length, the blade neatly slicing all his fingers off. The soldier's friend pushed his fiery torch into the highwayman's face and left it there, literally melting his face off. The Faceless Highwayman has been seen often over the years, stepping out of doorways, lying on the beds and very occasionally wandering along corridors, his face black and incinerated, his eyes white and lifeless, as he strides around the White Hart unable to find the door.

The Chambermaid

In the middle 1800s the White Hart was considered one of the more upmarket venues for the wealthy and well-to-do. The staff of such an exclusive establishment were very carefully chosen, and often came from middle-class families using the job as a stepping stone to finding a rich husband. Such was the case of Jenny, who came from a background of extreme poverty, yet had struggled to get a good education and was very well-spoken. Her dream was to meet a handsome young man with a decent income, to give her the things she would never be able to afford on the wage of a chambermaid. Jenny had long blonde hair fastened in a bun, a perfect figure and long legs, often giving a glimpse of curvy ankle to those men she found pleasing to her eye. She was what could be described as a 'good girl' and was determined to save herself for her husband. Despite the attentions of these men only keen for 'rumpy-pumpy', she kept a high moral tone. One man in particular caused her a great deal of harassment; he was the local rat catcher, though he described himself as a private businessman. He would visit the White Hart to gamble, and to try and persuade Jenny to sell her body to him. He had offered as much as £10, in those days a fortune, but she had rebuffed him as always. Then one night she met her Prince Charming, a local farmer's son, and she fell in love. To her surprise he seemed similarly smitten, and they would spend many evenings conversing and flirting. This annoyed the rat catcher who would get drunker and drunker to try to exorcise the pain he felt at not being able to have the wench he wanted. During a particularly raucous game of cards he let slip to his friends how he felt, and one said, 'Well, go on, be a man, get up those stairs and take her then! She's in that room at the top of the stairs.' In his state he would have tried to fly if someone had asked him. So he staggered up to the first floor and started trying the doors; at the third door it opened and out stepped Jenny carrying some used bedding. She looked into the rat catcher's face and saw a murderous lust. She screamed as he hit her, knocking her backwards on to a bedroom floor; there he attempted rape, but found that his drinking had put an end to that, so he strangled her to death. Poor Jenny is said still to wander the corridors and if anyone sees her, she appears terrified, as if the rat catcher had returned to kill her again.

The Lincolnshire Dandy
Stories vary as to who this gentleman was, a smartly dressed chap who used to stay at the White Hart while in Lincoln on business. He would often buy and sell antiques and used the Hotel safe to keep his purchases from the hands of the many rogues that even then made life a misery for the law-abiding. Legends differ as to his fate, some say a much-prized ginger jar was stolen, and such was the shock the old gent died.

Others say that the ginger jar was cursed because he had tricked an old woman out of its full value, paying her coppers for something that was worth pounds. So while he lay in his sleep the woman conjured up a shadowy spirit from Hell to come and strangle him as he slept.

He has been witnessed by hundreds over the decades and occasionally guests in that particular room have smelled cigar smoke.

The Floating Ball
Whether this is a ball of pure energy or a ghost without human form nobody knows, but staff in the 1960s swear that it once swept around the dining room 'for almost twenty minutes' before it just disappeared.

The Suicidal Man
In 1962 a young man staying at the Hotel was so depressed with his existence and a love affair that went wrong, that he took his own life. He had dined quite well on rainbow trout and brandy,

and had told the waitress serving him that it was his last supper. She made a joke of it, and they shared a smile. At the end of the meal he asked the waitress if she would go out with him to the pictures the following evening. She thanked him for the kind offer, but explained that she was recently married, saying, 'I'm not sure my husband would like that idea!' Perhaps he just needed some love and compassion and couldn't find it. He returned to his room, placed a pistol in his mouth and fired, splattering the walls and bed with his brains.

Some guests say they have heard sobbing coming from some of the rooms, and in 1977 Peter Prosser from Crowland said he woke up in the middle of the night because he heard a huge explosion, like a gun going off. He even popped down to the reception to ask what was going on. They had heard nothing.

The Poltergeist
In the 1950s the White Hart was named in another newspaper story when a couple claimed that their romantic meal was ruined by a poltergeist who had hurled all the cutlery off the table, and had dropped a full pepperpot into the girlfriend's soup. Midway through the main course, the steak he was eating leapt on to his lap. They swore that they were not just sloppy eaters; something was playing games with them.

All things considered, the White Hart has to be one of the most intriguing places to stay in Britain, if you can stand the pace.

WEST CENTRAL ENGLAND

THE MADMAN OF BURTON-UPON-TRENT

When King Richard II was told that 'the peasants were revolting' he could have added that some of them were stark raving mad too. Such a man was Jethro Orme, a hermit who lived on the outskirts of Burton-upon-Trent, relishing the reports from London of the Peasants' Revolt, how the mob ran riot in an orgy of destruction, rape and murder.

The summer of 1381 had been a particularly bloody time for all concerned. In London a peasant mob had ignored their own cause, instead looting shops and houses, beheading a judge and hacking into pieces eighteen leading citizens for no reason. Legal documents were burnt in an attempt to end the hated poll tax. In London in the 1300s there was a huge Dutch community, and the mob also chose to blame them for their own ineptitude and savagely butchered 35 men with scythes and axes, using their heads as footballs in a disgusting insane game. Not even churchmen were exempt from the crowd's bloodlust; Sudbury, the Archbishop of Canterbury, was dragged to Tower Hill where he was killed. His head was brought to London Bridge, and displayed on a spike, with his mitre nailed to it.

Finally the fourteen-year-old king agreed to meet the leader, Wat Tyler, but at their discussion in Smithfield, the Mayor of London drew his sword and killed Tyler.

All the gory stories excited Jethro Orme, and he started to do some most peculiar things. He would chase and kill any dog or cat he could find, and while they still lived he would try to eat his way into their stomachs. Once they were ripped open he'd rub himself all over with their blood.

Jethro was clearly mad, but as he had done no one any harm he was allowed to wander around Burton-upon-Trent singing, dancing on the backs of the flat carts and making faces. One day he told a soldier that he had been filled with the spirit of Wat Tyler, and was going to lead another peasants' revolt. The few troops stationed there paid him no heed, knowing him to be crazy. However, word of Jethro reached the King, who had suffered greatly during the rebellion, and had no wish to reopen old wounds. So he sent a message to the Captain of the guard, ordering that Jethro be 'despatched silently', and two soldiers were sent out to commit the deadly deed.

They found Jethro by the Trent fishing. They grasped him and held his head below the water until they felt him relax, allowing the water into his lungs. At this they let go and watched him float downstream. Not ten yards away Jethro jumped up to his feet and screamed, 'Fooled you!' and swam over to the other side. The soldiers waded into the river, the weight of their armour pulled them below the surface and they were both drowned.

The Captain couldn't believe that his men had been killed by this madman, and ordered his entire troop of twelve soldiers to hunt him down. Three weeks later he still hadn't been found, but the Captain had received a badly written note from Jethro. It read: 'Ye'll never catch me, those wot luk will dye. Do not luk and liv.'

The Captain was surprised Jethro could write at all, but he resented being taunted, and became even more determined to capture and kill the crazy fool. Within two months, eight of the soldiers were either dead or laid up with broken limbs, following a string of unbelievable accidents. One man had fallen from a building; another had died whilst atop of a whore at a local tavern; another was almost decapitated by a falling roof tile. The Captain was replaced and demoted.

Thirty crack soldiers accompanied their new military commander and cast a net across Burton; within 24 hours the madman was in custody. While he was imprisoned, several of the soldiers met with nightmarish accidents. One was set on fire in a bizarre incident with a barrel of tallow; another choked to death on a chicken bone; four men were injured when a carthorse ran amok, pinning them beneath a huge wagon, shattering ribs and breastbones. The new Captain was advised to despatch Jethro as soon as possible, to end his deadly influence. He ordered his men to build a bonfire in the town square. The following day Jethro was burnt alive.

*In the 1400s several visitors to the small town claimed to have seen a crazy tramp wandering around the streets. The Burton residents would say, 'No, that's just old Jethro!' He was accepted as a part of the town for almost 300 years. As Burton-upon-Trent became more sophisticated the legend seemed to fade.

*In 1911 something very strange happened. A note was received by Burton's modest newspaper, claiming that there would be another peasants' revolt. This time the note was impeccably presented. It read: 'It is time that I returned in my disguise as Wat Tyler. I will lead a revolution against injustice and my battle will begin in Llanelli in two days' time.' It was signed 'JETHRO'.

The newspaper took this to be a crank cashing in on a long-dead legend. It was 18 July 1911. On the 20th troops clashed in Llanelli with railway strikers who began looting shops and setting fire to railway stock. Nine people were killed, three of them shot dead by the troops, the other six were literally blown to tiny pieces when a railway carriage full of explosives and bottled carbide was caught by the rioters' torches. The soldiers only opened fire after the stone-throwing crowd had tried to board a train and take it over.

The Riot Act was read to the crowd and troops advanced on them with fixed bayonets. Looters raided the homes of the two magistrates and shops, forcing their wives and children out into the streets as they tried to set the property on fire.

Ten bodies were finally recovered; in the ashes of the exploded railway carriage there were the remnants of a body that was never identified. Some said it was a tramp hiding from the bloody battle in the carriage, others said it was Jethro, back to lead the rebels into the fray.

THE LUDLOW DOLLY BIRD

Five foot ten inches tall, long slim legs, boots, a tiny mini-skirt, a see-through blouse showing two shapely breasts, and long hair swaying down her back. Can you imagine a less likely description of a ghost? Yet around Ludlow in Shropshire they know this apparition well.

There are various suggestions as to who she is; the most likely sounding story concerns a girl called Jayne Jones who lived in Ludlow. During the 1960s she was the ultimate pop music fan and travelled all over Britain to see her favourite acts: Freddie & the Dreamers, Dusty Springfield, Brian Poole & the Tremoloes, the Rolling Stones, the Kinks, the Merseybeats. . . . She always wore the latest fashions, and was one of the sexiest visions imaginable. Many people at the time wanted to dress in an outrageous fashion, but in Ludlow few had the guts to do so and she was very much out on her own, and no one could fail to follow her with their eyes.

It was 14 May 1966, and Jayne was in London with a friend to visit the buzzing club circuit, hoping to meet the hordes of pop stars that flocked to it. However, unbeknown to them it was Cup Final day, and half of Liverpool and half of Sheffield poured into the capital to view Everton's 3–2 victory over Sheffield Wednesday. The number of remarks Jayne had to put up with, the countless times her bottom was grabbed, her legs stroked, or a man would rub past her 'accidentally on purpose', annoyed and upset her. The last straw came when she was in a bar waiting for a jive club to open at 10p.m., when it was invaded by football fans celebrating their team's win. A group of them grabbed her and pushed her around. The barman tried to intervene and was punched in the face for his trouble. The police were called and the bar was cleared. Jayne was in an awful state of panic, a simple girl, she loved music and she loved to dance, that was all. The first chance she got, she ran into the street; she was going home! Home where it was safe. Home where she could lock her bedroom door and escape into the music on her tiny record player. Home where she could burrow into the arms of her mum and dad and know that no one could harm her. She glanced up at a clock outside a jewellery store, it read 8.40. The last train home left at 9p.m. She would have to be quick. Jayne never gave her friend a thought, even though she was supposed to be staying the night at her flat nearby.

She ran through traffic as if she didn't see the cars and onlookers gasped at how close she came to being hit, yet each time the vehicles seemed almost to go through her. Her long shapely legs were now at full stretch, even though her shoes were far from comfortable for running in. She neared the station, and could see the clock – 8.57; if she sprinted, she could still make it, she already had her return ticket. She put on a spurt of speed and that was when her luck ran out. Yards from the station entrance an accelerating black taxi hit her head-on.

She was thrown like a rag doll almost twenty feet through the air, landing on the road to be hit by at least another two vehicles, which screeched to a halt. As she lay on the tarmac, still conscious, she looked up at the concerned faces; she was loosely aware that someone was calling an ambulance. She looked down and saw her beautiful legs, all smashed and bleeding, the white bones sticking through the skin, and blood spurting everywhere. She tried to move her arms, there was no response, she tried to move her neck, still nothing. She was completely paralysed.

Her thoughts were swimming, everything was a jumble and she couldn't even talk.

'Surely I am supposed to be in pain?' she thought, yet she could only feel as if she was wrapped in cotton wool. She had no awareness of her broken body being straightened and placed on a stretcher, none of the ambulance journey, none of the number of operations carried out. Finally she regained consciousness. On waking up she saw her mum and dad, who had remained at her bedside for months. Her mother nearly fainted with joy when Jayne uttered her first words: 'What are you doing here?' It seemed as if Jayne had forced all of the horrors of that dreadful night out of her mind.

They chatted for what seemed to be hours when Jayne said, 'All right then, let's go home!' She lifted up the hospital sheets and tried to swing her legs out of bed, without success. That's when it hit her like a hammer, that she would never walk again.

The chatty, fun-loving gadabout sank into a deep depression, and nothing her parents could do or say lifted her. Months of counselling ensued, and she remained dour, without any will to live.

Then, on Wednesday 22 March 1967 she heard George Harrison talking on television about the power of the mind, and how with the help of a guru he could travel the world, without ever leaving his bed. This struck a chord with Jayne, and she listened as news reporters told of something called astral projection. How some people believed that they could send their souls out of their bodies, to walk, run, even fly. She wrote to one of the 'experts' of the time, a Mr Roger Rees, a spiritualist in his late sixties. To her surprise he didn't reply to her letter – he actually walked into the hospital to see her. After a month he had taught her how to meditate, how to re-create the bridge between being awake and asleep, and also how to relax so completely that the spirit would be free to leave the body.

Her family didn't believe a word of it, and made arrangements to get Jayne a wheelchair, and to prepare a downstairs bedroom for her at home. Jayne finally returned to Ludlow on 31 August 1967. She soon settled in, and that's when her life changed for the better. All over Ludlow her friends would see Jayne strutting down the street, her long legs as fine as ever, and wearing mini-skirts or hot-pants. Her parents received phone calls from their friends saying how thrilled they were that Jayne had made such a full recovery. They couldn't understand it, as the furthest Jayne had managed to get was to the tiny patio in the back garden.

Then one day her father telephoned home to his wife, saying that he could see Jayne across the street from him in Ludlow, looking into a record shop window. Hurriedly, her mum ran along to Jayne's bedroom to find her fast asleep, in almost a trance-like state. She shook her daughter awake, then returned to the living room to tell her husband that he must be mistaken, to hear him jibbering like an idiot. 'Bloody hell, Betty, she disappeared. She's gone. Right in front of my eyes. The woman standing next to her nearly had kittens.'

After hours talking about this at home, they had no option than to believe that their daughter could travel astrally.

From that day Jayne was seen all over Ludlow, looking as solid as anyone else. The shocks came when someone bumped into her accidentally, because they would go straight through her. Countless car drivers were scared witless when a gorgeous mini-skirted girl stepped out in front of them, only to have the car go straight through her. Perhaps even more astounding was that it seemed that Jayne could 'project' on to herself whatever clothes she wanted to wear.

This amazing girl was able to tell her parents what certain movies were like without ever having gone to see them, in the accepted sense; and she claimed to have attended pop concerts, even to have travelled abroad – all in spirit. Far-fetched as it all seemed, Jayne's folks became as near comfortable as they could with her incredible abilities.

On several occasions the staff of The Feathers in the Bull Ring, Ludlow, saw this beautiful girl – and served stiff drinks to countless men and women who had watched her walk through walls, pillar boxes and parked cars. They were sure they had seen a ghost.

Sadly in the middle 1970s the miracle ended when Jayne took her own life. It was thought that her spirit had met and talked to a young man who worked in one of Ludlow's boutiques of the time. He had asked her out, and she wanted to more than anything in the world, but for obvious reasons had to decline. The legend has two versions at this point; one says that the spirit led the young man to her house and showed him the 'real' Jayne. He couldn't cope with the shock of it all, ran out and refused to have anything more to do with her.

The old sentimental me, however, wants the second version to be the real one. It tells of how Jayne taught the young man to travel astrally, and they decided that if only they could leave their bodies behind, they could travel the world forever in spirit. So they both cut the invisible thread that tied them to their bodies and now they walk the earth forever hand-in-hand.

*Jayne still pays regular visits to Ludlow, and you may see her, but you will think she's solid and real. This begs the question when we look down a bustling high street: how many of the people are actually there?

THE SHREWSBURY NINJAS

Of the many extraordinary stories to come to me is that of the Shrewsbury Ninjas. The Shogun, or military governer, of Japan in the 1600s was a vicious warlord called Iemitsu, who hated the British and the Portuguese. They were trying to establish better trade relations at the time but Iemitsu believed that Japan should be for the Japanese and all links with the outside world should be actively discouraged. His version of 'discouragement' was to chop off the heads of any foreigner he came across. In 1640 Iemitsu allowed 61 representatives of the Portuguese government to land, and they were brought to his palace at Nagasaki. They had come to try to persuade the Shogun to re-open trade links with their country. Iemitsu said only one word: 'No.' The Japanese ruler (for that is what he was – the Emperor was little more than a figurehead) believed that Portugal had tried to organise a Christian peasant rebellion at Shimabara some years earlier. Instead of sending these diplomats away with a flea in their ear, therefore, he ordered their public beheading. So the harmless civil servants were marched before a crowd of around four thousand people and on the stroke of midday 61 heads fell into wicker baskets.

Three Englishmen, cloth merchants from Shrewsbury come to try to purchase some of Japan's fine fabrics, witnessed this sight and decided to make themselves scarce. They escaped north to the small fishing town of Sasebo, where smugglers were paid to get them to one of the Ryukyu islands. There they sent word to the Philippines, where British vessels had regular links. It took the three men almost two years to get back home. They had spent a total of four years trying to achieve a working arrangement and had returned empty-handed – but lucky at least still to have their heads.

Three days after their return, one of the men, David Dunaway, was found lying in his bed, his head severed and his eyes pierced with skewers. The other two, Roger Friend and Simon Oliver, were more than a little concerned, for they knew that on the other side of the world the Shogun had ordered their deaths. Surely that threat carried no weight in quiet little Shrewsbury?

At the funeral Friend and Oliver were perturbed to see two Japanese men standing at the graveside, waiting for the lowering of the coffin. They were dressed in black in the fashion that we would now identify as that of the ninjas, hired assassins sent from the East. It seems that Iemitsu had the Englishmen's documents, so knew where they were from, and that in fact these Japanese killers had arrived in Shrewsbury almost four months before the men had.

Roger Friend informed the local magistrate, who took it upon himself to apprehend the two Japanese, but he could find no evidence that they were responsible for the killing.

The following week Roger Friend was in his basement room, when he heard his back door being prised open. Knowing the threat posed by the assassins, he carried a large sword with him as he set off to investigate. The back kitchen was a dark, foisty room, with lots of places where a shadowy figure could hide. Instead of chancing his arm in the shadows with trained killers, Friend bolted the kitchen door, and ran out of his front door for help.

He never saw the blade of the sword, he merely ran on to it, and it was so sharp his body kept running, while his head bounced along the street. It rolled down the sloping road almost a hundred yards before coming to rest in the centre of a busy street. Torrents of blood gushed from his torso down into the primitive guttering to paint a crimson river down towards that disembodied head.

When Simon Oliver heard of his colleague's murder, he rushed to the magistrate for protection. Soldiers were sent to apprehend the two Japanese, and expel them from the country. They had gone. Oliver refused to go home, in case he put his family at risk, and chose to live on the outskirts of Shrewsbury, staying in a cow byre, and buying food from the local farmer whom he had sworn to secrecy.

One morning he looked out of the wide-open window to the old farm building and saw the two Japanese walking along the edge of the field towards his hideout. He quickly grabbed a sharpened axe and prepared himself for their attack. It seems that the assassins had no idea that Oliver was there; they were keeping out of Shrewsbury to avoid arrest, and were looking for food. They sat against the wall of the byre and chewed away at some soily carrots.

Terrified, Simon Oliver was, he sat and trembled, his palms sweating and his heart beating so loudly he was certain the Japanese killers would investigate and murder him. It was only a matter of time before they discovered him. So he stood by the rotted wooden door, his axe at shoulder level ready to take one of their heads.

Seconds later the door creaked open and into the shadows walked a figure, and Oliver brought the axe down with all of his might. He felt his shoulder jar as the sharpened blade of the axe found its mark. As the body fell backwards he stared in shock as he saw the farmer almost split in two. Looking out into the field he saw the two killers racing towards the byre. Oliver tried to remove the chopper from the old man's body, but it was firmly embedded. The more he struggled to remove it, the more it seemed to stick, so in desperation Oliver turned to a hayfork, and ran towards his attackers, catching one of them at stomach level, lifting him off his feet, until he fell back to earth with a sickening bump. The other Japanese held a sharpened curved sword, and Oliver began to run across the muddy field. Although he had a ten-yard head start, the mud held him back and the lighter frame of the assassin saw him catch up fast. Oliver fell forward into the mire, and was trying to pull himself free when he glanced up to see the ninja standing directly above him. He looked up but could barely make out his shape, as the sun was directly behind him, and Oliver was blinded. He could see the form raise the sword above his head, and in blind panic punched with all his might into the assassin's groin. The sword was dropped and the killer fell to his knees. Oliver grabbed the deadly blade, surprised at how light it was. He was barely standing up when he brought it down on the neck of the poleaxed killer. The head was instantly detached, and Oliver lay in the field, breathing heavily. He had survived, and not only that, he'd killed the men sent across the globe to kill him. He dragged his weary body out of the mud, and was walking to the roadway, all set to return home, and to inform the magistrate. Then he heard a sound from the field. On turning he saw the body of one of the ninjas raise itself from the ground, and watched in dread as the headless body marched purposefully towards him. It held a sword in its hand, and Oliver stood agape as it came at him. He held up his hands against the barrage of blows rained down upon him. His hands and fingers were severed, littering the field with flesh and bone. Finally Oliver was on the ground, his arms merely bloody stumps, when the final blow was struck, and his head fell with a splodge into a mud puddle.

The following day the farmer's wife came upon the scene that would have been more in place in a slaughterhouse than in an idyllic country setting such as this. The authorities were soon in attendance and they found the dead farmer, the decapitated body of Simon Oliver, a Japanese killer impaled on a pitchfork and one Japanese head. Where was the body? A search was made, but no trace was ever found of the headless torso.

*Over the next 180 years there were many sightings of a headless man around the area. The story seemed to die out in the early 1800s.

*In November 1954 Mr & Mrs L. Kirke from Shrewsbury were looking for horse-chestnuts for their son to play conkers with, when they came across a man wandering through a small copse of trees. Thinking it was the owner of the trees Mr Kirke shouted out, 'I hope you don't mind but I'm just getting a few conkers for the son.' The man didn't reply, and when Mrs Kirke walked towards him she screamed, and passed out on the spot. When her husband revived her, she said, 'He's got no head!' She had to be treated at hospital for shock and neither of them ever returned to the countryside outside the town again.

THE BUTCHERED BABIES OF BIRMINGHAM

We tend to associate poltergeists with creaky old houses, but it seems that the vast majority of cases are in fact in new houses. On 9 December 1982 Mr and Mrs Michael Bryant of Halesowen, on the outskirts of Birmingham, were sitting down to a meal in their modest two-bedroom semi, when they heard an almighty crash from a bedroom upstairs. Darting to the scene, they found a heavy wardrobe full of clothes face-down across their bed, the clothes strewn all about the room. The window was closed, the doors were locked and the burglar alarm, which was switched on, was silent so this couldn't have been an intruder. As they stood there, a picture fell off the wall. Gillian Bryant screamed and ran down-stairs. They phoned the police who thought it was a wind-up and refused to come out. Things continued to happen – the long mirror in the hall shattered, items hurled themselves on to the floor, smashing into pieces.

Then things returned to normal – until 9 January, when it all happened again. The few items the Bryants had managed to replace over Christmas were all smashed, and they couldn't move without scrunching shattered china and glass into the carpets; their mongrel, Trudi, cut its paw badly and needed a vet to stitch up the wound.

Over the next four months they suffered massive disruptions every month, always on the 9th, and eventually they called in a gentleman who helped me research my previous book, Father Flanagan, who carried out a full blessing. The house was, as usual, quiet for the month, but when he returned on the 9th it was to find the malevolent ghost had too. He then invited Maureen St Clair, a spiritualist medium, to join him that afternoon, when they found themselves in the centre of incredible happenings. Glasses crashed against the walls, carpets flapped at the corners, a rumbling sound came up from under their feet, and all the while footsteps could be heard upstairs although no one was there.

Mrs St Clair walked around the house. When she got to the Bryants' bedroom she sat on the bed, where she felt unseen hands pulling at the bedclothes, dragging them out from beneath her.

Then she tried to contact whatever spirit was there. Suddenly all of the activity ceased, and Father Flanagan joined her upstairs. She was having a conversation but he could neither see nor hear anyone she could be talking with. Finally, Mrs St Clair stood up saying, 'Well, that's that!' She clapped her hands in satisfaction, and proceeded down to the fridge, opened the door and pulled out a bottle of wine, opening it and pouring herself almost a half-pint.

Father Flanagan asked what had transpired and she explained: 'Over eighty years ago two children were hacked to death on this very spot, in the house that stood here before this one. The mother is seeking her dead children because they still haven't passed to the other side. She believed someone was holding them in this house. I have swept the place and they are not here. So I wished the mother Godspeed in her search, and she won't be back.'

Father Flanagan is still not totally convinced that the story is true, but the Bryants had no further disturbances.

TUTANKHAMUN'S BIRMINGHAM CURSE

On 25 November 1922, in Egypt's Valley of the Kings, archaeologists unearthed a tomb that had been lost beneath the sands of time for some three thousand years. The leader of the expedition, Howard Carter, had searched for the legendary tomb of the Tutankhamun since he had first heard of its possible existence thirty years earlier. So we can only imagine his excitement as he excavated the sixteen steps down into the sand that led to a huge door marked with the Pharaoh's seal. To everyone's surprise it hadn't been interfered with as had so many others in the vicinity of Luxor. Carter sent for his sponsor the Earl of Carnarvon, and together they made a hole in the door, lit a candle and Howard Carter pushed the light into the blackness of the tomb to look upon what he could only describe as 'Many, many wonderful things'. Those treasures had been buried in the sanctity of that place for 3,300 years.

It may well have been the tomb of a Pharaoh, but it was still a grave, the last resting place of a boy king. Maybe fate intervenes when graves are robbed, however humble, however rich. For from the moment that the first items were removed, things began to happen. Several of the Arab workers fell violently ill and died whilst working in the tomb. Two of the expedition's cooks were found drowned in the Nile. In March 1923 Lord Carnarvon was stricken with some 'mystery' infection. The official line given was that a mosquito bite had turned septic; he returned to Cairo for treatment but contracted pneumonia and died on 5 April at the Continental Hotel. It is said that all the lights in Cairo went out at that precise moment and the city remained in darkness for some hours. A nurse at the time said 'This is a cover-up, they know the truth, but they are frightened to admit it!' Back in England, at the moment of the Earl's death, his dog gave a howl and dropped dead.

Stories spread like wildfire of the curse of the tomb, for written in hieroglyphics on the door of the tomb, it was claimed, were the words 'May death slay with his wings ye who disturb the rest of the Pharaohs.' Then a national newspaper in England printed a story that gave even greater credibility to 'the curse'. It told of another tomb, that of one of Tutankhamun's high priestesses, unearthed in 1911. This woman was said to have been gifted with magical powers, given to her by the gods to protect the 'son of god on earth', Tutankhamun. Her body and many rare and ancient treasures were being shipped from England to New York, and as they were beyond price, they were placed in a specially locked cabin directly behind the wheelhouse of the ship. Hundreds of Arabs had protested at the moving of the high priestess's body from her homeland, and had warned that death and destruction would follow. The authorities ignored their pleas and the ship sailed. The ship was named the *Titanic* and over 1,500 perished in the icy seas of the North Atlantic in the early hours of 15 April 1912.

It is easy to understand the reluctance of people to involve themselves in handling any of the treasures that were being brought daily out of the tomb. Those that did could not possibly have believed what would happen. A keen museum curator offered his expertise to help preserve and store the treasures. Within two months he died in a motor accident; his wife and child were to die from 'a mystery illness'. Two local police officers were murdered by Arab workers, three Egyptian clerks who were cataloguing the finds also fell victim to 'the curse'. One lost his wife to a snakebite, another lost an arm in a bizarre accident with a ploughshare and the third suddenly became blind.

It was 3 January 1924 when they finally entered a darkened room, and found the coffin, a magnificent gold sarcophagus. By mid-February they were ready to open it. Despite the fear that the curse had caused, scientists, tourists and local workers all gathered outside the tomb waiting in excitement for news of what was inside.

The gasps of astonishment at what Carter and his men found were clearly audible to the hundreds that stood out in the blazing heat, waiting for word.

The curse continued to cause consternation to those who chose not to believe in it. An aeroplane flying some of Tutankhamun's treasures back to England lost power in three out of its four engines, and had to make an emergency landing in London. The pilot returned home to find himself homeless, as his house had burned down. The navigator travelled home by motorcycle, crashed it and had to have one of his legs amputated. In the 1960s one of the crew who had excavated the tomb was being interviewed by a BBC television programme when the lights in the studio failed. On leaving the studio, he fell into the road and a London cab missed his head by inches. From that day until his death he refused ever to speak of the expedition ever again.

In 1970 the curse spread across Britain to Birmingham. An antiques collector called Mark Wright began a tour of the Midlands in search of old and rare jewellery. He visited flea markets, fairs, pawn shops and antique shops. It was in a market in St Martin's Circus, Birmingham, that he found a scarab brooch. Wright was very taken by it and bought it for £67, a lot of money for such a thing in 1970. While he walked to his hotel on Suffolk Street, he was stopped by a man in his middle seventies who ordered him to give up the scarab. 'It must be returned to the sand or it will take your life!' said the craggy-faced man. His name was Idris Fahoud, and he had been there on the day that the sarcophagus had been opened, appalled that foreigners should be allowed to plunder the graves of his country's ancient kings.

Mark Wright listened patiently to him over coffee in a small café near the Alexandra Theatre. Having just handed over £67 of his hard-earned cash, he was certainly not going to just give the brooch away because of the superstitious ramblings of this old Arab. So he gave him a polite but firm rebuff and proceeded back to his hotel, followed by Idris Fahoud.

Wright was due to return to London the following morning, and had settled his hotel bill, packed his cases and after a tot of whisky put his head down for the night. At eleven minutes past three a terrifying scream was heard, and fellow guests hammered on his door. Eventually the night porter ran upstairs with the pass key to find Wright sitting upright in his bed, eyes wide, his mouth open in a now silent scream, his hair standing on end. At that moment a huge insect, almost the size of a sparrow, proceeded to climb out of his mouth.

The porter ran to kill the creature, but it vanished and could not be found. At one point, the porter thought he had spotted it on the top of Wright's suitcase, but it turned out simply to be the scarab brooch.

The porter had the presence of mind to shut the door on the other guests and phone for the police and ambulance to take away the body. While he waited he pocketed the scarab brooch and helped himself to half of the money in the man's wallet – after all it was of no use to him now.

Idris Fahoud visited the police station that very day, to demand the return of the scarab brooch, that did not belong to Wright, it belonged to the people of Egypt. The police explained that a thorough search of the hotel room had been made and no trace of anything answering that description had been found.

Fahoud guessed that the porter must have the brooch, and visited the hotel again. The porter denied all knowledge of it, and told

Fahoud that if he continued making allegations like this he would call the police and have him arrested. So the Arab left the man to his own devices, having warned him of the possible consequences. Two days later the porter was in a Birmingham Accident and Emergency unit having swallowed some glass in some jam; his innards had been badly lacerated and he had caught an infection and was close to death. Fahoud visited him saying that his only chance was to get rid of the scarab brooch. In his weak state the man agreed, but rather than give it to Fahoud, he ordered his daughter to take it to the market and get what she could for it. This she did and it was bought by a dealer from Yorkshire and disappeared into the North Country.

Fahoud eventually returned to Egypt in 1978, taking with him a variety of trinkets that he claimed belonged to King Tutankhamun. He took them to the Valley of the Kings and returned them to the earth. He was interviewed on his death bed by a Cairo newspaper who reported: 'He swore that the curse would remain as long as the body of the Boy King remained above the sand. "Each article stolen from the holy shrine of the Son of God will bring death to anyone who takes possession of it. I must go now, I go to join my Lord, my task is complete!".'

If the curse is real, that scarab brooch is still travelling from market to fair, from antique shop to pawn shop, carrying death wherever it goes.

THE SEVERED HAND OF COVENTRY

In 1777 Jacques Théodore was released from Coventry prison, after spending eight years in a stinking cell for a crime he certainly never committed. He had been charged with attacking a young woman from Canley Ford, found guilty and imprisoned. Three days after his trial the girl, an amateur whore called Nell Vaughan, openly boasted of how she'd 'got that Frenchie put away'. There was a tremendous anti-French feeling in England at this time, and all that Théodore had done was to refuse to purchase Nell's sexual services.

While in prison in a cell shared by eleven other criminals – rapists, murderers, arsonists, thieves and cut-throats – the Frenchman, being small in stature, had his teeth knocked out and had been savagely buggered by many of his cellmates.

To survive eight years in prison was a rarity in itself, as Coventry Jail at that time was riddled with disease and vermin. One night the Frenchman woke up to find the man in the next bunk to his being eaten alive by hundreds of rats, that were ripping away at his flesh. Two of the other prisoners tried to help him, but the rats were utterly relentless, and eventually stripped the man to the bone. The other prisoners hid his death for a month using it as a way to get more food and water.

At last Théodore was released, a shadow of his former self. Wherever he went in Coventry he was shunned, for he was the 'foreigner who had raped an English girl'. Despite his innocence he was unable to find work to raise the money to return home to Lille in France.

His frustration finally got the better of him, and he kidnapped Nell at sword point and marched her to the local magistrate. There he ordered her to tell the truth. This she did, and then he struck her with the sword in the back and watched as she slowly bled to death. No matter how long she suffered it wouldn't add up to the terrible indignities that he had undergone in that scruffy cell. The magistrate swore that if he gave up his sword he would get a fair trial.

A trial was the last thing Théodore wanted. Instead he placed his arm on a table and with his right hand he swung down his sword, severing it just below the elbow. As the Frenchman staggered around, with his sword he flicked the arm at the petrified magistrate. To his horror the severed arm climbed up his nightshirt, leaving a trail of gore behind it. On reaching the throat of the old man it clenched it tightly, squeezing the life from him.

Soon the Frenchman was marching down the street cursing everyone who approached him and swinging his sword around his head. Blood spurted from his ghastly stump, and his head began to swim, as he swiftly lost strength. He knew he had to end his life or he would certainly be placed back in prison or face the gallows.

So he stood on Swanswell Street, overlooking the lake, balanced the sabre on its hilt and fell on to the blade. He managed to struggle to his feet and took a couple of shaky paces to fall face first into the chilly water.

The arm was never found and is said still to haunt Coventry, creeping up ladies' bedspreads late in the night, and stroking their cheeks. If the woman awakes it disappears.

THE LOST LEGEND OF THE HEREFORD WURM

The lucky researcher comes sometimes across a story that was a traditional legend that virtually disappeared, remembered by only a very few folk in the area concerned. Thanks to Mrs L. P. Johnson of Worcester who sent me a photocopy from a book written in the 1700s I learned of the Hereford (or Worcester) Wurm. A wurm is not as one might suppose a long wriggly worm; it is in fact a dragon, and this one was said to live beneath the fields of the Hereford countryside.

It all started in AD 372, when King Arthur's magician Merlin (who was well-known in the province long before his involvement with the young king) lived near Worcester and the land was being ravaged by a group of vagabonds who had organised themselves into a most efficient robbing gang. They waited until all the farm workers were out in the fields and then they would descend on a village where they would steal everything worth having, rape the women, and eat all the food, before moving off to their encampment near Hanbury.

These thieves had murdered over two hundred men and raped thousands of women, and had to be stopped. So the members of Worcester's primitive council of that time approached Merlin, despite having for years discounted his supposed powers. He magnanimously agreed to help, and went out into the countryside to face these animals who had preyed on villagers throughout the county for almost three years. He was unarmed and the councilmen thought he would not stand a chance against this murderous gang who were armed to the teeth.

It was by fate or by pure chance that Merlin was in a small village outside what is now Kidderminster when the farm workers said their goodbyes and headed out into the fields. Within the hour Merlin was sharing water with the older ladies of the village when a gang numbering between forty and fifty appeared. They started running at the women and grabbing them, when Merlin stood up and shouted, 'Unhand those women, lest I strike ye dead, varlets!'

The rogue nearest him laughed at seeing this long whiskered man facing up to such a heavily armed robber army, and lifted up his club to strike the wizard. But Merlin had protected himself with a spell. The club began beating the man, who held it until he lay dead on the ground.

Merlin continued: 'Should ye choose to harm me, your evil intent will destroy ye, not me!'

The robbers could not understand what the old man meant and ran at him with swords, axes and knives. And ended up stabbing and killing themselves. One of the gang's leaders strode forward saying, 'Ye may be able to protect yourself, but we'll have our way with these women, and should ye harm us, we'll kill them all!'

Merlin knew that he couldn't protect so many villagers, so began walking in a circle. The women screamed as the vagabonds started tearing at their clothes, when suddenly from nowhere came a whirlwind. It seemed to force itself from beneath the ground, as soil and clay parted and a huge dragon climbed from a fiery pit below the village. The gang scattered as the dragon snapped its jaws shut, killing three of them. The Wurm lashed out with tongue and tail, talon and fiery breath; one by one the thugs were killed until only the leader was left. The Wurm made its way back to its pit, as Merlin addressed the last man: 'Ye must go to the pit, Hell's flames await to punish ye.'

The rogue tried to step back but Merlin's magic was too strong for him and pushed him towards the entrance to the dragon's lair. He clung desperately to the ground but a huge claw burst through the ground and dragged him under.

It is said that should anyone try to bring fear to the people of the area the Worcester Wurm will rise from its fiery home and strike them dead.

THE WORCESTER BLUEBEARD

'Murder, bloody murder!' came the cry in 1638 when an old cleaning lady opened the door to the attic of Richard Dunwoodie's house. What had she found? The story began eighteen years earlier when Dunwoodie was travelling around Britain with the historian and cartographer John Speed. To say he was a ladies' man was rather like saying that Herod wasn't fond of children. Dunwoodie, a Lowland Scot with a gentle accent, was blond with steely blue eyes that could enchant at a glance, and he swept the fair sex off their feet.

His job was to help collate the first really accurate maps of England and Wales, and he had travelled throughout the country gathering information and breaking hearts. When the bulk of research was being collated, in mid-1609 he took a house in Friar Street, Worcester. The project he worked on was highly regarded and could lead to great things – the world was his oyster, or so he thought.

Then came Bess Armitage, a girl he had dallied with eight months earlier while passing through Winchester. She had traced him to his new two-storey house through his employer. She was at least eight months' pregnant and she demanded that he marry her, and she would ruin him if he didn't.

Dunwoodie said that he would and suggested she take a room in his house for the night, rather than stay at the inn where she had left her bags. Bess was very surprised as he had known her for less than a week, and hadn't seen her for months. She realised that she had the upper hand and had succeeded in her task of finding a husband and securing a father for the baby in one fell swoop. Bess had been a 'woman of easy virtue' from the tavern where he had stayed, and the baby could have been fathered by any number of men, but Dunwoodie's feelings of guilt made him an easy victim.

He helped her enormous swollen frame up to his bedroom while he bedded down on the couch. There was no earthly chance of him sleeping, as he certainly didn't want to marry this girl, but he had told her he would, and he believed the child to be his. He had one major problem, he was already married to three other women!

This is where fate took a hand, for as Dunwoodie tossed and turned on his couch, Bess awoke and shouted down to him, 'I feel queer. I need the lav.' As he rose to go to her aid she missed her footing at the top of the stairs and tumbled to the bottom. When he got to her he saw that her nightgown was covered with blood and to his horror the baby had begun to appear. He tried to wake her but she was unconscious. The baby slipped from her body into the dazed Dunwoodie's hands. It didn't move; it just lay there eyes closed, still attached to the mother by the umbilical cord. Blood was pouring from the womb on to the highly polished wood floor, and Dunwoodie placed the infant's motionless body on a table, and tried to stem the flow of blood with a thick towel. Still the blood forced its way through as he ripped down an expensive velvet curtain in an attempt to stop the relentless river of blood. It was probably only twenty minutes or so but it seemed like a nightmare lasting hours. He tried to revive Bess but she had lost too much blood and was dead.

Dunwoodie was up to his elbows in blood and he sat there totally stunned by what had happened. He was just about to notify the authorities when there was a cough and a tiny croak from the table; the baby was starting to move. In his haste to reach the child in the dim light of the early hours he tripped and knocked the table; the baby fell and landed with a sickening thud on the floor. Its tiny head was broken and it was dead. As Dunwoodie looked down at the helpless mite he could not help himself from being sick. What was he to do now?

If he went to the authorities would they believe his story? His career was just taking off and a scandal like this would surely ruin him. So he looked in his attic and found eight large trunks full of soil awaiting the variety of bulbs and seeds he had collected, as he was a most enthusiastic gardener. He took the two bodies into the attic and placed them in the cases. He believed that the soil would soak up the bodily fluids and blood. When he could get them out of the house he would.

The opportunity never did seem to present itself, so he kept the cases and his attic firmly padlocked. The following February his employer John Speed published the *Theatre of the Empire of Great Britain*, the first great collection of detailed maps covering England and Wales. Much of the reflected glory fell on Richard Dunwoodie, and many lucrative offers were made and readily accepted. It seems that his financial future was now secure, thanks mainly to Sir Fulke Greville, Speed's patron, who thought highly of the young Scot.

This is when Dunwoodie decided to travel to Ayr in Scotland to meet his first wife, to whom he had been sending money all the while. She had read of his exploits and wanted to come back to him without delay. So she packed up her belongings and returned with him to Worcester. Richard Dunwoodie had become rather wrapped up in his devil-may-care lifestyle and the thought of having this rather plain frumpy wife appalled him. He was in love with a Worcester lady from one of the richest families of the day, the Sheridans, and had led them to believe he was the most eligible of bachelors. He already had the deaths of two people on his conscience – what would another one be? As they arrived at his house in Friar Street, she was no sooner through the front door then he was planning her demise. He took her into the large kitchen where there was a huge cleaning area, large enough to prepare a whole pig or a boar. He asked her to stand with her back to it, because he had a surprise for her. He gently closed both of her eyes, as she chuckled in excitement.

She probably never felt the blow of the heavy iron pan as it flattened the top of her head and shattered the vertebrae in her neck. She fell backwards into the trough, the blood running along the white surface down into a tiny gully designed for that precise purpose. Dunwoodie ripped off her clothes and put them on the fire he had set in the huge kitchen grate. Once more, he found himself carrying a corpse up to the attic. He had had to place a sack over her head as its contents had been dripping out across his fine carpets. He then packed her rather stout frame into another soil-filled chest. Now he could continue his pursuit of a woman that he really loved, Elizabeth Sheridan.

However, his second wife, Amelia, who lived in Cornwall, had also read of his successes and sent a letter saying that she wanted to be reunited. Dunwoodie couldn't believe his bad luck: he was due to ask for Elizabeth's hand in marriage, but as he was now 'famous' his two remaining wives would be bound to hear of it if he were to wed, and once again his promising career would be ruined. So he sent two letters, one to Amelia, the other to Gwyneth in Manchester, asking them both to come to him as soon as possible. This they did; Gwyneth arrived first and Dunwoodie guided her to the kitchen and rested her neatly against the trough. One swift blow, an enormous cracking noise and she was soon stripped and on her way up to the attic to fertilise another trunk of seeds and bulbs.

It seemed that the more Dunwoodie tried to extricate himself from his past liaisons the deeper into trouble he was getting. His nerves were just getting back under control when a knock summoned him to the front door and there was his second wife Amelia, his 'little Cornish pasty', he used to call her. She was still beautiful and obviously thrilled to be in her husband's arms again. Dunwoodie knew she had to die, but he had forgotten just how attractive she was, and it was late in the day so he thought that he could perhaps entertain her for just one night. So after a rabbit supper and a tot of rum they were soon in bed together. The following morning they were still entwined around one another when there was a rapping on the door. Dunwoodie pulled a robe around him and waddled his weary bones down to the door. It had been a night where sleep was certainly not the priority and his sagging eyes and tousled hair testified to just how seriously this man took his lovemaking. To his horror it was his ladylove Elizabeth Sheridan and her brother Alexander.

'Good heavens!' giggled Elizabeth. 'Don't you know what time it is?'

'Oh – er, no,' stuttered the Scot. 'I've not been feeling too well.'

'Aren't you going to invite us in, then?' barked Alexander. 'Or do you keep your future bride and brother-in-law on the doorstep?'

Dunwoodie was now wrapped in stark terror, but couldn't think of a single excuse to keep them out. On getting inside into the drawing room, he excused himself and dashed upstairs where Amelia was beginning to wake. He flung himself across her and placed a pillow over her head, and began to smother her. She screamed and flayed her arms about, unable to understand how the husband who had been so desperate for her was now acting in such an insane way. At first she thought it was a prank; then the cushion was forced even closer into her face, the more she screamed, the harder. Hearing the commotion upstairs Alexander shouted, 'Is everything all right?'

Dunwoodie, who was clinging desperately to Amelia's frantic body, managed a reasonably calm 'Yes. I'll be down in a second.' Then grabbing a water jug from beside his bed, he drew the pillow away. There was a split second for her to scream and she didn't take it. The jug was swung down into her face, smashing her skull and crashing so violently that it cut Dunwoodie's hand and literally shredded Amelia's face. The blood began to seep into the bedclothes as Dunwoodie walked to the top of the stairs. He nearly jumped out of his skin on seeing Elizabeth a few steps from the top.

'What's wrong, Richard? We heard a crash,' she said.

'Oh,' said the startled Scot, 'I dropped the ruddy water jug, and I've cut my hand.'

Elizabeth guided him downstairs where the cut was bathed and bandaged. Alexander was keen to leave as he was due to meet friends at a nearby inn, so Richard kissed Elizabeth softly on the cheek, and bade her farewell. At the door she turned back saying, 'I think you're ill, Richard, you are shaking like a leaf. See a physician, my pet, or you'll not see our wedding.'

Richard nodded and closed the door behind her. He rushed upstairs, placed another sackcloth bag over Amelia's splintered head, and carried her upstairs and planted her with the rest.

The wedding was arranged and in due course Elizabeth Sheridan became Richard Dunwoodie's wife, the first he ever admitted to.

She moved into his house and never ever seemed to want to know what he kept locked behind that attic door. They had been married for sixteen fairly happy years when she finally persuaded him to join her for a holiday in Tuscany, where she had distant relatives.

Without telling her husband she hired the services of three cleaning ladies to go through the house with a fine-tooth comb, so it would be spick and span on their return.

It was then that Richard heard the scream 'Murder, bloody murder!' and ran to the attic, where a cleaning lady was sitting on the floor in a panic. 'There's a dead body up here!' she said.

Dunwoodie said, 'Don't be stupid, woman, there are some old bones belonging to the family that we're waiting to put in the family tomb. Nought for you to worry yourself about.'

The old cleaning lady left the attic room muttering to herself.

Quite how Dunwoodie managed to remove the chests from the attic no one knows, but three days later they were gone.

Alexander Sheridan arrived at Dunwoodie's house to wish him 'bon voyage' and said that his maid had heard that there were dead bodies in the attic. Dunwoodie dismissed the story as a flight of fancy, saying that he had told the cleaning woman that because she was 'knebbing into his private things'. When Sheridan asked to look into the attic to 'see what all the secrecy was about', the Scot had no qualms about taking him up, and there was nothing in the room that was in the least bit incriminating. There was a painting on the wall that looked lifelike, and Dunwoodie explained that she had seen that and frightened herself in the darkness.

All was well, Dunwoodie and his wife enjoyed their holiday, and returned refreshed. It is believed that in the night Dunwoodie had taken the bodies to the local park and had buried them where they still lie. Many believe that it is only because of the 'human fertiliser' that the gardens have such a fine show every year.

Dunwoodie made a full confession on his deathbed to a priest as his wife Elizabeth sat by his side. On his death she said he was rambling, and his mind had left him.

His last words were 'Oh my God, they're waiting for me. . . .' then he died.

Were his wives lying in wait for him, hiding behind death's curtain for vengeance? We'll never be sure, but his ghost is still seen walking the avenues and alleyways of Worcester.

*In the mid 1930s there were reports of a ghost – 'an amorous spook' the local press called it as only young girls were ever pestered by it. It sounds the kind of thing Dunwoodie would be prone to do. Maybe he has to remain on earth to avoid the attentions of his battered wives.

THE PHANTOM COACH OF RUGBY

Hooves thundered along the country lanes around Rugby as a jet-black carriage driven by the old squire made pheasants fly from the hedgerows and rabbits scamper to safety. The squire's passion was speed, and no matter how tight a corner it was, he would chance his arm time and time again at increasing velocity. Eventually, disaster struck and the cart crashed into a stone wall throwing the squire into a field where he landed on sharpened slate which severed his arm.

Rather then deter the old man from driving his coach at speed again, it seemed to spur him on to be even more reckless. He had been known to trample any peasant foolish enough to be in his way. Now with only one arm, he'd hold the reins in his teeth, cracking a long black whip with his single hand. His broad, jowly face was always black with fury as he drove as if the Devil was on his tail.

The legends vary as to how this sour-faced chap met his doom; some say he drove his horses off a cliff, others that they sank into a bog, the latter is most likely in light of more recent stories.

Throughout the years following his death the one-armed squire would return almost every night, driving his ghostly carriage down the country lanes, terrifying the locals and forcing some residents to leave the area altogether. There were several attempts by the local clergy to rid themselves of this ill-tempered spirit. Some tale-tellers claim that an exorcism was carried out in the mid-1700s, yet throughout the late 1700s people still heard the phantom coach and four, so it can't have been successful.

The story goes that the squire was addicted to Drambuie, and found it hard to come by. So one night in the early 1800s a seance was held, with the great-grandchildren of the old squire in attendance. The medium managed to raise the cold-hearted gentleman from his grave, and his shadowy form hung over the table. The assembly froze in fear seeing the twisty-faced old swine growling from the beyond. He looked as unsavoury as ever as the medium, aptly named Miranda Sessions, told him that they had brought him a last tot of Drambuie. If he wanted it it was in an open bottle on the table. The people around the table were stunned as the bottle seemed to fill with smoke while the shape of the one-armed squire evaporated. In front of their eyes they saw the Drambuie apparently disappear into the cloud of smoke that swirled inside the bottle. Quick as a rat up a pipe, the medium pushed a stopper into the bottle and then poured holy water over the bottle. She claimed that there in the bottle was the squire's tainted soul.

Some say the bottle, now firmly sealed, was hurled into the River Avon, others that it was lobbed into nearby Draycote water. Whatever, the errant phantom coachman was gone for ever, or at least that's what they thought.

It seems that about sixty years later a fisherman from Church Lawford swept up a strange bottle in his net, and couldn't make out the writings on it. When he mentioned it to his friends they warned him not to uncork it, but it was the first thing he did. He tasted the sour liquid inside, and rammed the stopper back in. The landlord of an inn at Newbold on Avon told them that the bottle belonged to Brownsover Hall, where the seance had taken place. The bottle was duly returned, but ever since the one-armed squire has continued his nightmare journeys along the country lanes. Another seance was attempted and once more the unruly squire did appear, but he just laughed at their futile attempt to catch him again.

*Brownsover Hall is now a hotel and all manner of ghostly apparitions and noises have been heard, including the clacking of horses' hooves on cobbles late in the evening as the one-armed squire charges by.

*Frank Manners used to live in Coventry and in 1971 he was driving to Rugby when he stopped at a petrol station. There he saw a woman in her forties who had collapsed on the forecourt, screaming, her hair was standing on end. He managed to calm her down enough for her to be able to relate a story that sounded far-fetched but was told with such conviction that he found it hard to dispute. She'd pulled over to the side of the road just outside of Long Lawford, where she watched a hawk fluttering above the verge and then swoop down on a young rabbit. She had run out of the car to try and rescue the little creature. This was at about 5.45 p.m., the light was just on the wane, and the night beginning to creep in. The rabbit did escape, and then she heard a rumbling noise. At first, she thought it could be a heavy tractor or some construction machinery coming along the lane. Her car was on the verge and she waited to see what it was. To her shock a black coach with four white horses flew over the rise directly towards her. There, sitting atop this speeding carriage was a plump man in

115

a black hat, holding the reins in his teeth, and cracking a whip above the horses' heads. She said that she was directly in their path and tried to move but couldn't. She wanted to scream too, but no sound could escape from her frightened throat. The coach hit her head-on, and went straight through her. As she told of how it felt she was violently sick on the garage forecourt. She explained how she felt as if for that split second something evil was actually inside her body. It was as if she had been raped. Once more she vomited, and Frank suggested that she go to hospital to be checked. The woman shook her head, and begged just to be helped home to Redditch. Frank agreed to follow her home to make sure she was all right, which he did.

Three weeks later he called at the same petrol station, where he asked if the woman had been back in. She hadn't, but the attendant told of how dozens of people every year see this spectral joyrider and come in to tell him about it. On one occasion a coachload of students from Birmingham saw the phantom, and couldn't believe it was a ghost. They presumed it was a stunt for a local fête. It wasn't.

*Alfred Evans, a retired farmer, hadn't witnessed anything quite like the picture that presented itself to him in August 1982. He was out with his two old Border collies near Cold Ashby, just off the A50, quite late in the evening, when he heard a noise similar to that of a cow extricating itself from mud. He looked over a nearby hedge and saw a black shape trying to fight its way out of a mire. He had often had to help cattle and sheep in similar distress so marched over to lend a hand. On getting there he saw it was not just one horse, but two, and then three, finally a fourth, all pushing themselves from the ground. Surely no field swamp could possibly be that deep?

Then to his shock he saw that the horses seemed to be pulling a coach, and a coach with a figure still aboard. As soon as the entire carriage was out, the horses were chivvied into action by the driver, and they thundered across the field. Alfred yelled, 'Slow down, you madman, you'll hit the wall!' The driver ignored his cries, and hurtled flat-out towards the old stone wall and went straight through it without disturbing a single brick. Alfred Evans went to the nearest pub and told his story and was dismissed as an old fool so took it no further.

THE EAST MIDLANDS AND EAST ANGLIA

THE ALTHORP CANDLESNATCHER

Althorp House is the family home of the Earl and Countess Spencer, the late father of the Princess of Wales and her stepmother, and it has a most friendly ghost. Rather than frighten people, this ghost is said to keep the house safe and cut down on the electricity bills. The spirit is said to be that of an old butler who goes around late at night switching off any lights that may have been left on. The phantom is worried that a candle left on its own could start a fire, so is eternally vigilant.

It is said that on the day that Earl Spencer died many lights were left on on purpose that night. In the morning they were all out.

TOM, THE PEEPER OF CORBY

An old cobbler used to live in Corby and was generally considered to be a dirty old man. Once he was badly beaten up by the men of the town after he was caught peeping through the bedroom window of a fifteen-year-old girl as she was undressing. He was well-known for his voyeurism, having told what few friends he had about how he enjoyed looking through keyholes. Eventually, he started groping girls at the local inn and was barred. Finally, he was chased out of Corby after attempting to rape the fifty-year-old wife of a parson, grabbing her as she bent over a grave, placing flowers on it.

The cobbler, whose name is unknown, lived on the outskirts of Corby but each night he'd return to peep in people's windows while they were undressing, or in the bath, or making love.

When people experienced that common feeling of 'someone walking over their grave' the people of Corby would say 'Tom the Peeper's about'. His very last glimpse of female flesh came in November 1757 when he was staring at the bulging buttocks of

117

the wife of the local blacksmith, totally unaware that the husband was standing behind him at the time. Tom's feet were lifted off the ground as the gigantic blacksmith carried him into his workshop. There in the centre of the forge hot coals were still glowing red, and in his jealous rage the blacksmith hurled the hapless old cobbler on to the fire face down. With one gigantic hand pressing his chest deeper into the coals, his other hand pumped at the bellows, increasing the temperature. Tom screamed in agony and tried to scrabble his way out of the furnace, but each time he put his hand down on the red-hot coals his skin was burned away.

It took a sickeningly long time for him to die. Finally, when he'd stopped moving, the blacksmith left him there, his clothes almost completely incinerated and his skin black and cooking with an aroma similar to that of roast pork.

The following morning the smith told the authorities that he'd found Tom in his furnace when he awoke, and had no idea how he got there. They surmised that he'd been trying to reach an upstairs window to peep, and had fallen into the fire.

Cooked Tom was buried in Corby cemetery, but it is said that wild dogs, attracted by the smell, managed to dig him up and had eaten him, leaving only a handful of bones and the skull. His arms and legs had a lot of meat on them, so it seems likely the dogs ran off carrying them in their mouths.

*Almost 250 years later it is thought that Tom may well have returned to Corby, if the story about the Knights Lodge Inn is true. One of the tenants claims to have a sex mad spectre causing havoc in the public bar. Women have had their bottoms nipped, their breasts fondled and have felt hot and smelly breath on the back of their necks. One of the newspapers picked up on the story and listed how women had been tickled by some strange invisible being. Sometimes female bar staff have felt someone lifting up their skirts showing their undies to everyone.

*In various places throughout Corby, particularly pubs and clubs, women have claimed that they felt as if they were being watched when in toilets or changing rooms.

Mrs Lorraine Stanton from Corby was in the local leisure centre when she felt someone looking at her. She turned quickly and saw a small old man with what she described as a 'black kizzled face'. As soon as she looked at him he disappeared.

REBORN, ONE OF HISTORY'S MOST EVIL MEN

Arthur William Hull moved to Northampton from Wolverhampton in February 1887 and had a house on Denmark Street, regularly attending spiritualist meetings at a terraced house owned by an elderly lady called Cordelia Smith in Victoria Road. Yet after regular meetings covering almost twelve years, he was told that he was no longer welcome because he was possessed by an evil spirit. Hull thought that she was being petty because he had argued with her over the cost of the sittings, so he took counsel from another spiritualist lady who lived on the other side of Northampton, in Lower Harding Street. Within the first meeting, she screamed and demanded that he leave. This frightened him and he found himself visiting his physician who was an amateur hypnotist. Hull wanted to know if he had lived before or whether he was possessed by a demon.

Hypnotic techniques were in their infancy, but the physician had studied Chinese relaxation exercises and had placed people in a trance before. So they agreed to try hypnotism, and Hull went back on 4 January 1900. To the physician's suprise as soon as he was taken back he started talking fluent French. The physician understood a little of what was being said, but interrupted the exercise to fetch one of his colleagues to interpret. As soon as the French doctor heard what the man was saying he became pale, and had to sit down whilst he wrote page after page of Hull's outpourings.

The hypnotised Hull claimed to have been Gilles De Laval, one of France's most respected and beloved knights. Yet much of the talk had been about the sodomy of young children, murder and rape. So, having returned Hull to consciousness, the two doctors arranged another appointment, and then set off to the library to research into this man Gilles De Laval. The French doctor had heard the name, but couldn't remember in what context.

Eventually, they saw the name linked with that of Joan of Arc, for he had been one of her commanders. As his own personal power grew he built up a private army that did whatever they wanted. He found enjoyment in watching children being tortured, and would collect any children he found in whatever part of France, taking them home to be tortured and killed. He particularly enjoyed watching his men bugger children as young as three; those between eight and fourteen of either sex he would take to his own bed and rape. Whenever his men gathered for a feast a child would be placed in a torture contraption to suffer throughout the meal. Sometimes a youngster would be perched with a spike up his rectum, then as time progressed gravity would force his weight down on the spike and it eventually penetrated the full length of his body. Other times a youngster would be tied to a table and each guest had to cut off some part of his body without killing him. Fingers, thumbs, the penis, an eye or an ear. The man whose amputation killed the child lost a substantial wager to Gilles De Laval.

The turn-around had been amazing: this sainted and holy man, who was renowned as a friend to beggars, patron of the Arts and the embodiment of all things chivalrous, had become one of the most evil men ever to walk this Earth.

De Laval had used his 'holier than thou' image to act as a smokescreen for his other interests, too; in black magic, for instance, and he was a skilled alchemist. His hero was Caligula who had put many of the perverted and disgusting ideas into De Laval's mind. In October 1440 he was eventually made to answer for his sins of heresy, sodomy, sacrilege and up to two hundred child murders. In the public square at Nantes he was placed in a wooden chair and garrotted to death.

This mindboggling discovery made Hull's next hypnosis particularly interesting, as he became De Laval almost instantly. It seems that Hull's alter ego lay just below the surface of his consciousness, and seemed to be growing in power. The two doctors began writing a paper on their astounding findings. They proclaimed to friends that this was proof positive of reincarnation.

Then a Northampton newspaper told of how a little boy had been attacked and sexually molested by a man who was still at large. The doctors were disgusted, but didn't believe for one minute that Hull could possibly be responsible. He was a quiet, unassuming man who was very gentle and kind.

Yet as the sessions continued through the year, eight children had been attacked or raped, so the doctor decided to ask Hull if he had assaulted them. They felt sick in their stomach when De Laval answered them in French saying, 'Those guttersnipes deserve such treatment, their lives are only of use when they are tools of my desire!' Inadvertently they had loosed this sick man from a bygone age upon the innocent children of Northampton.

The physician had an idea. 'Perhaps if we take Hull to the point of De Laval's death we can exorcise this monster's presence from him.'

The French doctor agreed it was worth a try and they began taking De Laval through his life, hearing disgusting stories of insane treatment and murder. Then finally, after a sickening review of his bloodsoaked life, they talked to the recumbent Hull about the wooden seat he sat on at the public execution. Hull sat up as if he was in that seat and his voice boomed out De Laval's words of confession. How he was a confirmed Christian and that his own execution was a fitting punishment. As he had confessed he would still get to Heaven and sit on the right hand of God.

The physician then asked him what had happened next, and at that very moment they could clearly see Hull's neck tightening; his face twisted in agony and he began to gasp. The next split second was shocking and horrific as an invisible garrotte sliced through Hull's neck and his head lolled down upon his chest and his clothes became awash with blood. The physician clapped his hands and clicked his fingers to bring Hull round, and did so just in time to see Hull's eyes trying to comprehend the torment he was in. He held his hands up to his throat and to his horror they both slid inside the open slit. He tried to scream but his windpipe had been severed and blood was pouring into the open hole and he was choking on his own blood. Hull fell headlong on to the floor and the pool of blood widened to surround their feet as they both screamed with disbelief. When they had regained their composure they thought of contacting the authorities, but how could they? Surely no one could believe such a story? So they cleaned their room, removing all traces of blood and the late Mr Hull, and put the body in a big lockable trunk, which they took on a cart to where Becketts Park meets Midsummer Meadow, close to Bedford Road. There they offloaded it, waited until dusk and buried the body deep, so it would never be found. They even took the trouble to plant prickly bushes over it as discouragement to the interfering eye. The doctors had already told close friends about Hull, so began explaining how they had confronted him about the child attacks, and how he had denied it. However, as Hull had refused to attend any further sittings they presumed him guilty and in hiding. They even notified the police, who tried to find him for questioning. In 1937 the story got out of how the doctors had murdered him, but it was never followed up. The child assaults had stopped and parents could rest easier in their beds.

*There have been a few strange sightings at Midsummer Meadow over the years, but Hull's body has never been found nor disturbed, and in light of who else is buried with him, perhaps it's just as well.

MARY QUEEN OF SCOTS IN OUNDLE

An old monastery in Oundle, Northamptonshire, was transformed into an inn, and it is claimed that many additional building materials had come directly from Fotheringhay Castle, which had been demolished by King James I after his mother Mary, Queen of Scots, was executed there. The innkeeper, a bit of an Arthur Daley of his time, decided to pay the men demolishing the Castle to save the best bits for him, secretly carrying them to Oundle in the dead of the night. Roofing joists, timbers, wood panelling, even the staircase, were all saved and used in the building of what is now known as The Talbot Hotel. The bannister is said to bear marks made by Mary's Royal seal ring, as she walked down the stairs each and every morning.

The hotel is a very atmospheric building, and it is easy to see how any self-respecting ghost would be more than happy to choose it as its home. It is believed that not only did those workmen supply the inn with materials – they also brought the spirit of Mary, Queen of Scots, for she has been seen many times over the decades.

*The first plausible sighting was recorded in a newspaper in 1865 by a feature writer called Thomas Case. 'At almost midnight on the 27th of February,' he wrote, 'I was passing under an archway towards the entrance to an Oundle Inn when I saw a phantom. I hesitate to tell of my tale lest you think me addle-brained, but I saw the figure as plainly as you see this newspaper. It was of a slight woman in a long black Elizabethan dress. She wore pearls and a long beaded crucifix around her neck, a neck masked by a heavily ridged collar. She seemed to be leaving the premises and so convinced was I that she was real, I even exchanged pleasantries. She walked past me and I was less than a yard from her, and saw her face clearly. She was very pale, her hair swept away from her face, and pinned behind her ears and kept in place by a skull cap. Although she did not reply to my "good evening" she looked uncommon calm, and passed by me with the hint of a smile on her lips. She turned right under the archway, and so intrigued was I that I took to following. Yet as I reached the turning she had vanished, there was no sign. I asked a fellow reveller, and he claimed to have seen no one.

'On arriving at the inn I was entranced by a painting that stood centrally on the inn wall, the painting was of the phantom. On seeking the name of such an enchanting creature I was told it was Mary, Queen of Scots. You know I have oft been critical of such matters, but now I have witnessed this magic I declare myself eternally a believer.'

*Tourists have commented on how they have heard noises, sobbing, anguished muttering and footsteps in the night. Some visitors have even felt something pushing them down into the bed. Once a man was taking the mickey out of the ghost stories when the portrait of Mary fell with a crash onto the bar floor, silencing his jibes in one fell swoop.

A BIT OF ROUGH LUCK

The class divide in days gone by ruined many a romance, when the rich could only dally with the lower classes, never marry them. Lady Elizabeth Gray, however, decided to cast caution to the winds and marry her coach driver. It was obvious that no local clergyman would carry out such a service, as her father would not permit it, so they would elope. They met one evening at the George Inn, Silsoe, in Bedfordshire, swore their love for one another and packed the coach in readiness for their escape. Before they left, though, Lady Elizabeth's maid arrived in great haste at the inn to warn them, that somehow word had leaked out and her father and his friends were out searching for them.

So, without fully checking the carriage, the couple dived aboard and galloped off into the night. However, their desperate effort to evade capture was too hasty, and the carriage was far from safe. On a sharp bend in the road, the horses turned and the carriage didn't, sending the coach and its occupants crashing through a fence and into a lake where they both drowned.

The lake is now regularly haunted by Lady Elizabeth Gray, who is said to walk across the surface of the water, glowing in a pinkish light.

In the past twenty years over fifty sightings have been documented. The coachman doesn't seem to appear at all.

*George McIntosh from Hertford was fishing in the lake when he saw something heading toward him. 'It was just like that advert on the telly, where they eat porridge and it makes them glow. A woman walking on the water with a blue glow right around herself. I started laughing at first, believing that I was seeing things. Then as she got close up I could see her dress clearly, peach-coloured ribbons and lacework. A hat tied beneath her chin, and what a beautiful face she had. I got totally lost in her. Then she just turned and walked back across the lake. Once she'd disappeared I took it for granted that I'd nodded off and imagined the whole thing.'

THE GIBBET AT CAXTON

One of the busiest men in old England was the hangman at Caxton. It was his duty to 'see to' those that needed their neck stretched for crimes ranging from the theft of a chicken, to mass murder. In the 1600s the penalty seemed to be fairly standard. Whatever crime you committed you'd likely as not be hung by the neck until you were dead.

The Caxton Gibbet was of the T-shaped variety, so two could swing at the same time. Different hangmen had different techniques. In the early days they would stand the victim on a wood block, then kick it out from under them; later they had special trapdoors made, so a decent job could be done.

The site of the gibbet is said to be haunted by thousands of men, women and children who have all lost their lives to the hangman's noose. Many are said to have been buried beneath, or close to, the gibbet itself. According to legend one of the ghosts said to be there is that of a small child, aged about seven, believed to be the youngest to be hanged there. In the early 1700s the child, whose name was Mary, found herself charged with murder. A local nobleman called Ramsey was thrown from his horse and broke his neck on a stone wall. Mary's dog had been playing nearby and it was claimed by other riders that the dog had attacked the horse. No one can be sure what the truth actually was; however, by the time the story reached the court it was that Mary had set her dog on Ramsey's horse, causing his death. Mary was sentenced to death, yet on the day of her execution protesters had to be restrained by soldiers to allow the hanging to go ahead.

A tiny noose was placed over her head, along with a black hood, her minute hands tied with a velvet ribbon. Men and women alike were appalled by the murder of an innocent child right before their eyes. When the child's body fell, suspended by the knotted rope, her hands suddenly became free, and she reached up to rip the black hood from her face. Women fainted in fear, men turned and ran, including several of the soldiers who were supposed to be securing the area. Many claimed that the child started singing, and that rather than appearing to be in the agony that was part of such a barbaric death, she looked calm and happy, smiling at those who stood and watched.

Until the middle 1800s, children used to chant the rhyme:

> 'Mary, Mary, how you swing,
> On a hangman's rope and still you sing,
> Your neck is broke, your candle out
> Yet you smile instead of shout!'

Visitors to the Caxton Gibbet have heard the weeping of a child, or seen a tiny ghostly infant hiding around corners, or peering out from behind trees.

*There are countless other ghostly sightings made on a regular basis from around that area, spirits of all shapes and sizes. It is a regular challenge for charity to drive out there and remain through the hours of darkness. This became a less popular activity after Malcolm Hilary from Caxton, while leading a ghost hunt one night in 1976, suffered a heart attack in his car.

*The pub nearby, called the Caxton Gibbet, suffers various visitations including an ex-innkeeper whom some believe was the very last man hung on the gallows there. It is said that he had over the years murdered and robbed a number of guests (some say as few as three, others as many as twenty-eight) and had disposed of their bodies in the well that stands at the foot of the stairs. After his arrest various parts of severed bodies were recovered. That landlord is said to visit rooms in the pub in search of valuables, and if anyone tries to stop him he turns nasty and throws things around.

Strange footsteps are heard, and knocking sounds from the walls; in the 1960s Rosemary Barton from Cambridge claims to have heard a scream come from the well.

UNREQUITED LOVE, HOLYWELL

There is an ancient saying that 'too much love will kill you', and that's exactly what happened to a beautiful nineteen-year-old Huntingdon lass called Juliet Tousley (or Tilton as some tales tell).

Her father had arranged that she marry the local poultryman, although she had made it clear that she hated the old bugger. She was already in love with a local woodsman called Tom, whom she had been seeing on the quiet for almost eight months. Tom, however, was not in love with Juliet, but was quite happy to have sex with her at every possible opportunity. That was until 1050 when he declared his undying love for another girl who lived in Holywell.

This bombshell totally destroyed Juliet, who could see an unhappy future with the fat and sweaty poultryman. To make things worse every single day she would see the man she loved in the arms of another woman. On the day that Tom was due to be married she hanged herself from a willow tree, and was buried beneath it, a terrible end to a tragic love.

*Every 17 March Juliet's ghost appears, sometimes hanging from a bough, other times dancing around the area.

*In 1987 Marion Ross took her three sisters for a meal at the Ferry Inn in Holywell, built on the original site of the willow tree. In the middle of their meal one of the sisters screamed – in the centre of the room she saw a body swinging in mid-air, the eyes wide open and staring, the hands clutching at the heart. She did not know of the legend. The date – 17 March!

CROMWELL AT ST IVES

If there really is such a thing as a ghost, then the busiest of them all has to be that of Oliver Cromwell. Many places claim to be regularly visited by him. One of his most regular haunts is the Golden Lion Hotel in St Ives in Cambridgeshire. The building had been used as his headquarters, and during the 1800s there were literally hundreds of reports of Cromwell's ghost walking in the grounds, most generally seen next to a tall oak tree. In fact, it became rather like a shrine for those of his followers who still supported his views long after his death.

In the writings of one Philip Pope is this bizarre report: 'I believe not in the after-life, yet I have myself seen Cromwell stirred from his grave at the oak at St Ives. He was as solid as we, and stood facing me at a distance of no more than twenty paces. Those with me gasped, and others turned and ran away. It was certainly he, and I viewed with others until after almost thirty minutes he slowly faded away. Did I dream it, nay I did not. Was I afflicted with drink, nay nor can I say 'twas that. If ye have no life beyond death how does that dog Cromwell still walk this earth?'

The phenomenon seems to have ended in the 1870s, for since then the only ghostly sightings in the vicinity have been of a troublesome kind. The Golden Lion claim a 'lady in green' sweeping along the corridors and frightening guests. There have also been several reports of poltergeist activity, including doors bolting by themselves, bells ringing, taps being turned on, bedclothes being pulled off beds and an ashtray that flew from the bar narrowly missing the landlord.

Oliver Cromwell would surely never bother with such trifles, particularly as he chose to show himself to thousands a century and a half before.

VENGEANCE ON ACLE BRIDGE

Throughout history killings have always led to more killings and this was certainly the case when a well-known brute called Josiah Burge started his murderous trek around the county. It was thought that even as a child Burge had pushed one of his seven-year-old playmates into the path of a horse that trampled him to death. As a village tough he was universally despised, and the local girls all shunned him. Word spread of the kind of thug he was, and he wasn't made welcome anywhere.

So desperate was he for a woman that he decided he would pounce on a girl as she walked home along a quiet country road. Her heeled shoes clicky-clacked along the roadway while he stealthily pursued her on the other side of the hedge, keeping just out of sight. Then suddenly out of the corner of her eye she spotted the shadowy figure and started running. Burge dived over a stile, knocking her into the ditch where he struggled to restrain her. She was swearing and cursing at him until the rogue's patience snapped and he slammed a fist down on to her face, hammering over and over again. Even when she no longer fought back, Burge kept hitting her, unaware that he had broken her neck. The attack may

127

well have started as an attempted rape, but ended as a bloody murder. Burge didn't give her another thought, he made no effort to hide the body, he simply walked away. He had murdered before, he would again, and it seems that he had no concern that he might be found out. He'd been a bully from the age of five and no one had ever dared to face up to him. He was well over six foot and almost as broad, and he had a face similar to that of a bulldog eating a wasp.

The murdered woman had a brother who was told that Burge was boasting to his guttersnipe mates about how he'd killed 'a snotty bitch' and left her in the hedgerow. The brother began to shadow Burge and late one evening, under a crescent moon, he followed him towards Acle Bridge. Burge's boots crunched along the gravel pathway, as the brother mirrored the murderer's pursuit of the sister now long underground.

As Burge started crossing the bridge the brother plunged a knife into his back. To his horror, Burge turned around and threw him to the ground. The knife clanged across the road, forcing the brother to scramble after it on his knees. No sooner had he picked it up than Burge kicked him in the stomach, lifting him clear off the ground. He was about to hoof him again when the brother grasped his leg and slit the tendons behind his knee bringing Burge crashing to the ground. As Burge howled in pain the brother slit the other leg too, leaving the murderer lying helpless on the ground. The brother then picked up a huge stone and crashed it down on the man's chest. Burge, his lung punctured, gasped for breath. The brother was so exhilarated by his success in gaining revenge on his sister's murderer that he grasped the killer's head and slit his throat.

Some believe he reached inside the gaping wound and pulled Burge's tongue through the hole, creating the 'Devil's necktie'. Whatever the case, the killer had been killed. The brother was never brought to justice because no one locally could blame him for seeking vengeance.

Exactly one year to that day, the brother walked back to Acle Bridge and was taking a swig from a hip flask, when a huge skeleton came towards him, clenching his throat between bony fingers, squeezing the life from him. That's how the legend goes; others claim it was one of Burge's associates paying him back.

They say that every year on 7 April blood begins to well into a puddle on the very spot that Burge was killed.

THE GHOST PUB OF HORNING

Many very reasonable explanations have been given for sightings of ghosts and spirits, yet very few could come up with anything to explain the bizarre occurrence in February 1950 in Norfolk.

William Baxter was returning to his home county after living in Australia for almost six years. Like so many others he'd gone off to war in the early 1940s serving in Burma in the almost impossible conditions fighting along the Mayu Peninsula on the Bay of Bengal. His regiment was instrumental in the capture of Maungdaw in 1942, and he was mentioned in Despatches for his gallantry. After the war Baxter, who was not married, wrote to his parents, who lived in Sea Palling, telling them he wasn't going to return home, as one of his best mates, an Australian soldier called Frank Dobbs, had offered him employment in Brisbane.

He had been away from home for years and had nothing to go back to, so he took his chance and he helped build up a small but successful engineering company.

On getting back to Norfolk Baxter, along with his business partner Dobbs, decided to spend a night out before landing on William's parents. So they went out to the pub that had been his favourite, the Ferry Inn in Horning, and had a skinful before rolling into the boarding house they'd booked into that morning. Next morning they returned to the Ferry Inn for a swift half before driving to Sea Palling. They couldn't find the pub.

They'd spent almost four hours there the night before, singing with Chalky the landlord and about two dozen others. Baxter put their inability to find the place down to the thunderous hangover he had, so instead of having the hair of the dog, they set off for his parents' home.

On getting there, to a tearful welcome from Mum, they settled down to lunch, and conversation came around to their night at the Ferry Inn. 'You must've been drunk. It's not there any more!' Mr Baxter declared. William thought his dad was joking and went on to say, 'We were both there last night. Chalky looked the same as the day I went overseas.'

At this his father rose and proceeded to dig through the top drawer of his sideboard, pulling out a collection of newspaper cuttings.

'I collected these for you over the war years, son,' he said, 'to keep you posted about what was happening here at home.'

Sorting through them, he handed a yellowing front page to his

129

son, on it a headline read: 'Nazi Bomb Blasts Pub'. The piece told of how a huge German bomb had landed on the Ferry Inn on 26 April 1941. The building had been completely destroyed and 22 people were killed, including the barman, Peter 'Chalky' White.

William Baxter and Frank Dobbs were both frozen to the spot, for they knew that they had spent the entire night in a public house that was no longer there. Their hangovers were real, their memories of the night before identical, yet it seemed that all of the people that they had named as having seen there were killed in that blast nine years earlier.

*The Ferry Inn was rebuilt in 1956 and the only ghost haunting the Ferry Inn now is said to be that of a young girl who was raped and murdered nearby in 1916, and returns every twenty years to the place where she was so ruthlessly despatched.

THE NOOSE OF BILDESTON

Whenever I hear of yet another pub that claims to be infested with ghosts I am always sceptical, yet the Crown Inn, in Bildeston, Suffolk, does seem to have an interesting track record. To be honest, I was about to exclude the place from the book until I received a story from Jacqueline Marr from Romford. It told of a member of her family who suffered a tragic death at an inn on Bildeston's High Street in the 1800s. Although in her letter there was no mention of the Crown Inn, it does seem to tally.

So let's away to rural Suffolk, in the days of the old man at his plough, women planting in the fields and the old squire living a life of leisure in his mansion. There seemed to be no escape in those days, if you were born poor, more than likely you would die much the same way. Yet Helen Marr had higher ideals, she had been raised on the writings of such as Walter Scott, and dreamed of being waited on hand and foot, of being swept off her feet by her very own 'Sir Lancelot' who would carry her to his Castle and protect her for ever more. She was wise enough to realise that it was most unlikely, but she could dream, and dream she did.

Miraculously, she met a young man in Bildeston on market day, and they struck up a close friendship. To her shock and utmost delight she discovered he was the local squire's son, and heir to his fortunes. He had returned some months earlier from Spain, where he had fought alongside Sir John Moore to repulse Soult's French battalions. The young man's name was Frederick Morton, and he had been wounded by grapeshot, and returned to England to recuperate.

The two didn't know how long they would be together, so they made sure that they would squeeze the most out of every single second. They would ride together around the Morton estate, picnic, travel to London, journey along the coast, always clinging to one another. They were the very picture of love in bloom. It was then that Frederick received his orders to return to his unit. This hit them like a hammer, their immediate plans crumbled away, as they proceeded to prepare for the parting. Frederick spoke to Helen of love, marriage and children, of how he would write every day, and on his return they would never be parted again.

Squire Morton, Frederick's father, was less keen on this union, as Helen was from a poor family with nothing to offer the rich Morton bloodline. He saw the girl as merely a mercenary money grabber, interested only in his son's wealth and position. Nothing could have been further from the truth; Helen really loved young Frederick and it wouldn't have mattered if he was penniless, such was her pure and undying love.

After a tearful farewell Helen was driven in a coach back to her father's tied cottage close to the edge of the Morton estate. The entire journey was an earbashing from the Squire as to how 'these childish infatuations' had to be put into perspective. How Frederick was promised to the daughter of a wealthy family in a neighbouring borough. Helen could see then that she was being frozen out, and could only hope and pray that Frederick had meant all of the things he had said to her.

A few months later the United States declared war on Great Britain and Frederick Morton was one of the men ordered to journey to 'the New World' with his regiment. The year was 1812 and no one believed that Britain, one of the world's great colonial powers, could possibly be defeated by a rabble of a nation such as America then was. Helen had hoped to see Frederick before he left, as she had some important news. However, Squire Morton had met Frederick in London and had escorted him to Southampton where the regiment joined its ship for the horrendous journey across the Atlantic towards Baltimore.

On the Squire's return he was surprised to see the Marr girl waiting for him in his study. Her important news could wait no longer. She was pregnant.

She removed her cape to show that she was at least eight months, and the Squire's grandson was to be born a bastard. Old

131

man Morton tried to take this in his stride and offered her a bribe. When this didn't work he tried to avoid any scandal by sending her to a private hospital in the country to have the baby. Helen did visit the hospital, but returned after a week, when staff told her that the baby was to be adopted. This was Frederick's baby, and she wanted to keep their child.

Finally the Squire threatened to run her family out of the shire if she refused to cooperate.

Over the next few weeks he tried every conceivable tactic to intimidate. Helen's old dog, a golden labrador called Ben, had its throat cut, was disembowelled, and its intestines trailed the full length of the fence around the Marrs' garden.

In the early hours the family discovered the house was on fire; they managed to save most of the building, but the roof needed to be entirely rethatched.

Helen's father was beaten unconscious by some of Morton's farm labourers.

Every day there would be an incident, until finally the Squire decided that Helen would only relent if she herself was threatened. So, reluctantly, he ordered two of his most loutish workers to catch her when she was alone, and force her out of the county. They followed her for almost two days. One evening she was heading home through Bildeston as darkness crept across the August landscape, and they snatched her. One with his hand over her mouth, the other clenching her legs tightly, they carried her into the stables of an inn around the back of the High Street. They locked the door, and lit a lamp. There on the straw lay the pregnant girl, terrified that her struggling may have harmed her unborn child.

The men spat threats at her, and she spat curses back at them.

Helen was a most attractive girl, and this gave the thugs another idea. One of them held her hands, and the other began to unbutton her long dress. She tried to scream, only to have a gag tied across her face. 'You caught the Squire's son by opening your legs, so now you'll have to open your legs to us too!' She panicked and struggled, fighting as best she could. All the while the verbal assault continued. 'We'll say the baby could be ours, you slut, then where'll you be?'

Finally when the dress, already stretched as far as it could be, was opened the huge stomach could be seen. Surely the baby was due in only a matter of days. Even these disgusting louts couldn't have sex with a woman in this condition. They were running out of ideas, so they tied her hands behind her back and placed a noose around her neck, hurling the other end of the rope over one of the roof joists.

'All right, bitch,' barked one of the toughs, 'unless you swear to leave the county you'll swing this night!'

Still Helen refused to leave, saying, 'When Frederick returns you'll both pay for this with your lives!'

At that one of the men lifted the pregnant woman off the ground, returning her to her feet with a bump. 'That's a warning, lady, we don't want to hurt you, but hurt you we will. Just get yourself gone and you'll not be hurt.'

Still she shook her head. The thugs were at a total loss as what to do, so finally they both pulled on the rope lifting Helen right up into the air, so high she was almost up to the roof. They were just about to bring her back down, suitably scared when the weight of the baby and the shock of the noose began the birth process. Both of the louts were unaware of this until to their horror the baby plummeted to the stable floor with a sickening splat. The men let go of the rope and Helen's choking body fell the fifteen-to-twenty feet on top of the baby. Her hands were still tied and she rolled helplessly around the blood-sodden stable floor. Behind the gag she was screaming over and over again. The men knew that they would pay with their lives if they were discovered party to this, so they grabbed the rope and pulled her back up by her throat. She kicked, wriggled and writhed for almost thirty minutes until finally the life was choked out of her. All the while she was gazing down at the child, created by their special love, who had been killed in such a senseless manner.

Before the men left they cut the ropes that had tied her hands, removed the gag, and left the body hanging, as if she had committed suicide.

The Squire was appalled to hear that she had taken her own life, but deep down was glad that both she and the baby were no longer a problem. Now his first grandson would come from the upper classes, thus guaranteeing the blue-blood of the Morton family line.

His happiness was soon brought to an end by a letter from the government saying that Frederick Morton had been killed within days of his arrival in America in a battle to capture Fort Detroit. The Squire was the last male in the family line; ironically he had been the man behind the death of the only child with any claim to the estate.

133

*Whether the stable concerned was that of The Crown Inn, Bildeston, I can't be sure, but they do have a ghost, supposedly that of a woman found hanging in their stable.

*If you visit the Crown Inn they have as many as four phenomena. The ghastly experience of the stable, a most eerie place in the candlelight. Two young children from the late 1800s have been spotted by customers. There's a ghostly old man in the bar, and a swishing sound, perhaps the crinolines of Helen Marr as she tries to escape from her torturers.

THE COTSWOLDS TO THE THAMES

BOSSY BETTY, THE GOOD WITCH

If ever there had been a popularity contest in Gloucestershire in the middle to late 1700s it would certainly have been won by Elizabeth Bastre, known to everyone as 'Bossy Betty'. This strange woman in her fifties had the ability to cure the ills of the beasts of the field. She grew a variety of strange herbs and plants from which she had been known to create 'magical potions'. It is without doubt that she had saved many lives. She was also Cirencester's midwife for many years; almost half the town had been brought into the world by her.

In 1786 a 'witchfinder' came into town, but was unable to find anyone that fell even loosely into the category of heretic. Those self-proclaimed 'witchfinders' were often basically wicked. Their reputation was that of being a murderous brood, using the name of God as an excuse to murder, rape and plunder. Any young girl who refused to have sex with the witchfinder or his officers often found herself tied to a stake and burned alive as a witch. The homes of those charged as witches were considered 'spoils of their Holy war'.

They would never have heard of Elizabeth Bastre, had the witchfinder not complained that his 'vitals were aflame'. So 'Bossy Betty' was summoned and when he dropped his trousers, she saw at once that the witchfinder had syphilis in its late stages. At that time there was no cure, only a variety of poultices that could reduce the pain. Betty was not known for holding her tongue, and whilst applying a compress made from various leaves and berries, she told this so-called 'soldier of God' a few home truths, explaining that no true holy man would ever suffer such a complaint. She suggested in front of his own men that he should be burned at the stake for any serious good to come out of his existence. Within two days she was arrested and charged with being a witch.

135

The people of Cirencester and its surrounds got up in arms, demanding that she be freed at once. They refused to allow a stake to be put up in their market square, and each time wood was collected, they would scatter it. On one occasion Betty was brought out and a fire started, and hundreds of townspeople brought out buckets to extinguish the flames.

Finally they chose to hang poor Betty. Before life finally ebbed from her she cursed them, and said wherever she was buried she would remain to haunt it for ever.

She was buried at a crossroads outside Cirencester that is known as Betty's Grave.

There have been sightings of floating lights around the crossroads, perhaps it's 'Bossy Betty' still casting her spells.

THE OXFORD LEPERS

Throughout the Napoleonic wars various sites in Oxfordshire were used to house hundreds of French prisoners. Many were injured or diseased, and those instructed to care for them were disgusted to uncover several dozen cases of leprosy.

John Morgan and his wife Thelma were charged with running a house where some of these lepers were to be held, four to a room in the large residence. Such was the fear in those days of contracting leprosy that the Morgans had holes cut into each door so they would not have to breathe the same air as 'the doomed'. The lepers were never given food that needed a plate, and each had his own cup, which each day would be filled with water. For all their caution, however, one day Thelma, a rather addle-minded blonde overkeen on the ale, unlatched a door, and one of the fitter French lepers escaped. Rather than admit to their mistake, they claimed that he had died and that they had buried him.

The Frenchman hid in the fields around Oxford, until one day, while sleeping in a field that had been allowed to lie fallow, he was trampled by a plough horse, and cut in two by the plough. The farmer was horrified, thinking he had accidentally killed a traveller. Times were dangerous, so the farmer merely dug a deep hole at the side of the field beneath the prickly hedge, and placed the two halves of the Frenchman's body into it, covering it with rocks and soil.

For that day on, the ghost leper of Oxford has walked its streets late at night. There was a rhyme recited by children in the streets while skipping that became well known in the 1800s:

'Pierre, Pierre,
Are you here or are you there?
In the bed or in the chair?
We see you were cut in two,
Now whatever can you do
Poor Pierre, Pierre.'

*In 1947 Donald Smart from Osney Lane off Hollybush Row, Oxford, was walking through the Botanic Gardens near Magdalen Bridge when he saw someone hiding in bushes. The figure seemed to be glowing, a grey misty figure with a well defined shape. Donald walked closer and as he neared it, the crouching man turned and rose to his feet. The figure's face had been eaten away, the skin from his nose had completely gone, leaving a deep hole in his face and you could see the inner workings of the mouth and throat through the gap. One eyeball hung on a long thread bobbing around his flaking cheek. The man began to speak and his teeth were so loose in his head they seemed to wave from side to side. If the man had spoken Donald didn't wait to hear what he had to say, he was off like a scalded cat. He had no knowledge of the legend of the 'Oxford Leper' and thought it was some kind of monster he had stumbled upon. Donald died in 1977 still swearing that he had witnessed this ghastly apparition.

*In 1956 three ladies were walking along Oxford High Street having visited a café for early morning tea, and about to begin some serious shopping, when one of them tripped over an uneven paving stone. Whilst on the ground she spotted a human finger. On bringing this gruesome discovery to the attention of her two friends they decided that they had better report it to the local police. They knew there was a police box near the prison off New Road, so gingerly they picked up the rotting finger, placing it in a handkerchief and walked on along Queen Street. It was there that they found themselves confronted by a crouched man who blocked their path.

One of the women shouted at him, but he wouldn't budge. He spoke in a mumble, keeping his head behind his arm. He beckoned as if he wanted something from them. All they wanted was to be past him, so they could get to the police. Finally Mrs Taylor decided to shock this old tramp, so she opened up the handkerchief she was so carefully carrying, and showed the man the finger saying, 'See, we've got to take this to the police, so out of the way!'

At that the tramp held out his hand and the middle finger was missing. The three ladies screamed, dropped the finger and rushed back along the High Street. Later, accompanied by a policeman, they returned to the spot but the finger was gone.

*The house used as the leper prison may well be the building known to those in Thame as The Bird Cage, on the Cornmarket. It is said that one of the lepers held there was stoned to death by a mob, and returned to the building as a most discontented ghost. Some nights a pounding can be heard. Many have heard a pounding on the walls, and objects have been seen rising and falling. No amount of investigation has come up with any explanation other than that it must be a poltergeist.

THE DATCHWORTH PIEMAN

One of the earliest recorded Freemasons in Britain was a Hertfordshire butcher called Clibbon. He helped collect the first major lodge in the early 1700s. By 1717 there were about 1,300 Freemasons in Britain, and Clibbon was a high-ranking Mason in the Grand Lodge based at the Goose and Gridiron Tavern in London's Covent Garden. Each week Clibbon would travel from Hertfordshire to attend a meeting.

However, Clibbon was not as wealthy as he had boasted to his Masonic colleagues that he was, and he needed money to help pay for his travelling and overnight stays. So he began selling his pies in Datchworth Market, and using the extra money to support his masonic duties. The Grand Lodge was full of some of the richest men in London, and Clibbon was at full stretch to keep up. Eventually, the Masons opened a gambling club and this frittered away even more of Clibbon's money, so he became even more desperate not to lose face. So each week after Datchworth Market, Clibbon would put on a disguise, cover his mouth with a mask and rob a fellow stallholder of his hard-earned profit. Over eighty robberies took place before Clibbon was followed home and reported. He was arrested on his return from London and, such was the outcry in Datchworth, he was sentenced to death. The Freemasons were asked to gain his release, and they were successful, and a Royal pardon was sent to Hertfordshire. However, the letter never reached the magistrate, as the delivery boy read it and delayed it until after his execution.

The thieving pieman was tied to a horse by his wrists, and the horse was ridden at speed through the town until he was dead. It took almost 45 minutes of tortuous agony before he breathed his last. His chest was skinned down to the bone. His body was left lying in the road for the street dogs to devour.

*Clibbon's ghost is said to be seen around Datchworth, still bound at the wrists and dragging chains behind him. Late in the evening deathly screams are often heard too, especially near the station.

THE WICKED LADY

Any movie fan will remember the fabulous film *The Wicked Lady* starring Margaret Lockwood and re-made very well by Faye Dunaway, both playing the part of Lady Katherine Ferrers who was greatly loved throughout Hertfordshire until they discovered she was also a highwaywoman who had robbed thousands of travellers over a period of several years. They say that her ghost still roams around the St Albans area; the juiciest story comes from 1965 and came to light through a church magazine.

I was sent a copy of the report by Malcolm Edwards who had been a verger in his younger days, and, having heard one of my radio ghost hunts had decided to share his collection of phenomenon stories with me. The highlight was a bizarre story from his church magazine: 'My Meeting with the Spirit' sent in by one Harry J. Lewis. It follows:

As a member of this parish you will know that we believe in the Holy Spirit but are forsworn not to have dealings with anything else as we consider it unGodly. Well, I came face to face with the ghost of what I believe to be Lady Katherine Ferrers, and I am ashamed to tell the full tale. I was visiting a friend's home and as it was a sunny day they suggested a picnic. So we filled a hamper with chicken roll sandwiches, flasks of coffee and lemonade for the two small children.

We decided to go to the hill on the outskirts of the City where they executed the Roman soldier known as Alban in AD 209 for saving the life of a Christian and hiding him in his house. He became Britain's first ever Saint, so it was of interest to us as Christians.

We were lying on the rug from the car when we mused over whether we would be frightened if a ghost of the old Roman should come out to meet us. We decided that we had nothing to fear, for if the man was a saint in life he could be nothing less in death.

It was at that moment Douglas, aged seven, came running from a small copse of trees to say that there was a lady in the woods. His mother, my friend's wife, told him to leave the lady alone. At this Brian, Douglas's brother chipped in saying, 'It's great – you can see right through her!'

We thought the twelve-year-old was merely funning, until the seven-year-old said, 'I bet she's a ghost lady!' So all three adults decided to go with the children and investigate. We had not been drinking, none of us is prone to exaggeration, as any of our friends will know. Yet what I am about to tell you is true, I swear to my Lord God.

In the bushes I saw a lady dressed in a long fine gown, and she was slowly getting undressed. She appeared solid and yet from time to time you'd catch a glimpse of light that seemed to go right through her body. On removing her dress and petticoats, wearing only underwear, she proceeded to put on pantaloons and a grey shirt and jacket. Then from a bush she placed a mask over her eyes and added a tricorn hat. Then she walked through trees and hedges and disappeared. We all couldn't believe our eyes and then suddenly through the thicket a horse appeared with the rider aboard and it ran completely through us and over the field. We never felt a thing, but the children were laughing and thinking the experience a wonderful one; as for us we were mortified.

I know we saw a ghost and it flies in the face of my beliefs, but all five of us saw the same thing. The phantom seemed not to see us at all, it was as if we weren't there. The only lady highwayman known in these parts is Lady Katherine Ferrers, and we are all sure that we witnessed a rewinding of history. Perhaps her image was being repeated on the very spot where she readied herself for her criminal exploits.

THE BASILDON THUMBER

If you had a ten-pence piece for every youngster from London who thumbed a lift to Southend-on-Sea in the summer you'd be a very wealthy individual. Yet it was exactly that unspectacular act that caused the death of a youngster, whose spirit is still seen very often indeed.

A young girl, believed to be called Alison, had been dropped off by a truck that had carried her from Brentwood to Basildon. There she had walked for miles, in the wrong direction as it happens, and found herself at the Wickford roundabout where the four roads lead to Basildon, Brentwood, Chelmsford, and her ultimate target Southend. A sea fret had smothered the land, crawling across the countryside, turning the early evening into darkest night. The fog was as thick as you could imagine, and there was no chance of car drivers seeing a figure at the roadside. So once again Alison decided to try to reach the next village before it got too late. Barely one hundred yards from the roundabout a truck driver ploughed through the mist, crushing the poor girl's body beneath its wheels. She was killed instantly.

Ever since, many drivers have stopped to pick up a pleasant-looking hitchhiker, wearing jeans, T-shirt, and with her blonde hair tied in bunches. Each time they do, when they look around the girl is gone.

*This story also ties in with a mystery told to one of my colleagues in London. He heard that a Mr Trevor Howe from Wilmington near Dartford was driving his family to Southend for a day out when, as he accelerated out of a roundabout in South Benfleet, he drove straight over a young girl. He watched in blind terror as her helpless body disappeared beneath his Jaguar XJ6. He got out of the car and although he had felt a thud there was not a mark on the car itself, and no sign of the girl. They searched the hedgerows, in fields, across the road and there was no one there. Trevor told a magazine at the time: 'If I imagined her, how come my wife and three children saw her too?'

THE BRENTWOOD POLTERGEIST

If you believed all of the reports to come from Brentwood in Essex you would think that every building had a ghost. However, one of my ghost-hunting team seems to have found the root of much of the trouble.

The story begins in Cawnpore in India back in 1857 when John Francis from Brentwood was serving with General Havelock, using his commission to find his brother, who had been serving in India for the past three years. India had risen up against what it described as its 'insensitive' rulers, one of the Indian soldiers' grievances being that cartridges were greased with pig or cow fat, thus offending both Moslems and Hindus. Thousands of Indian soldiers had mutinied in May and had marched on the Indian capital Delhi. The British had heard that the mutiny would take place, but they refused to believe that anyone would dare take arms against the British Army. That arrogance would cost thousands of lives. The final straw was when British officers court-martialled 85 Indians from the Third Cavalry Regiment because among other things they refused to handle the new cartridges the British had issued. After their arrest and conviction their fellow soldiers broke into their prison and set them free.

India became a living hell for the British at this time, they didn't know which of their Indian soldiers were loyal to them, and there was a dagger waiting for them in every shadow. The next major setback to the British cause came when General Havelock's company entered Cawnpore to discover the mutilated bodies of 200 British men, women and children thrown down the local well. The Indian rebels had lined up all of the British in the main square and one by one they were pushed to the ground and while they were still conscious they were hacked into pieces, and hurled down the well, all in full view of their families. Rebelling Sepoy riflemen had been ordered to chop the British to pieces, but they refused and the local Cawnpore butchers were summoned to carry out the inhuman work. John Francis knew that his brother Terence had been serving with General Hugh Wheeler, and that most of the soldiers had been massacred after surrendering. Those who had escaped being massacred survived only to become part of that bloody porridge down the well. When General Havelock and his men entered the city the street where the killing had been done was awash with blood; tiny fragments of clothing, hair and sinew swam in the gore, and the stench had drawn swarms of flies and beetles by the thousand, maggots and all manner of vermin. John Francis refused to believe that his brother had been killed, and volunteered to take a party of men down the well to retrieve the bodies of those unfortunates.

We can only surmise what these men must have felt being lowered into a broth of blood, bone and tissue, neckerchiefs wrapped over their noses against the sickening odour. Bit by bit, piece by piece, the bodies were brought to the surface, where they would ultimately be placed in a mass grave, as no one would be able to put together the right limbs with the right torso. Thousands of bucketfuls were drawn from the well as John Francis searched right down to the actual base of the well. It was there that he saw a head, one of over 200 that had been found, that he knew. With a wood baton he drew the head towards him; as it bobbed in the water the face turned towards him, and he let out an almighty cry. It was his brother Terence Francis, his face contorted in such terror and agony that in that very second John Francis's hair turned white. He was winched up, cradling his brother's head in his arms. They tried to take it from him, only to have him scream at them and pull his pistol. General Havelock is said to have ordered a guard on John Francis, as he sat in the corner of a room, looking into his brother's dead face. Eventually he fell into a deep and troubled sleep, giving them the chance to remove the head, and bury it along with the others.

John Francis woke up barely a shadow of his former self and was returned home to Brentwood. There he went to his bed and was dead within three months. Before he died he told his few remaining friends that he was disgusted at how little the people of his home town cared about what was happening in India. His last words were 'If I can I'd like to come back and haunt them; they deserve a taste of the horrors that we went through for them. Damn it, I will come back and upset their pretty lives!'

*All was quiet until the turn of the century when a lady called Mary Matthewson was plagued by a series of noisy disturbances at her home in the centre of Brentwood. Chairs would be pulled out from under people just as they were about to sit, items would disappear and the worst incident saw a pan of boiling water being taken from a stove and hurled down the back of a male guest.

*In 1921 a visiting doctor called Walker from London told colleagues that he had seen a ghost in his bedroom, a backroom belonging to a local pharmacist who had put him up for the night. In the middle of what had been a cosy night's sleep he was stirred by a very powerful draught of cold air. When he opened his eyes he saw a shape at the bottom of his bed, and getting attuned to the darkness his eyes could pick out two faces, and he called out. At this a man stood up. He was holding a human head in his hand. The good doctor promptly passed out. As he did so he fell backwards and cracked his head on the wooden bedpost, needing treatment at the hospital he had come to Brentwood to visit. He believed the apparition to have been merely a dream until, some months later, he received a letter from a local schoolteacher telling of the story of John Francis.

*The Fountain Head in Ingrave Road in Brentwood suffered a variety of poltergeist phenomena in the late 1960s. So much so that a local newspaper wrote: 'The most haunted pub in Essex is undoubtedly the Fountain Head, following a number of most frightening disturbances including beer bottles exploding in the hands of customers and furniture moving!'

The White Hart Inn and the Swan Hotel, both on the High Street, have a history of doors mysteriously locking, windows and doors opening, furniture tipping and strange knocking. The Golden Fleece on London Road and the New World Inn on Great Warley Street claim similar disturbances. Some say they are haunted by their former owners, but most of the phenomena exhibited fall in line with the curse of John Francis.

*Between 1951 and 1968 another pub, the Seven Stars, also stood on the High Street and suffered the worst poltergeist hauntings. A barman, Frank Harrison, said, 'I had to pack it in, things got really crazy. I would be upstairs and I'd hear crashing from the cellar. I would know there was no one down there, but still the crashing kept on. The tenant used to say it was me wrecking the place, but I always asked customers to witness the fact that I was nowhere near the place. This cost us a fortune in stock, and the brewery wouldn't believe it was a ghost doing all this. I was with the Guv'nor one day and he heard the crashing about and ran down. He came up white as a sheet saying that something had pushed him down the stairs, and he saw bottles lifting out of crates and flying across the room. He left, I left, and eventually nobody would work there and it closed down. It's a bakery and offices now, and bloody good luck to them.'

*In 1987 Donna Knighton from Brentwood was walking past the Abbey National Building Society offices there towards the White Hart Inn, where she was due to meet her boyfriend. She looked in the window of the building society and saw the reflection of a man in the window. The man looked as if he was standing behind her, so she swung around but there was nothing there. So she looked back into the window and saw the man was holding something in his left hand hanging down by his side. She looked closely at the reflection and saw that the object was dripping down on to the street. When she looked behind her there was still no one there, but on the path beside her there was what looked like a pool of blood appearing from nowhere. She took to her heels and raced

144

into the White Hart Inn and raved her story to everyone, and was promptly dumped by her boyfriend!

She still swears that the story is true, and she now has a boyfriend from Braintree who believes her.

THE SPIDER OF STOCK

It is very rare that two legends seem to run side by side, but there is such a case in Essex. The first legend begins in 1777 when Arthur Trumble returned from Brazil to his home in Essex following the takeover of the country by a most wicked man, the Marquis of Pombal. Trumble was a botanist and naturalist, and returned from the Americas with a huge collection of insects and beetles. By the time he got home many had died, and he was left with a handful of living specimens including one gigantic spider from the Amazon jungles. At first, everyone was fascinated by his tales and stories of mysterious creatures who lived on the other side of the world; his lectures and talks were always full of interested members of the public hungry to learn. However, one day Trumble reached into his case for his huge spider, to discover the box open and the spider long gone. This caused intense panic throughout the neighbourhood. One old lady died of a heart attack, and people claimed that as she had been fit enough she had obviously seen Trumble's spider and had dropped dead on the spot. The reality was that even in the southern winter the spider would most likely be dead, but reports of sightings kept coming in for years.

Almost 150 years later stories of the ghost spider crawling up people's legs, dropping down on to heads from springy webs and climbing up the bedclothes of sleeping people became a popular late-night activity. The most recent tale comes from a Mrs Gloria Craven from Hedingham who claimed that in 1974 she saw a huge spider, the size of a dinner plate, climbing up her husband's jacket. She grabbed a book and swung it at the beast, only to catch her husband a firm blow to the back of the neck. She swore on a local news programme that it had been real and a divorce was avoided.

Trumble lived in Stock in Essex, and the 'Spider of Stock' remained an established legend until a man called Charlie Marshall appeared to steal its thunder. Charlie worked on many of the farms thereabout as an ostler, tending to horses and ponies. It was in Stock that Charlie Marshall found a way to cash in on the legend and make a few bob in the process. He decided he would become not the 'Spider of Stock' but the 'Spiderman of Stock'.

He thought about climbing up the local church tower, but couldn't gain permission from the local vicar. One night whilst enjoying a drink at the Bear he chatted to the landlord who was complaining how bitterly cold it was in the room. Charlie asked him why that was, because he had huge fireplaces in each room. The landlord explained that the chimneys were actually too big, and a lot of the cold wind would blow down each one, cooling the place to a bitter chill on occasions. This planted the seed of an idea in Charlie's mind. He was a lithe and slim fellow, and perhaps he could climb up a chimney. This tiny eccentric figure did a lot more than that, his party piece would be to climb up the chimney in one bar, and down the chimney of the bar next door. This he would only do provided the assembled company put enough money into his small bowler hat. On one occasion he was making his way down one chimney when his friends lit a fire, forcing him to turn around and climb up again, reappearing in the other bar blackfaced and angry.

Charlie Marshall would perform this precarious stunt as often as twice a week, for any new visitor to the pub, until one day he climbed up a chimney, and failed to reappear. Many looked up the chimney, they even had it swept on a dozen or more occasions, yet no sign of Charlie Marshall was ever found. He is still wedged up one of the chimneys of the Bear in Stock.

Countless sightings of his ghost have been reported, others see strange falls of soot, black footprints across the carpets, and on some occasions Charlie's face hanging down from the chimney breast.

THE BUMBLERS OF HAMMERSMITH

When discussing the endless possibilities of life after death it is often considered that if human beings have souls, and can become ghosts, then surely so must every other living creature. There are very few examples of this, and most creatures said to have been seen in phantom form have been dogs, cats and the occasional bird and horse. However, Hammersmith in London has an extraordinary story from the late 1790s.

At the centre of the tale was Frances Murdoch, the wife of Patrick Murdoch who had been one of the clerks during the court martial of the Bounty mutineers in August 1792. They lived in

Hammersmith and managed a basic existence on his pittance of a wage. Frances was a rather loud woman fond of several glasses of stout and prone to aggressive behaviour when drunk. And drunk she most certainly was on 15 August 1797.

She had been to a local inn with her husband where he had played chequers, while she had sat with the other ladies getting completely sozzled. Half-way through the evening one of her friends told her that she was having problems with a neighbour who had a beehive in her back garden. Frances Murdoch had had more than enough stout to be able to solve any problem, so without telling Patrick where she was going, these three drunken women set off to Lillie Road, to set these bees free. On reaching the garden, owned by a tiny old lady, they proceeded to crash through her fence and set about the hive, all much too drunk to worry about being stung. The bees were utterly confused and buzzed around them, as the hive was totally wrecked.

The noise of this fracas woke the owner, who rushed into her garden and screamed at the women to leave her property alone. She was ignored until she started tugging at Frances Murdoch's shawl and was promptly punched in the face by her. Two of her teeth were smashed and she was so dazed she couldn't get back to her feet.

The following morning neighbours were asked what had happened, but no one knew anything. The old lady had died, possibly of a heart attack, and remained on that back lawn. The three women were horrified and eventually went to the authorities, telling them that the old woman's hive was a public menace and they had gone to her to ask her to do away with it. They said that she had promised to do just that, and then they had left her. This certainly didn't explain her bruised face and the missing teeth, but as they wanted the case solved the police presumed she had fallen on to the hive, destroyed it, hurt herself and died of the shock. It doesn't sound in the least bit convincing, but it was convenient and kept the case closed.

Three weeks later the old lady's cousin, Hester Cecil, arrived from Ireland, and began trying to sort through her affairs. In an old tattered book she discovered that her cousin's young neighbour had been persecuting her, and had even struck her on several occasions. Hester was a large woman, almost six feet in height, and more than capable of looking after herself. She hammered on the neighbour's door and as it opened she stormed inside armed with a small wooden club. The woman's husband strode forward only to be hit firmly on the skull and knocked unconscious. Then Hester proceeded to strike the wife on the arms, the legs, in the stomach, across the bust, demanding to know the truth about her cousin. As the woman lay screaming on the floor, Hester sat on her chest and brought the club down on her mouth, smashing her teeth into splinters. The woman almost passed out, her mouth swimming with blood and tooth fragments, and she finally told Hester the truth. Hester stood up, threw a white towel from a nearby hand basin to the woman on the floor, and then went out to the back garden. There she chanted, skipped and danced around, attracting quite a crowd. They thought that she had gone mad, then there came a loud humming sound and one by one bees began to gather around her. At first only a few dozen but as her strange jig continued, dozens became hundreds, hundreds became thousands, thousands became tens of thousands and, the story goes, ultimately it was millions. The dancing Hester was all but lost black cloud of bees. The people who had come to watch were now fleeing in terror. The jig became faster and faster and then finally Hester stood there arms stretched up and screamed 'Frances Murdoch!'

Bees cannot understand English, nor can they identify any human by just a name, and they do not usually gather by the million if someone dances a jig. Something miraculous was happening, something far beyond our understanding. The bees suddenly began flying at speed away from the back garden and along the road, some folk say it took almost a half-hour for all the bees to pass them. No one was stung.

At that moment Frances Murdoch was walking along the Goldhawk Road on her way to the butchers. At first she saw just a few bees flying around her, then she saw the swarm as it flew towards her. She opened her mouth to scream and forty or more bees poured into it. She had no time to grasp what was happening to her, bees were flying and landing on her, climbing into her nostrils, into her ears, stinging her as they did. To sting means suicide, yet here they were, killing themselves by the thousand to attack Frances Murdoch.

In less than ten minutes she was dead. She was left swollen and deformed, so many stings under her skin that it was blackened. Every square millimetre of her body had been stung. It took almost an hour to shovel up the dead bees. A drunken murder had been avenged in a terrible fashion.

Hester Cecil was charged with assault, but never brought to

justice as she returned to Ireland and was never located. The house remained empty until it was sold 23 years later.

*In 1877 there was a march through London by early suffragettes in support of contraceptive campaigner Annie Besant, who was then facing imprisonment and heavy fines for indecent and lewd behaviour. They marched through Hammersmith and were attacked by a swarm of bees. The local press covered the event, saying that 'the procession dispersed amidst screams of terror, as the swarm of bees descended upon them'. Despite lashing out, not one single bee was hit, not one woman stung. How could this be possible? Could it have been the ghost swarm?

*Another protest march through Hammersmith, in December 1936, was also disrupted by an enormous swarm of bees. A group of over three hundred men and women were carrying placards that read 'We Want King Edward VIII' after he had announced his abdication over his love for twice divorced Mrs Simpson. They travelled through Hammersmith on pushbikes and on foot chanting the name of King Edward VIII, when the swarm made a beeline for them. The local newsman on the radio reported: 'People scampered in all directions, some hiding behind garden walls. Women were pulling their coats over their heads to avoid the attentions of the bees as they were constantly bombarded.'

Again, not one person was stung, not one bee killed. One woman Mrs Rose Pearson said at the time, 'I was lashing out with my placard, but it seemed to go straight through them. I really can't understand it!'

Perhaps those tens of thousands that died there still return from time to time as tiny insect ghosts.

THE CAPITAL OF THE GHOSTLY WORLD

Near the centre of London lies a trendy pub called the Grenadier that has been described as the most haunted pub in the world. During my time I have heard several places described in such a way, yet the weight of evidence at this place is quite phenomenal.

My first task was to discover who the ghost was and they told me that it is that of a young Grenadier guard who was murdered. This is convenient for the pub, but doesn't seem to have any real substance. Far more likely is the legend I have been given by three sources, that all seem to follow the similar pattern. I have chosen the most interesting version, which also seems the most plausible.

Most of the inns and pubs in London were also used as gambling dens, where all manner of games were played, cards being the most common. The legend goes that a man called Hobbs (or Faraday, or the errant Grenadier guard with no name – as I've said, accounts differ) was gambling and had suffered particularly bad losses one evening, yet was holding a very good hand. The stakes had overtaken him, and no one would accept his IOU. One of the men at the table had a particular fancy for Hobbs's daughter and said, 'Your daughter is of marrying age, and I want to wed her. If you lose promise me her hand.' Every gambler believes his luck is going to change, and although Hobbs knew his daughter disliked this man intensely he promised and put down his hand. To his horror he was beaten by a full house. Foolishly, he alleged that the other fellow had cheated. The argument became violent with counter-allegations being made against him. All the men at his table turned on Hobbs, considering him a scoundrel as he was reneging on his bet, cheating and making false allegations. They tipped over the small wooden card table and promptly gave Hobbs a sound beating, then proceeded to take him to the top of a flight of rickety stairs, from where they hurled him down. Instead of suffering the expected scrapes and bruises Hobbs hit his head on a solid post and died. They all claimed Hobbs was drunk and had fallen to his death; as all four told the same story they were believed.

His daughter cursed all of the gamblers and refused point-blank to marry the man her father owed.

Since that weekend his ghost has made regular appearances in a variety of disturbing ways.

*In the late 1890s a report supposedly made by Sir Arthur Conan Doyle told of a 'hostelry plagued by ghosts in Wilton Row'. It is almost certainly the Grenadier.

*Fielder, Thompson and Marshall, authors of a biography of Houdini, wrote that he held a séance at the Grenadier because he was desperate to find out whether there was life after death.

*In 1952 a Mrs L. Morton told of how she had watched a glass 'slide across the bar as if an unseen hand was pushing it.'

Following that story several other customers reported hearing strange noises, a knocking on the walls and occasionally the lights dipping.

*In 1955 two customers, a husband and wife, told the then land-lord that they had seen a man wearing a military-style coat walking through the tables and chairs as if they weren't there.

*In 1956 a member of the landlord's family claimed that customers regularly saw strange glowing shapes floating around the building. Some described them as smoky apparitions, others as dark shadows.

In November 1992 one of my team visited the Grenadier with its tell-tale sentry box standing outside, and made enquiries of the locals, who told various stories of ghosts. A Mr Woods told my colleague that he had lived overlooking the pub from 1948 until 1966 and had seen the ghost 'thousands of times'.

Woods was now retired from an accountancy firm in the City, and didn't seem the sort to invent tales of this sort. We asked him to jot down what he had seen. He sent us the following letter.

I will attempt to inform you of the many strange experi-ences I had whilst living close to the public house known as the Grenadier, in Wilton Row. If you wish to use the following in your book you have my full permission provided you do not give my address. Following my divorce in 1954 I lived quite a lonely existence and spent many evenings looking out of my window at the mews, often watching the people swarming to and fro. To my surprise most evenings around two in the morning I would see what I thought to be lights being reflected around the pub. At first I thought them to be car headlights and yet the lights seemed to glitter, like an expensive Christmas card. Before retiring to bed I would watch these lights and then one day I got out my binoculars and focused in on this patch of light. I was amazed to see the shape of a man in the very centre. He seemed to have the ability to fly.

I told some friends and they thought me to be jesting, but I swear that I have witnessed this 'ghost' many times. Always in the early hours of the morning. On the several occasions that I invited people to my lodgings to see the spirits, none

151

have turned up, yet the very next night they were there again. It was most infuriating.

Yet one night I decided to walk down to the Grenadier at almost two in the morning and I met some people I knew, Pauline and her fiancé Richard. We were no more than fifty feet from the Grenadier when Pauline said, 'What on earth is that?'

Before I looked I knew what it would be. The ghost had appeared and was swooping and diving around the door of the Grenadier. They were mortified with shock, and I had to take them in for a sherry before they got a taxi to their respective homes.

I still drink at the Grenadier from time to time and have seen the figure as recently as August of this year [1992]. This public house is certainly haunted; as soon as you enter it you know that for a certainty. Thousands have seen the ghosts yet no one seems to catch anything on camera. I did on three separate occasions, yet each time I had the photographs developed they either didn't come out, or were blurred. Only one showed anything different. Around where the figure had been there are two red dots on the photo. As if the ghost's eyes have reflected back at the camera in red, as often happens when we take pictures of friends or family. I took my story to a newspaper in 1988 and they didn't believe me. They discounted everything I told them without any investigation whatsoever.

I hope this account has been of some use to you. . . .

THE COCKNEY CURSER

One of the most bizarre stories to come out of London has to be the story of a pearly king called John Good. He was in his mid-seventies when he met a Geordie building worker called Derek Walker, who had moved from his home in Wallsend to Riley Road in Bermondsey. The building trade had started to pick up after the recession of the early thirties and London, being the capital, was climbing from the depression faster than the provinces.

January of 1935 seemed to see a series of marches through London, one by the British Union of Fascists led by Sir Oswald Mosley, another by pacifists against the German Brownshirts and the threatened war in Europe; and then, astonishingly, the Pearly kings and queens took to the streets. London has always loved the cockney characters who always gave a smile and a cheery word in troubled times. The rabble-rousing Jew-hating demagogue Adolf Hitler had stirred up all of Europe attempting a coup in Austria the year before, and everyone knew that he would not stop there. So to see a glitzy parade of friendly faces was a most heart-warming sight.

One of the leaders was a hobbling John Good, riddled with arthritis but determined not to miss the parade. They stopped at a pub for lunch before the return march and this is where he met Derek Walker. They talked for almost an hour then as the old Pearly King got up to leave he noticed his wallet was missing. The pub was searched and finally it was located in the toilet, empty of the six pounds it had previously held. The finger of suspicion firmly pointed at the Wallsender who denied that he was responsible. The police were called and despite the Northerner having £12 on his person (a lot of money in those days), nothing could be proven, so it was advised that Derek Walker make himself scarce, lest the other Pearlies should rearrange his face. John Good shouted across the public bar, 'Pay heed to me, you thieving git, for I curse you and your family, and it shall not end for twenty long years. You shall know it's over for I will make your entire world turn to ice!'

Walker ran out of the pub and legged it back to his home, and there he considered himself lucky to be in one lump and still with the £6 that he had stolen from the Pearly King.

He never gave the curse another thought yet every January from then on strange things began to happen.

In January 1936 King George V died and Walker was laid off work as the site was near Westminster Hall. He was later sacked.

In January 1937 he had his nose broken and three teeth kicked from his head in a row at a pub with the British Union of Fascists. (Just one of many incidents that would ultimately lead to the Public Order Act coming into force banning political uniforms on British streets.)

In January 1938 his wife Valerie left him, taking their two children.

In January 1939 he was in the centre of London when an IRA bomb exploded as he queued to pay his electricity bill at the offices of the Central Electricity Board at Southwark. He was knocked off his feet and had to have glass fragments removed from his cheek and arm.

In January 1940 he was called up to join the forces as World War II continued; he tried to avoid it for health reasons, but his claims were denied and he joined the Cheshires.

In January 1941 while he was serving on the South Coast he received a letter saying that his house had been bombed flat by German bombers.

In January 1942 Walker's best friend Colin Hunter was blown up in front of him in Italy when one of his own mortars exploded for no apparent reason.

In January 1943 whilst back in Britain on leave he caught a sexually transmitted disease from a London prostitute and the condition stayed with him for the rest of his life causing him great pain and discomfort.

In January 1944 Walker was guarding a German prisoner when the Nazi turned on him, whipping his face with a pistol and smashing his nose.

In January 1945 Walker was with his regiment in Bastogne as the Battle of the Bulge drew to a close. He suffered frostbite so severely that the little finger on his left hand had to be amputated. This led to him being returned home to London.

In January 1946 his cousin died in a rail crash at Lichfield in Staffordshire.

In January 1947 he was made redundant from his new job as a steelworker because there was a shortage of coal.

In January 1948, with the nationalisation of the railways, he was paid off from his job as a railway porter at Paddington.

In January 1949 Walker was arrested for stealing a bicycle and on his release after 14 days' imprisonment he was attacked and badly beaten up by the family of the bike's owner.

In January 1950 Walker returned to Wallsend to live, couldn't find accommodation and was forced to sleep in parks and the countryside.

In January 1951 his new fiancée, a 42-year-old called Lucy Davies, suffered a fire at her home in Jarrow and was badly burned.

In January 1952 Lucy left him, three weeks before their planned wedding, taking all of his money, his car and his gold watch. She told friends she was moving to relatives in Morecambe and was never seen again.

In January 1953 he suffered another family tragedy. Frank O'Neill, Walker's uncle and his only remaining close relative, was killed when a car ferry sank off the coast of Ireland. He was one of over 120 people aboard the *Princess Victoria*, a British Rail car ferry that had just left Stranraer when mountainous seas forced open the cargo doors and flooded the ship until it sank.

In 1954 Walker was in hospital and both his testicles were removed due to complications caused by his sexual disease.

In January 1955 Walker was aware that it was the last year of the curse, and the Pearly King had sworn it would end with a big freeze. To Walker's amazement it was the coldest it had ever been on Tyneside: -26 degrees. The River Tyne, a huge and mighty river, was completely frozen in several places. Only one vessel, the *Princess Wilhelmina*, a Dutch coaster, braved its way into the river cutting through the ice to find its way to the coal staithes.

Never was there a man so glad to see a Monday morning as Walker was on 1 February. He was wrapped up warm and walking along the banks of the Tyne towards the steel stockholders where he was working when he slipped on the ice and hit his head. He was taken to hospital where he died almost four months later.

COOKED TO DEATH

When researching this book I kept being told a story time and time again, yet in each case the names and locations were different – a true urban myth. I'll share it with you without naming specifics for that reason alone.

One of London's top hotels decided to invest in the latest technological breakthrough, the microwave oven. It was a very basic model but the very first large industrial microwave. The chef was thrilled to have the advantage of cooking so swiftly, and created countless wonderful recipes, knowing that the microwave would guarantee that each dish would be piping hot when served. The man given the task of using this equipment was a young commis chef, training with the master after taking his City & Guilds certificate at college.

This young man loved cooking, but increasingly found himself leaning up against the microwave oven, waiting for the timer to 'ching'. He'd done this for six weeks when suddenly he collapsed in the kitchen. An ambulance was called, but he died before reaching the hospital.

It seems that the old-fashioned industrial microwave had not been properly sealed, so the rays were escaping. The young chef had been leaning against it and the microwaves had cooked his kidneys while he was still alive.

Huge sums of money were paid to hush up the incident, and the microwave company were made bankrupt by the out-of-court settlement.

THE GHASTLY FIREFIGHTER

In the late 1800s a fire station stood on Park Street in Croydon, and it seems that old habits die hard. Maybe they don't die at all.

Stories differ, but the most gruesome appertains to Jack Bell, a leading fireman in his day, who was transferred from the Westminster to the Croydon division. He was described by those who knew him as 'a man of vulgar habits'; those who disliked him (almost everyone) said he was 'a right bastard'.

He stuck to the letter of the rule book, no flexibility at all, and those that transgressed the written word were thrown out on their ear. He had sacked several people for being five minutes late, for leaving equipment in the yard and even for 'backchatting'. He was known as 'the Sod' to all at the station. Fate has a way of giving such people their come-uppance and Jack Bell's was long overdue.

One day a fireman, Harry Redpath, asked for the afternoon off because his wife was giving birth at the local hospital. He was told to 'wet-nurse his brat in his own time'. Saddened by his boss's response he sent a young lad to the hospital to tell his wife that he would be sacked if he were to leave work. The boy was instructed to gather the family together to give his wife some support during the labour. They didn't get there in time. It was a breech birth and there were complications. Both mother and child perished.

Harry Redpath in the meantime was doing his best to keep his mind on his work, but he couldn't help thinking of his wife who at the late age of 38 was giving birth to his very first baby. They had tried for so many years without success, and then the miracle occurred. His wife was so desperate for a baby and they had both thanked God for allowing them the chance to raise their own child. Redpath was already seething at 'the Sod' and was taking his frustrations out on the fire engine. He polished and polished until it seemed the paint would come off it. Then he glanced to the side of the machine and caught a glimpse of his old mother with the young street boy he'd employed as a messenger. He knew something was wrong.

He stood up and walked slowly towards them, reading every line of their faces, then the truth hit him without a word being spoken.

'My baby is dead then?'

His mother, with tears streaming down her face, gave a heavy-hearted nod and said, 'It's Theresa, she's gone too.'

Harry's legs buckled and he fell to his knees, his mind unable to take in the full weight of the tragedy. He'd been married to her for over fifteen years, all his adult life, and he couldn't imagine living a single day without her. His mind was swimming in the grief that descended upon his life like a blanket of nails, each one tearing at his skin. At that moment Jack Bell walked in to see him sobbing, and strutted across shouting, 'Redpath, get back to work! We don't pay you to sit on your fat arse!'

Redpath turned to him and, leaping to his feet, pinned him to the wall by his lapel, shouting: 'You bastard, it's because of you they're both dead, you heartless sod!'

Bell looked shaken and pushed Harry away, saying, 'Well, you'll have things to see to, so off you go.'

How Harry restrained himself from smashing his fist into Bell's face even he didn't know, but his mother took his arm and together they returned to the hospital. There he cradled his wife in his arms and refused to leave for over three hours. He never once saw the child that had lived less than ten minutes.

The funeral was two days later and at ten in the morning Redpath's wife and child were laid to rest. He returned to work that lunchtime to be met by two policemen, who instructed him that he had been sacked for assaulting a superior officer. In those days it was quite an achievement to become a fireman as it was a well-paid position with status in the community. It had been all that Harry Redpath had known since he was fourteen. His wife and child were dead and now his job had been taken away from him by a man who was too wrapped up in his own sick power trip.

The policemen were based nearby and kept vigil to make sure that this 'troublemaker' reported by Jack Bell didn't return to cause any problems.

The plot begins to deepen when you learn that Harry Redpath and Jack Bell died within two days of each other in 1892.

On a chilly January morning Jack Bell's body was found trampled to death in the fire station's stables. It was claimed that the docile horses used to pull the fire engine had been spooked and had kicked him to death. Bell's body was almost unrecognisable, what remained was barely more than a sort of human mush. All over the beaten body were literally hundreds of hoof prints. Never had there been such a violent trampling; indeed, horses try to avoid stepping on people. It took eight people almost two hours to collect the pieces from the ghastly place.

The following morning Harry Redpath was found dead at his home in Elmers End. He had slit his wrists while sitting in an old tin bath in front of his fire. He had drunk almost two full bottles of whisky as if celebrating, then in his stupor cut deep into his arms, allowing his liquor-soaked blood to flow into the hot water of his bath. Some say that the neighbour who discovered him found a huge wooden club with a horse shoe nailed on to it, but hid it before he called the police. Revenge had been Harry's and not the horses'.

*Opinions vary as to who the ghastly fireman of Croydon is. Some say it's 'the Sod' Jack Bell, others that it's the anguished spirit of Harry Redpath. In the early 1900s there were dozens of reports from people nearby of hearing a man sobbing in the early hours of the morning. Others swore that they could see the sad figure of Harry Redpath pacing up and down outside the Park Street Fire Station with his head in his hands.

*The King's Cellars pub claims to be on the site of the original fire station, and a variety of strange things have happened there. This includes electrical equipment working on its own accord, glasses filling with beer without anyone touching the pump, and strange cloudy apparitions floating through the restaurant. The local newspapers have regularly been called in, particularly in the 1970s, when plates would rise from tables, glasses smashing off walls, more apparitions, extreme coldness in heated rooms and a mixture of sobbing and laughter from various rooms. It became such a haven for ghost hunters that a television documentary was made of the strange phenomena that persist today.

THE GHOSTS OF DRURY LANE

Many of Britain's great theatres claim to have ghosts, yet the one most commonly spoken of is none other than Drury Lane. Over the decades hundreds of people have claimed a wide range of experiences, ranging from women who feel a feather being drawn across their bare shoulders, to those who see actual ghosts passing through walls in the auditorium or foyer.

On chatting to theatre staff I was told that the most famous of their ghosts is said to be that of arguably the greatest pantomime clown of all time, Joseph Grimaldi, who made his very first and last appearances at the theatre. Many actors and actresses have seen his clown face floating across the footlights; others have merely felt his presence spurring them on.

*In 1986 an American called Thomas Marx was standing in the theatre's bar when he saw a man walk past him. He turned and stared at the figure, who was dressed like a waiter of the 1890s, and to his horror the man walked straight through a wall. Mr Marx asked the barmaid if she had seen the figure, she said she hadn't but wasn't surprised, explaining: 'It's a bloody funny place to work. You see all kinds of strange things. It's not natural!'

THE LONDON LOVERS

One of the saddest of Britain's legends comes from the capital, where a Thomas Marston lived and worked for a merchant who traded with the West African enclave known as the Gold Coast. It became a Crown Colony in January 1821, and Marston's firm was one of many companies trying to exploit it for as much money as they could.

Marston had many female admirers as he was gallant in the extreme and yet had never married. His best friend was Michael Porritt, a socialite from a wealthy Suffolk family, who lived in Connaught Road, E16. He had courted and married the daughter of an impoverished tailor from the East End, a small brunette called Constance, known to friends as 'Stancy'. The match was not considered a good one as it was well known that she had long held a candle for Thomas Marston, and had married Porritt very much as second choice.

The marriage was rocky from the very beginning, and bitterness crept into their relationship in the same way that condensation spreads across a badly ventilated window. Soon they could see nothing between them clearly except for the unpleasantness. It became a sick game between them to try and hurt each other a little bit more each day. She would put salt into his tea instead of sugar, tear a hole in his favourite shirt or embarrass him in public; he would smash her favourite ornaments, deface paintings she was fond of, and he even sold her favourite horse to the knacker's yard. Everyone knew of the animosity between them and wondered just how far it would go. Divorce was unthinkable among London's rising social figures, so they had no option than to put up with the atmosphere of hatred that fermented like rancid milk. A sour marriage with two sour people, each one searching for some pleasant conversation, a smile and a little peace.

Porritt would spend as much time at his work as he could, knowing that when he returned home it meant another bout of endless arguing. She had sworn to leave him time and time again, yet still she remained to plague his existence. He had even suggested a separation, with him buying a house in the country for her. This was also completely outrageous, as Stancy was well known around town, and she quite liked the position, having come from the dark and dingy back alleys of East London.

Porritt was heartily sick of putting up with the tantrums of his wife, and was trying to find a post overseas so he could get away, when he spotted Stancy chatting to his best friend Marston outside the local pie shop. He watched them for almost fifteen minutes, laughing and joking, before parting with a kiss. This enflamed Porritt to such a degree that he followed Marston back to his place of work, and attacked him with his silver-topped cane. Despite having been badly bruised by him, Marston remained calm, explaining that they had been friends for many years, and that he looked upon her as nothing more than the wife of his very dear friend.

Porritt felt ashamed at ever doubting the man with whom he had been at Oxford all those years before, and apologised profusely. But the tiny worm of doubt had entered his head, and on occasions of severe stress, common sense and reality tend to go out of the window. Three weeks later his jealousy overcame him once more, and he decided to follow his friend late one afternoon. Marston was off to get a fitting for a new suit, and ended up at the shop belonging to Stancy's father, and purely by coincidence she was sitting at the window drinking a sherry. Once again Porritt saw his wife exchange a kiss with Marston, and saw her face beaming with happiness as they chatted. His mind was tumbled and whirled; he didn't know if he should be happy that she was seeing someone else, as that rather took the heat off him. Maybe he should demand vengeance from his friend for having these 'secret liaisons'. This time he kept it to himself, and what had genuinely been an accidental meeting was used as the foundation on which his paranoia built a gargantuan case against his innocent wife. Admittedly, she was guilty of giving as good as she received in verbal encounters with her husband, but she had not betrayed her husband. Every time she went out shopping Porritt decided she must be seeing Marston, each letter she received from her family was a *billet-doux* full of flowery romantic phrases. Stancy took to reading the poetry of Keats, Shelley and Byron – this was a certain sign, Porritt thought, that she had fallen in love with Marston. Whatever she did was more proof for her twisted husband to jump to entirely the wrong conclusion.

Ironically, Stancy had told friends that she had decided to try and 'start afresh' with her husband, as the aggressive atmosphere at home was not right if they were to raise a family. Stancy believed that if they were to have children a degree of normality could perhaps return to their marriage. They had not had sex since a month after the wedding, as they were far too keen on spitting venom at one another to exchange embraces. That evening Porritt returned home in a foul temper, a wheel had detached from his carriage, his shoulder was hurting and his paranoia was suggesting to him that his wife could have been responsible for the accident. He entered the house slamming the front door behind him. When his housekeeper Mrs Knight came running, he promptly dismissed her, saying that he was moving to Somerset and would have no need of her services.

The house was empty except for Porritt and his wife, who was in her bedroom fixing up her hair, hoping that this was to be the night of their reconciliation. She appeared at the top of the stairs in a long flowing gown and moved elegantly down the stairs towards the hall. There she saw the glowering face of Porritt almost crimson with rage. He was going through a cupboard hurling boxes and ornaments onto the floor with a crash. He turned to look at this beautiful lady in front of him; for a moment he was lost in her loveliness and did not listen properly to what she was saying.

'Michael, let's enough of this fighting, let us start a family, let us have a baby and a new beginning,' she had said.

Stancy was sincere in wanting to try again, but Porritt in his anger had misheard, believing that she was going to have a baby. As there had been no sexual relations between them he instantly concluded that she was going to have Marston's illegitimate offspring.

He turned back to the cupboard, yelling, 'You'll not birth a bastard in my house, you whore!'

Stancy was speechless, as her husband ranted and raved uncontrollably. Then to her horror she saw that he had a sharp pair of tailor's scissors in his hand. She had no time to move and before a sound could escape her throat he plunged the scissors deep into her gullet. She couldn't lower her head as the handle of the scissors was sticking out under her chin. She staggered around the hall dizzily as the air escaping from her windpipe gurgled and hissed as the blood bubbled its exit from her body. Finally blackness overtook her and she fell backwards on to the carpet in convulsions. It took almost ten minutes for her to die, Porritt kneeling over her for all of that time, and for a further twenty minutes after she had died. In his madness he dragged her dead body to the bottom of the stairs, tied a rope around her punctured neck and raced up to the balcony, winching his dead wife to her feet. He positioned her with precision at the foot of the stairs, and her lifeless body standing there in her beautiful amber gown covered with gore. Night was approaching and he opened his front door and promised a street urchin five shillings if he would run across London to summon his friend Thomas Marston at his home. The youngster readily agreed and returned about two hours later in a carriage with Porritt's friend. The child was paid and as darkness fell Marston was invited in by Porritt who was still covered with blood.

'Good heavens, Michael, have you had an accident?' asked Marston.

'No, Thomas,' said Porritt in a frighteningly calm monotone, 'but your worst nightmare is about to happen!'

Marston laughed nervously. 'What do you mean?'

Just then he spotted Stancy standing, or so he thought, at the foot of the stairs, so he went across to embrace her. He kissed her cheek and through the darkness saw the blood dripping down her gown, marking his brown suit. As he jumped back with a start her body started swinging and he leapt towards the door in terror. Between him and the outside stood Porritt holding the scissors.

'What have you done, Michael?' said Marston as tears ran uncontrollably down both cheeks.

Porritt was as cool as a cucumber. 'You and Stancy had betrayed me, she always loved you and you'd been meeting her in secret. The final straw was that she was about to have your child. Deny it if you wish but no matter what you say you are about to pay for betraying me with your life.'

162

Marston's eyes were as large as dinner plates as he watched Porritt walk towards him. Marston knew he was innocent, and that therefore Stancy was innocent, yet she was swaying on the end of a rope with her throat cut. His heart sank as the realisation hit him that he was about to die. He fell to his knees in prayer, clasping his palms together in a last desperate plea for salvation. The prayer was never finished let alone answered for Porritt pierced the base of his skull with the scissors shattering his nervous system with a single blow. Marston was dead but his body was writhing and spinning around the floor, finally ending up beneath the swaying body of his friend Stancy. The truth was that Marston had remained single because he was homosexual and in a secret relationship with an actor from one of the West End theatres.

The bodies of Marston and Stancy were never seen again. Porritt sold the house on Hackney Road, moving to Somerset as he had said. He told friends that his wife had run off with Marston and if he caught them he would 'flay the hide off the pair of them'. Friends and colleagues believed this to be understandable behaviour from a betrayed husband. The actor did go to the police telling them that Thomas Marston would not run off with any 'woman', but the police dismissed his testimony.

*The legend gave no address on Hackney Road, yet recently I was told about the ghostly problems suffered by Ye Olde Axe a pub on that street. Customers have spoken of moving glasses, tables shaking, strange bumping noises, disembodied screams and the classic phantom footsteps. Many pubs claim this kind of activity, particularly those that are a good age, yet this has rather more substance than most. Nothing can give us more goosepimples than when a legend bumps into fact. I have since discovered that in 1979 the new landlord of Ye Olde Axe was ordered by the Health and Safety Executive to install a fire escape, so the workmen were called in. On digging a trench to lay the foundations they found two skeletons and a rusty pair of tailor's scissors!

TURPIN'S SAFE HOUSE

Anyone interested in legends of swashbuckling derring-do should visit an inn that Dick Turpin, the notorious highwayman, used to use as his safe house whilst in the south. The Spaniards Inn, Spaniards Road, London NW3, will take you back in time to an age filled with pirates, smugglers, rogues and road bandits.

There are several stories about this fine establishment, including one that claims to be of the only time Turpin was ever identified as a murderer. The legend begins with Turpin travelling down to London on his horse Black Bess to spend some of his loot and to meet one of his contacts who had been receiving a variety of smuggled goods from ships off the northern coastline.

He was staying at the Spaniards Inn and was in a downstairs kitchen ravishing a prostitute on the table, when a group of soldiers walked in on him and started laughing at the sight that met their eyes. Not even a rogue like Turpin could complete this manoeuvre with an audience and he pulled on his trews and began shouting at the men for interrupting him so rudely. The soldiers were drunk and spoiling for a fight, and Turpin was in just the mood to oblige them. The girl tried to scurry back into the inn but was grabbed by one of the soldiers who said, 'No, don't run away, my poppet, you've been paid by this jackanapes, so the least I can do is get his money's worth!'

He started fumbling with his belt buckle, while holding the frightened girl tightly by the arm. Much as she screamed the inn-keeper ignored her cries. In those days the tenants knew that it was the customers who paid the money, the girls had to look after themselves. By this time Turpin was being punched and kicked on the kitchen floor, as the sergeant had his way with the young prostitute.

Turpin regained consciousness some hours later to find the girl sobbing in the corner of the kitchen. The innkeeper had tended to Turpin's cuts, but the girl had been totally ignored. Her face was battered and bruised and a trickle of blood ran from the corner of her mouth down her chin, gathering into a stain on the shoulder of her dress.

Miraculously, none of the drunken troops had recognised their victim as Dick Turpin, for there was a sizeable reward offered at that time for his capture. His ribs ached and his jaw clicked each time he spoke and his every movement caused him extreme dis-comfort. He peered through a gap in the door and there at a table in the centre of the room sat the soldiers laughing and drinking. He heard them say to the serving girl, 'Before we leave we'll all have you too, my girl, so be swift with our ale!' Another braggart shouted, 'If you tarry we'll kick the landlord to death like we did that peasant in your kitchen!'

They thought he was dead. Turpin was a wily and calculating man, he never bit off more than he could chew, yet here was a group of seven trained soldiers who had hurt and humiliated him. He decided that he would cast caution to the wind, but would bide his time until the moment was right. The ale flowed merrily and in the early hours of the morning the soldiers were paralytic, hardly able to walk when they left the Spaniards Inn. The sergeant was dragging a plump lady from the inn shouting, 'I promised you a serving, and that's what you'll get!'

The innkeeper was begging him to leave her alone. 'She's my wife, sergeant. Please. I can find you a woman if that's all you want.'

'A woman be damned,' barked the soldier. 'I'm having this fat bitch, and if you say any more I'll run a sword through your gizzard!'

Tears were running down the man's face as he watched his wife being dragged towards the inn's dilapidated barn, screaming and yelling as she went.

This was Turpin's moment. He covered his mouth with his neckerchief, mounted Black Bess, and with a pistol in each hand rode into the open.

Seeing the imposing highwayman trotting towards them the soldiers froze on the spot, too drunk to react in any sensible way. Turpin rode into the middle of them pistol-whipping one and cracking his skull in the way you'd open a coconut. The others began to run, stumbling and falling as they went. Turpin rode them down seriously injuring at least another two. Then, galloping back to the inn, he heard screams of terror from the barn, dismounted and walked inside. There he saw the innkeeper's wife, her clothes ripped from her back, wedged in a corner as the fat sergeant taunted her. She had defended her honour as best she could, but was fighting a losing battle with the brute. Turpin shouted at the beast of a man, who was partially undressed. As he turned he saw the highwayman in his tricorn hat, cape, riding boots and mask, waving two huge pistols towards him. The sergeant surprisingly didn't seem unduly alarmed saying, 'Get you away, fellow, lest your neck will be stretched before morning!' Then he turned his attention back towards the terrified woman who was covering her nakedness with a dirty horse blanket. This angered Turpin even more, and he stepped behind the soldier and gave him an almighty kick in the pants. This finally caused some reaction from the lusty soldier, who growled like a bear and turned towards him. 'Listen, you rogue, we've stretched many a neck of thieves like you. I have this woman to attend to, so ride away. You'll not get another

165

warning this night. Who the Hades do you think you are? Dick Turpin?'

The sergeant's chin dropped when the highwayman replied, 'Yes!' Suddenly his ardour had cooled and his eyes betrayed the fear that ran through his body like iced water.

'All right then, the woman can go. Better still, we can both have her – eh?' The sergeant tried to laugh, but it fell from his mouth with no great conviction. He began running off at the mouth: 'Look, I am like you – this very night I killed a man, right here in the kitchens!'

At this Turpin pulled the mask away from his face baring a bruised chin that was every colour of the rainbow. 'Aye,' he said, 'you're as grand a lover as you are a killer!'

By this time the innkeeper had wrapped his arm around his wife; the young prostitute stood beside them watching this showdown. Turpin pointed at the young girl and said, 'I think you owe the girl an apology!'

The sergeant spat at the ground. 'I'll not apologise to that young slut. She merely got what she was paid for.'

Turpin was being wound up like a spring. When he robbed people on the road he had relied on their fear, yet he felt this man seemed to have little if any trepidation. Almost as if the sergeant could feel that the highwayman's confidence was on the wane he stepped towards him saying, 'Turpin, you've never killed a man, have you?'

The road bandit froze, for he had not; he'd threatened it regularly, but the nearest he had come was wounding a tallyman in the arm from over forty yards. Yet here he was, almost eye to eye with a man who was a trained killer. Suddenly the balance of power had shifted; the sergeant began walking towards him talking all the while. 'You're just a coward who waves guns around, you don't use them. You know if you were to kill one of the King's men your life would be over. So I will take you back for trial and pick up a handsome reward.' He was smiling now, gaining courage with every step as he continued his barrage at Turpin. 'Trying to wet-nurse these peasants, were you? Well, if they're in league with you, we'll have to have their necks stretched too as a warning to others!'

The young prostitute's face went white; not only had she been attacked and molested, now she was sentenced to death. Turpin heard her scream: 'My God, we're all dead!'

Realising that he had scared them the soldier started laughing, and stood within a foot of Turpin who held both pistols at his face.

'Hand me the pistols, you wretch, or I'll finish you where you stand!' A grand boast from a man armed only with small knife in his belt. 'Here is the gentleman thief,' continued the soldier, 'the polite, well-spoken rogue who has captured the country's heart! You're no gent, naught more than a thief!'

Turpin didn't answer, and silence fell like a net. The only noise that could be heard was the wind howling through the barn and the whimpering of the teenager whore as she was consoled by the innkeeper's wife. It was a battle of wills. The sergeant was deciding whether to attack the highwayman, his mind whizzing through the possible outcomes, while Turpin's brain, too, was swimming as the silence seemed an eternity.

Then finally Turpin jerked his knee into the sergeant's groin with such force it lifted him off the ground. He fell to the floor moaning and Turpin said, 'You bastard. Here am I listening to your threats, yet you are the offender this night not I!'

The sergeant cursed Turpin, reiterating that he was charged with thievery but not murder, his life could depend on what happened that very night.

Turpin was still undecided about the whole idea. 'If I let you live will you leave these people alone?'

The sergeant was holding his vitals and breathing heavily as he nodded, and Turpin knew that this man was as trustworthy as a scorpion. He looked at the three people scared witless, their lives hanging in the balance, walked towards the sergeant and placed both pistol barrels against the man's lips and said, 'Swear it on my pistols, for if you break your word I will surely kill you.'

The sergeant smiled, saying, 'You'll kiss my arse first!'

Turpin's hands were shaking as he clicked back the hammers of his pistols. The sergeant was at his most menacing when he said, 'You'll hang, my lad, and I'll see that this nest of rogues is burned to the ground with everyone still in it. You're all going to Hell.'

'After you!' answered Turpin, letting fly with both pistols, blasting a hole in the sergeant's skull. His body flew backwards as if he'd been fired from a cannon and hit the barn wall with a sickening crunch. He was dead.

Shakily, Turpin turned to the others, saying, 'I done him and no mistake. Now when word gets out, I'm a dead man too.'

'I saw nothing, sir,' the prostitute said.

'Nor I,' added the innkeeper.

Turpin was surprised at this. 'But his body will be found.'

The innkeeper began wiping up the blood with straw which he dumped in a barrow. 'Get yourself down the road. We'll clean up here and we'll take his body a few miles away. You were never here this night – you're in our book as Thomas Wastrell. That you'll always be. We'll say we saw you chase off the soldiers, but nothing more!'

'Aye,' said the girl. 'If we all say the same we'll be safe!'

Turpin mounted his horse and rode off into the night.

The innkeeper was true to his word, and Turpin returned three times to the Spaniards Inn; and at one time very nearly married the young prostitute.

It is said that the innkeeper was so grateful to Turpin that he redesigned the inn so that the highwayman could leave from one of the upstairs windows, to drop directly on Black Bess's back, should anyone ever track him there.

The boastful sergeant was right about one thing: he said that Turpin would be executed, and he was, on 7 April 1739.

*Apart from the occasional footsteps, the Spaniards Inn doesn't seem to be haunted, but it is still worth a visit. They have a variety of items that belonged to Turpin, including pistols and keys, and maybe if you ask nicely you can have your supper using the very cutlery used by the rogue.

*Several people have claimed to have heard ghostly hooves galloping across nearby Hampstead Heath. Whether this is Black Bess or someone else going to the newspapers trying to flog a dead horse, I don't know.

My researcher visited the Spaniards Inn and said that he felt a presence in the bar, as if someone was watching him. He mentioned this to the bar staff and they said that many others had felt the same thing.

THE SOUTH WEST

BLACK IN BATH

One of the commonest ghostly experiences you can have is that eerie feeling that someone had just sat on your bed. You lie there quivering with fear, too petrified to look around to see whether your worst fears are confirmed. It is out of precisely this fear that the Freddy Kruger character was created. It is in that netherworld between being awake and being asleep, that all kinds of strange things have been known to occur. Literally hundreds of thousands of people claim they have seen shadowy shapes at the bottom of their beds. Some say it is their departed relatives watching over them as they sleep, others that it is evil spirits ready to attack as soon as you lost consciousness.

One of the most amazing stories comes from a lady called Joyce McFaddon who lived in the beautiful city of Bath. Her home was very close to the River Avon and in an idyllic setting. She didn't have a care in the world until September 1954 when 'it' moved into her house.

All of her friends loved visiting the McFaddon home, and did so even more when Colin, her husband of eighteen years, died of a heart attack. They rallied around, and Joyce herself was very brave, and always tried to have a cheery word for everyone.

It was a dark, misty evening, and through her lounge window she could see the twinkling of lights ascending the hill towards the suburbs far above the city. Her two friends, Margaret McCartney and Claire Brown, had passed comment that it was a 'spooky' night, and perhaps they should try a ouija board. Joyce wasn't really too keen, but she could see how excited her friends were, so she allowed herself to be dragged along.

Once all of the letters had been cut out, and placed on the table the game began. Innnocent questions were answered with either a 'Yes' or 'No' and to all intents and purposes it was an innocent evening's entertainment. But when they asked 'the spirit' to identify itself the small glass they were using rattled and vibrated so violently that their hands were thrown off it. Margaret screamed and the glass exploded into a thousand pieces. Joyce ran to the light switch and clicked it on, only for that lightbulb to shatter too.

She ran into the hall and switched on that light, yet it still remained pitch black. Margaret and Claire were crying into each other's arms in mortal fear when Joyce strode across the living room to the curtains, and pulled them back so the room could have some light from the street lamps. As the curtains opened, there, standing behind them, was a huge black figure of a man.

Joyce recoiled in terror and when Margaret saw this towering black shape she passed out, dragging Claire with her to the floor. Joyce screamed until her voice trailed into nothing.

At that moment there was a hammering on the door, and Joyce rushed to open it. It was her neighbours who had heard the scream and had come running. Joyce blurted out what had happened and the neighbours did their best to calm her jangled nerves. They switched on the hall light, then they walked into the living room and switched on that light too. The girls were amazed, for they had watched the bulb shatter before their eyes, yet there it was back together again.

After some strong coffees and some straight talking it was agreed that they had all let their imaginations run away with them, and the ouija papers were thrown into the toilet and flushed away.

Margaret and Claire went home, leaving a still shaky Joyce to tidy up, wash the dishes and make her way to bed. When she lifted the toilet seat, there in the bowl were a few of the letters used in the ouija game: they spelled out D-E-A-T-H.

Joyce tried to rationalise it, but she could feel her stomach turning over and she jumped into bed. She tossed and turned unable to sleep, when she suddenly felt that she was not alone. Gathering what little courage she had left, she glanced over her top sheet to see a huge black shape standing at the bottom of her bed. She tried to scream, and the more she tried, the less sound she made. The figure approached her and sat beside her. She couldn't make out a face, but she could see shapes that could have been eyes. She backed towards the wall as it moved closer to her. In a letter to Claire she wrote: 'It came back. It trapped me in the bed, so I decided to run out of the house, but it was in my way. So I ran at it and went straight through the black shape. The thing is I felt it go straight through me too. It was the strangest feeling, as if for a split second it was inside me!'

On switching on the light the creature had gone. Ever since that night whenever she switched out the light the figure returned, sometimes with other shadowy figures that would lurk at the bottom of her bed. Yet when the light was switched on they just disappeared.

Joyce died in 1977 and her old friend Margaret received a very strange letter.

Dear Margaret
I know I am ill and don't have long left so I must tell you not to be afraid when you see me next. We were very lucky all those years ago, I know we scared ourselves, but now I'm off to join them. I always thought Heaven would be all clouds and angels, yet it seems our spirits are shadows that travel the earth. I have had years of fear, the spirits refused to leave me alone, and I'm frightened they'll come to you.

If they do I'll move them for you, first I have to find Colin and he'll help me. So watch the shadows, don't be frightened, they can't hurt you. I have always loved you, Margaret, and you have put up with so much. Remember me in your prayers.
Love for ever,
Joyce

Three days later Joyce was dead, and during her burial the sky clouded over, and it was as black as night. Margaret swears she caught a glimpse of shadowy shapes as her coffin was being lowered into the ground. That night Margaret was really frightened to go to bed, sleeping with the light on just in case. It was a balmy night but the wind was sweeping through the eaves of the old Georgian house and woke her up. The luminous dial of her alarm clock showed 4.30 a.m.

Margaret wondered how come it was dark, as she had left the light on.

On looking towards the end of her bed she saw countless dark shapes and she shrieked uncontrollably. It looked like the silhouettes of at least twenty people. Margaret screamed, 'Go away, leave me in peace!' and then broke down into a flood of tears.

At that moment a smaller shape began pushing these shapes towards the door, a tiny black shadow like a whirlwind sweeping away the strange creatures. The door slammed shut behind them.

Margaret was frozen with fear when the door opened again, feeling as if her heart was going to seize up altogether. The small dark shadow floated towards her and this is what Margaret had to say about it: 'I just watched this grey black cloud approaching me, and the tears just poured down my face. As it got really close I had to close my eyes and I felt something touch my face. It was so tender, it could've been a hand, it could even have been a kiss, and at once I knew it was Joyce.

'She comes back to see me from time to time, she can't talk or anything, but I know it's her. So now when I see a shadow I always smile, because I know I have a friend looking out for me. I think we must all become shadows, I don't believe in ghosts!'

THE FLASHER FROM BATH

There are few more beautiful cities in all of England than that of Bath on the River Avon. It is famous for the fact that the Romans exploited its mineral springs, calling it Aquae Sulis. During the eighteenth century stone squares were built to re-enhance its reputation of being a fashionable and trendy place to visit 'to take the waters'. Over the centuries it was made even more popular attracting the likes of dandy Richard 'Beau' Nash and others of society's élite, to the place 'that everyone had to visit'.

I don't have an interesting legend to tell you, merely a tale of a playful ghost that has made himself known over the past hundred years. If I were to tell you that another ghost of a Roman soldier had been spotted, you'd not be too surprised. Many cities with any historical background can claim an array of spectres that fit precisely with the history they are immersed in. This ghost is different from any other – he's naked!

The very first reported sighting was supposedly told to Queen Victoria in 1885. One of her maids had visited Bath and as she had taken the waters a man completely naked had walked over to her. She had screamed and called for help, as she was in a 'Women Only' area. Help arrived and as everyone looked at this bare-bottomed man, he turned to face them. Some of the women covered their eyes, others strained to get a better look through the steam, and at that very moment he just disappeared.

Two women fainted, one having to be rescued from the water by an attendant. On being told this, Victoria is said to have said, 'Tell me no more, I have enough scandal to deal with this day with our Salvation Army friends!'

(This I believe to be William Stead, a member of the Salvation Army, who had published naked pictures of underage girls in his magazine the *Pall Mall Gazette*. He had also catalogued cases of sexual degradation, prostitution and exploitation. When dealing with the white slavery issue, he had bought a naked thirteen-year-old girl for £5. His critics said he was a puritan totally obsessed with sex.)

*Since then there have been other sightings, including a lovely tale I was told on the *Night Owls* phone-in on Metro FM. It came from Mrs Irene Turnbull from Crook in Durham, whose grandfather was a policeman in Bath in the 1930s, where Irene and her parents lived until the middle 1970s. Her grandad had served with the police in Newcastle and had transferred to Bath when he married a girl from Wells Road in the city.

This is exactly what Irene told me: 'He was a bit of a one, my grandad, and he spoke broad Geordie, and this caused the people of Bath a bit of a problem understanding him. Well, he was patrolling on the beat around the Roman Baths and Pump Rooms and he heard a girl scream from the area around Abbey Church, so he dashed across. There was a group of young lasses aged about fifteen screaming their heads off and there in front of him was a blond-haired man completely naked. He did not seem in the least bit concerned at the effect he had on the girls. When my grandad saw him, he shouted, "Hey, you dirty bugger, get away from them bairns!"

'At this the naked man began to run down Pierrepont Street and Manvers Street with my grandad in hot pursuit. He was a fit man, he used to run for the Harriers, and he was determined to catch this pervert. My grandad couldn't believe it because this fellow actually had the gall to run stark-naked straight past the police station. It was about 11 p.m. and there weren't too many people around and finally he cornered the man in an alley leading to where the bus station now stands. The first thing he noticed was that the naked man wasn't out of breath despite having sprinted for almost half a mile.

' "Don't play silly buggers, son, you're coming with me," said my grandad, and the man didn't react one iota. So, as any policeman would have done, he reached across to apprehend him, and his hand went straight through him. My grandad told me that he kept pushing his hand through his body time and time again, but there was nothing there. He still looked solid, but his hands vanished inside him. He went back to the station, where his colleagues asked him if he had caught the flasher, and my grandad simply said no. He was too frightened to admit what had actually happened in case they thought he was mad. To his dying day he swore it was true.'

*In 1975 Mrs Mary Henderson from Torbay was visiting Bath for her summer holiday when she phoned the police saying that she had seen a naked man in the ladies' baths. When asked for a description she said, 'He was lovely and very well made.'

*This is the only naked phantom I've heard about, and certainly the only one that could run! Maybe this nude phantom has stopped flashing, or perhaps he'll stick it out a while longer.

THE POLTERGEIST OF BATH

The Garrick's Head Hotel in Bath is easily one of the most haunted sites in all England, with phenomena reported from the middle 1700s.

The hotel had been used by many rich and famous visitors to the city, including Richard 'Beau' Nash, who knew that a great deal of high stake gambling could be found there. Yet it would be love not money that would lead to the first ghosts taking up residence, if legend is to be believed.

There are many versions of the incidents concerned, I make no excuses for selecting the juiciest.

Philip Dunwoodie was a fairly successful local businessman, dealing in fine silks and materials, and gambling was his passion, much to the chagrin of his beautiful young wife Isobel. Despite her loathing of the game she would accompany her husband to the hotel, and would jolly herself with the other wives who would drink tea or share a sherry in the hotel drawing room. It was there that Isobel struck up a friendship with Dunwoodie's best friend Michael Creighton. The liaison began with fluttered eyes across a crowded room, and over the months it progressed from respectful nods, to muted 'hellos', to full-blown conversations. Creighton, a sworn bachelor renowned for his string of conquests, had finally fallen in love, ironically with his best friend's wife.

Despite being quite a Casanova, Creighton was an honourable man, and had often thought of telling his friend of his feelings, but he knew this would shatter their twenty-years friendship. But finally, whilst surrounded by dozens of people in the Garrick's

Head Hotel, he whispered to Isobel, 'I can bear this love no longer, I want you and let's damn the consequences!'

Isobel blushed, and she felt as if everyone in Bath was being warmed by her red cheeks. She was excited by the explosion of unbridled passion shown by a man who had always acted with such reservation, but deep inside she was frightened. Frightened of her husband, who was standing less than ten paces away. It was a Sunday evening in November, a dark and fierce night with the rain pelting down, and Dunwoodie's card game was a big one. Despite Isobel's protestations he refused to leave it, as, like many gamblers, he was determined to win back some of the money he had lost.

Creighton bowed out saying that he was tired, and left the back room where the gambler's club assembled, and walked straight in to Isobel. He offered to take her home if she was unhappy being in the hotel after hours, and she informed her husband that she had accepted the offer.

Dunwoodie was annoyed and the couple had a short exchange, then he beckoned Creighton to him saying, 'Look after her, Michael, see her home safe.' Creighton nodded and helped her with her shawl, then they made their way out into the street. The Dunwoodie house was only five minutes' walk away on Henrietta Road overlooking the park. However, Creighton suggested that they go to his room upstairs in the hotel first. Whether the argument with her husband had been the final straw, or if it had been the lust building up inside them both, they kissed, a long, passionate embrace. Even before it had ended, they knew they were to end up in bed. Creighton swept Isobel's tiny form into his arms, and he carried her upstairs.

'What of your husband?' asked Creighton.

'He loves his gambling far more than he loves me,' replied Isobel. 'He'll not be home until the early hours.'

Reassured, and really wanting to believe that, they began to tear at each other's clothes, and to make love.

Dunwoodie in the meantime, was in a foul mood. He had lost badly at his beloved cards, he was feeling quite sick after over-indulging in roast pork and stout, and he knew he had to face another argument on his return home.

His wife had left barely an hour before, and he believed that they could at least talk things over. On getting home, he found no sign of Isobel, and it was obvious that she had not returned, as there would have been footprints on the varnished wood floor. It really was a stormy night, and Dunwoodie decided to visit his friend Creighton at the Garrick's Head, to find out where his wife was. It had not crossed his mind that there was the least chance of them having an affair, but he was concerned as their last words together were in anger.

Arriving at the hotel, he strode up the stairs and was just about to knock when he heard his wife's voice say, 'I must get home now so he won't suspect.' It took Dunwoodie seconds to take in what he was hearing, and fury began to build inside him like a volcano. He looked around the hall and spotted two sabres crossed on the wall. He reached over and grabbed one, then using his shoulder he burst into the room. Creighton was naked in bed, and the force Dunwoodie had exerted on the door had thrown him literally on top of his best friend.

'You bastard cur!' screamed Dunwoodie, and then using both hands he forced the point of the sword down through the neck of his best friend. It didn't stop there, it went through the primitive bed and rammed into the floor beneath, the hilt hard against Creighton's throat.

Blood gushed from him soaking the pillows that had been, only moments before, home to a passionate love. Creighton was still alive and tried to speak without success, the hole in his throat merely bubbling and frothing as the words turned to air. His eyes had time to sweep the room.

There stood his best friend soaked in blood, and next to the window Isobel, the only woman he had ever really loved. He looked at her and his eyes tried to tell her how much he had really cared, how sorry he was and how powerless he was to help her now. It was as if she was reading his mind. She took a step back, pushed open the windows and threw herself out into space. Dunwoodie gasped in horror as he caught a glimpse of white, and she was lost into the storm. In a panic he tore down the flights of stairs and out into the street, and there was his beautiful wife, impaled on the railings that surrounded the hotel.

Over the years that followed many people claimed to have seen a grey lady gliding along the passageways, even visitors to he theatre next door often would see a pale figure silently moving along the dimly lit corridors.

*In 1952 Malcolm Docherty was having a pint when he glanced into the mirror in the bar and saw a small young woman standing behind him. On turning around there was no one there. Yet when he looked again into the mirror he could see her clearly.

*Jean Richardson from Newcastle upon Tyne contacted the *Night Owls* phone-in on Metro FM in 1987 with a story from the early 1960s. She had been visiting Bath and had stayed at the Garrick's Head Hotel. Very early one morning she was woken up by a noise, and saw that her window was open. So she secured it and returned to her bed. Once again the windows opened, and she assumed that in her sleepy state she'd merely made a poor job of closing them the fist time.

However, when this happened a third time she actually barked, 'Look, just shut the bloody things and let me get some sleep!'

At this the windows closed, and Jean screamed so loudly that staff rushed to her room.

*Various tenants of the Garrick's Head have suffered poltergeist activity of one sort or another, including articles being moved, doors opening and things literally flying around. In 1963 the landlord Bill Loud watched as his cash register flew into the air and hit a hard wooden chair, smashing it into matchwood.

*The most frightening story came from a Dutch tourist Johannes Van Veeran who was dining at the hotel with friends when suddenly he saw something and couldn't talk. It was a busy Saturday night in 1982 and staff thought he'd had too much to drink. He rushed from the hotel and refused to go back in. On returning to Holland he told the following story to his local newspaper, under the headline 'BLOODY GHOST FRIGHTENS TOURIST'.

Johannes Van Veeran (27) from Amsterdam was visiting Bath in England when he came face to face with a ghost. The local landscape gardener saw what he claimed to be the ghost of a young girl who had suffered horrific injuries to her stomach. Van Veeran said 'She just stood there in a white gown ripped in the middle, I could see her stomach torn open and her intestines hanging out. She was bleeding all over the floor, and I pointed to her but my friends could see nothing. I had to run out of the place. I had not been drinking and know what I saw!'

Van Veeran was dining at the Garrick's Head Hotel in Bath, a place well known for its ghostly phenomena.

MINEHEAD'S WHISTLING WIDOW

Those who live in Minehead in Somerset are sure to have heard of the Widow Leaky, the 'Whistling Spectre', a ghost who wanders the streets in the early morning.

As always, stories differ as to the ghost's origins. The most interesting story claims that she is the ghost of the mother of a 'streetman', Francis Leaky, whose job was to wander through Minehead shouting the time. 'Three o' clock and all is well!' he would call to inform and reassure the townsfolk.

His widowed mother had lost her husband while he was doing the selfsame job. One day Leaky senior had come upon two brigands robbing a fellow, and had waded in. His throat was cut and his head smashed through a bullseye glass window slashing it beyond recognition. The widow was determined that such a fate would never befall her only son. So when he went out to work, she would follow him, whistling loudly so that everyone would know that he was not alone.

By the time Francis Leaky had reached his fifties his aged mother had become quite a serious embarrassment, but he couldn't very well criticise her for looking after him so well, especially as he had never married.

At this point the storyline diverges. Some believe that to escape his mother's smothering, Francis left Minehead to seek his fortune in London, leaving Widow Leaky still whistling around the streets trying to find him. Others say that the widow died in her sleep, but every night her ghost continued to follow Francis around the streets, protecting him from beyond the grave.

*About fifteen generations later Widow Leaky's shrill whistling can still be heard, and they say anyone who hears it will feel their hair stand on end.

THE DEVIL IN THE PARRETT

In 1477 a mercenary soldier returned to his home in Somerset after fighting for Charles the Bold, Duke of Burgundy. His pay was stopped abruptly when in January of that year an Italian servant found the Duke's body lying naked in a frozen pond, half-eaten by the packs of ravenous wolves that lived in that part of Switzerland. His skull had been smashed in two by a battle axe, and so badly eaten was the corpse that he could only be fully identified by the many telltale scars on what remained of his body. Charles the Bold had wanted to be another Julius Caesar, and may have met a similar fate – killed by one of his own men.

This brought Alan Downton back home, to the very thing he hated most, peace and quiet in Bridgwater, Somerset. He had spent most of his money in London trying to gain another financial commission in the fighting forces of other armies without success. So this trained killer decided that he would bring the battle to Somerset. He began killing people, robbing them of what little they had. His favourite ploy was to swim along the River Parrett, dragging fishermen into the river with their own nets. He would entangle them, then drown them. Then when the bodies were found no one was suspicious, it looked like an accidental death. Who would know if their pockets were a little lighter?

He carried out at least a dozen murders when he made a mistake, and dragged a young girl into the river, killing her. She was dressed like a boy, and it was ony when he was rifling the youngster's pockets that he discovered what he had done. As a soldier he had always prided himself on never killing any women or children, something almost considered sport at that dreadful time in our history. He was so downhearted he committed suicide by tying heavy rocks to his body, then letting himself fall into the River Parrett.

Locals say that Downton's ghost still lurks beneath the surface and will claim at least one life every year, grabbing someone who swims or slips into the water. Once its victim is in the ghost's territory, it holds him under until he's dead. However frightening the legend there it is rare that a year goes by without someone paying it no heed and the river claiming its victim.

THE DREADED OAK OF STOGUMBER

When King James II took complete control of England, he sought vengeance on the supporters of the Dukes of Argyll and Monmouth, and it was a terrible revenge he took. In Somerset, in a small village called Stogumber, 48 soldiers were taken out to the Heddon oak tree. Instead of being hanged one at a time, they were strung up in groups of ten, while the bodies of the previously executed were allowed to remain on the tree. Finally from a distance it resembled a Christmas tree, dressed with death. The bodies were allowed to remain there until the birds and beasts had eaten away all of the flesh. Since that day in 1685 the tree is said to be

179

cursed. Anyone who stands beneath it will feel as if a noose is being tightened around his or her neck.

*In 1967 a young girl called Clare Donaldson, from Watchet, suffered an asthma attack whilst sitting under the tree, and had to be rushed to hospital, where fortunately she made a full recovery.

*In the early 1970s a group of schoolchildren were in the area doing a project on the West Somerset Railway, when the teacher made a detour to the tree. Four of the children happened to stand under the tree, and soon all four began to turn purple, as if they were being choked. The teacher put them straight back on to the minibus and they left immediately.

THE TAUNTON FIDDLER

A great many injustices have been caused over the years by the differing attitudes of British monarchs. King Charles II was a man who seemed far too wrapped up in enjoying himself, surrounding himself with sexual conquests and expensive playthings, to look to the good of his people. So when the frugal and plain living James II took over in 1685, the country really didn't know what to make of him. To ensure that he was able to rule unhindered the King ordered that the Whigs be kept out of office, so that the Tories would be re-elected. This caused an outbreak of rebellions mounted by the Duke of Argyll and Charles II's illegitimate son, the Duke of Monmouth.

The King was determined that nothing would stand in his way, so he called upon Judge Jeffreys to hold the 'Bloody Assizes' where 320 of Monmouth's followers were hanged, and over 800 sent to the colonies as slaves. One of the men to be hanged was a peasant known as 'Tom the Fiddler', imprisoned in Taunton for criticising the King. A balding man in his middle forties, with gentle eyes and a small ginger beard that seemed glued to his stubbly chin, his only crime was to say, 'That King James is a queer'un.' A soldier overheard and he was sentenced to death at Judge Jeffreys' court.

When the day came round he was given the chance to speak to the crowd who all knew Tom as an honest and decent man without the least hint of treason in him. Instead of making a speech he asked if he could play his fiddle for one last time. He played for almost fifteen minutes and even had the soldiers joining in with hand-clapping. Finally, they asked him to give up the fiddle. Tom refused saying that he wanted to play to the very end. A bizarre request but one the Taunton-born officer in charge gave in to, not wishing to incite the crowd to rioting. A black hood was placed over Tom's head, followed by the noose. At that moment Tom began playing a fast jig and once again the crowds began clapping. Half-way through the tune the officer gave the executioner the nod and the floor fell away, leaving Tom dangling in mid-air. Still he played on, his legs kicking in the air. Rather than the jig ending abruptly, it speeded up, and got so fast that no one could keep up with it and their clapping fell away.

Some say that he was snatched by the Devil who made him play a tune to gain entry to Hell. Others that the angels held his feet and allowed him to finish his tune, before guiding this innocent man to Heaven.

*The tune he played was 'Jig-A-Jig', which would be recorded by a group called East of Eden in the 1970s.

*There is a room in the beautiful Castle Hotel, in Taunton, called the Fiddler's Room where many people are said to have heard phantom fiddling late at night. It is thought that the room was once used by the murderous Judge Jeffreys, and that perhaps Tom the Fiddler had returned to haunt the old swine.

THE HAND THAT WALKS

One of Dorset's most told tales concerns a fight in the late 1870s, when a gamekeeper employed by a rich landowner who owned much of Chettle Down and the nearby Cranborne Chase came upon a poacher carrying a stringful of rabbits. He gave chase, catching the villain near Farnham. On bringing down the rogue the gamekeeper found that his adversary was a huge man, and was carrying a rabbit-skinning knife. So not wanting to be gutted by this brigand, the bailiff reached inside his pouch and pulled out a huge knife of his own. The two men wrestled, each trying to avoid the other's blade, and suddenly found themselves at the top of a steep grassy bank. Before they knew what was happening they were tumbling down, going head over heels into the gorge below. When they reached the bottom the poacher stood up clutching his arm that carried no hand, just a bloody stump that pumped blood into the air. In a shocked daze he ran into a copse, where he bled to death. He was eventually found lying among the trees and his body was transported to London for burial. The hand, however, was found later and interred in Dorset.

This is what seems to be causing the problem: the hand wants to be reunited to the body. Late in the evening many people have seen a bloody hand crawling across fields in search of its body.

*In 1986 Martin Stubbington from Portsmouth was touring Dorset with his caravan, and he caught a glimpse of what looked like a disembodied human hand crawling across a road. He stopped his Volvo estate and put his headlights on main beam to see it disappear into the verge.

*In 1991 a young couple were out for a cycle ride in the sunshine around Salisbury when they stopped for a drink and some sandwiches. They were not sure precisely where they were but they were heading towards Sixpenny Handley, off the A354. They sat leaning against a wall, and the young man, Keith Marshall, put his arm around the shoulder of his girlfriend, a student called Lorraine. Then she felt something touching her ear. Keith had a sandwich in one hand and her shoulder in the other, so she jumped up and saw a hand touching her from over the wall. She yelled, 'You pervert!' and then she saw that the hand was not attached to an arm. The flesh was still bleeding and sinews and veins hung limply from the wound. Lorraine fainted clean away. When Keith looked around to see what had had this effect on her he saw nothing.

THE HANGED MAN OF LYME REGIS

It is said that more than two hundred men and women were hung on Broad Street, Lyme Regis, the main place of public execution in the area. One of the weirdest legends I've come across tells of the 'Hanged Man' a John Robert Evans. He was sent to the gallows in the late 1600s for garrotting his neighbour Malachy Ellis with whose wife he was in love. However, the wife, Esme, didn't feel the same about Evans, and was not pleased to find him standing behind her husband with wire wrapped around his spine, and blood covering both of them.

Evans was taken to the gallows and hanged.

His neck was snapped but he just wouldn't die. He hung there for almost eight hours before he was cut down. The authorities believed that this was a sign from God that his life was to be spared, so he was set free. He could no longer hold his head up straight, it lolled around his shoulders, rolling from one side to the other. Everywhere he went he was shunned for murdering a good husband and father, the children made up insulting rhymes and pelted him with mud, and no one would sell him anything.

Evans decided that he would move to another town in Dorset, hoping that he could make a fresh start, and he packed up what little he had and moved to Wimborne (now Wimborne Minster). Word travels fast, however, and a group of children spotted him and ran into the village yelling, 'He's coming, the Hanged Man is coming!'

Men, women and children came out of their houses and pelted him with mud, rotting vegetables and stones. Once more he was forced out of the village, and back on the road. It was as he was walking away from Wimborne that he came across a carriage pulled by a single horse. The occupants asked if he was journeying far and offered him a ride. During the trip through Dorset an argument started and Evans hit the driver on the back of the head with a meat hook, which penetrated and remained in his skull. He died instantly, and his two daughters ran off into the countryside. Within 24 hours Evans was arrested and once again sentenced to be hanged.

'You'll not kill me, for I have God on my side,' he boasted, as for the second time he climbed up to the gallows in Lyme Regis.

The trapdoor swung open and down he went, but still it didn't kill him. The executioner even climbed down and swung on his legs, but to no avail. The crowd gasped at how he was even able to talk to the crowd while he dangled in the noose.

In a croaking voice he told them how he would keep on killing, because God obviously wanted him to. At that moment Evans saw that a woman had climbed on to the gallows and was now standing next to him. She carried a huge filleting knife with which she hacked at the rope. It snapped and Evans flew down through the trapdoor cracking his head on the wood frame on the way. He lay on the cobbled street bleeding from the split head, both of his legs broken. On looking up he saw it was Esme Ellis, the wife of the man he had murdered. She hurled herself down on top of him, landing with both her feet on his chest, smashing his ribs, and piercing his heart. The Hanged Man was dead.

Esme Ellis was arrested, but was eventually released when the executioner stepped forward and declared that he had asked her to help him carry out the execution. He hadn't, but public feeling was so strong the court realised that justice had been done in a very roundabout way.

The ghost of the hanged man is said still to walk down Broad Street in Lyme Regis, his head lolling from side to side as he wanders along the roadways, usually in the early hours.

*Malcolm Edwards from Poole was in Lyme Regis selling double glazing back in 1988 when he saw a man in a sweet-shop doorway. He approached him to ask if he was all right, and the man lurched towards him, his head wobbling from side to side uncontrollably. Malcolm backed off, and to his horror the man walked straight through him. 'It was as if someone had walked across my grave, and I shook with fear for almost three weeks. My boss thought I'd been on a bender, but I'd never touched a drop.'

*As recently as December 1992 the Hanged Man apparently showed himself again. Three girls were returning from a Christmas party at their department store on Christmas Eve, when they spotted a ragged man with his head rolling around his shoulders. As it was Christmas they felt sorry for him, so scrambled around their purses and were about to give him £15, when he ran at them. He hit them too, knocking two off their feet, and pushing the other into a lamppost, badly bruising her shoulder. Strange that four years earlier this phantom could walk through Malcolm Edwards, yet was a solid entity when he met the shop girls!

THE CRIPPLED CHILDREN OF POOLE

Whenever people talk about how things were so much better in 'the good old days' I think of stories like this, from the mid-1800s. It involved a landlord of an old inn near Market Street in Poole, whose wife gave birth to two children. Sadly, they were both born handicapped, one had a cleft palate and a paralysed leg, the other had a huge growth on his face and a twisted arm. The landlord was disgusted by the appearance of his children and decided to hide them from everybody by locking them in a back room while they were small. However, by the time they were six and eight, he felt that they were more bother than they were worth. His wife loved her children, and begged her brutish husband not to do them any harm, and reluctantly he promised not to, saying he would take them to a local convent and let the nuns look after them, as they had done with local orphans on occasion.

184

So, the landlord wheeled them away in a straw-laden handcart, leaving a very tearful mother sobbing on her bed, knowing that she might never see her children again. However, such were the man's feelings of revulsion for his children that he took them to the disused stables some hundred yards away from the inn. There he carried the children up to an attic room, where he strangled them. He left them there and sealed the room, taking off the crude door, and blocking off that corner. The stables were old and foul so the smell of rotting corpses would merely mingle with the nearby cesspit and garbage heap.

Many believe that the landlord was made an offer for the inn and its outbuildings some years later, and it was too good an offer to refuse. So one night he crept back up to that boarded attic room, gathered the remains into old blankets, then disposed of them in a bog nearby.

The landlord decided to use the money from the sale of both inn, stables and barn to move his family to Shaftesbury. This caused his wife great consternation, and she determined to see her two sons once more before she left. Without telling her husband she visited the convent, where to her horror she was told that they hadn't ever seen her sons.

In a raging fury she rushed back home and clouted her husband across the head with a copper cooking pot. In a daze, he was quizzed as to where her children were, and managed to cobble together a plausible story about how a passing tinker had agreed to care for the children. He added that much of his money was sent to them, when in fact it was a card table in a friend's house that had been responsible for his financial losses.

Suitably sorry and reasonably placated, the wife left Poole with her husband to start a new life.

That is when the troubles started.

All manner of incidents occurred in the stables, horses were untethered and set free, straw was set on fire, saddle girths were mysteriously cut and strange voices were heard from the attic. Many people said they could hear children laughing and giggling; strange, floating lights were often seen at night, and a few people actually saw the shapes of two deformed children limping down Market Street in Poole.

*Brian and Michelle Murray stabled their daughter's pony Willow at the stable from 1921 to 1924 and suffered a variety of mishaps.

They finally removed their animal after their fourteen-year-old daughter Briony fell, paralysing her leg.

*In 1966 the stable was converted into a discotheque, and this certainly didn't seem to please the spirits of the two sad children, so savagely murdered by their own father. Not only did they terrify dozens of people but they made the front page of the local newspaper. They started playing the piano in front of customers who could see the keys going down, but could see no one there. Then, even after bolting and padlocking doors, the owners would find the doors wide open when they returned. The business didn't last too long.

*The Crown Hotel on Market Street still has troubles. The voices of small children screaming in pain are often heard, and tiny troubled footsteps are heard rushing along corridors, as are creaking stairs and whispered voices in this busy and friendly establishment.

THE DORSET VAMPIRE

Anyone interested in the folklore of Dorset will know of Doggett's Corpse, of which several stories exist. I make no apologies for choosing the most gory.

In the small village of Tarrant Gunville stands a fine house called Eastbury, once one of the most sought-after residences in all of England. It was there that a squint-eyed man called William Doggett worked as steward. His duties included preparing the master's clothes, making sure the horses were ready and generally acting as a non-military batman.

Living in such a fine house gave him considerable standing in the community, and opened many a lady's bedroom door. Doggett was a sluggish man, his shoulders always hanging forward limply as he slouched his way around the county. He was well known for having no sense of humour at all, once thrashing a young boy who hit his leg with a snowball. He used to visit the local inn, sitting quietly by the open fire of an evening, spending all night over one foaming tankard of ale.

In 1827 the first body was found, in a copse of trees near Shroton. The corpse was that of a young servant girl from the inn, her clothes had been removed and her stomach was ripped open. Some maniac had not only dragged her insides out of her body but teethmarks could clearly be seen on her liver. There were many bloody footprints that seemed to lead back to Sutton Waldron, so a full search was carried out in that area.

Later that same year a six-year-old girl was discovered in Ashmore, stripped naked and impaled on a tree, part of the flesh from her arm had been eaten away, and her eyes had been removed.

Quite understandably everyone was terrified, and when a madman was captured in Shaftesbury, everyone breathed a sigh of relief, believing him to have been the killer. But the strange deaths continued. A 75-year-old lady was found dead in her bed at Spettisbury. She was known to be frail so her death would have been no big surprise to the locals – except that the artery in her neck was severed and yet there was no sign of blood. The lady was found with the knife in her hand, but where was the blood? The authorities dismissed this, but locals believed that a vampire was on the loose and it had drank the old lady's 'juice'.

Between 1827 and 1843 there were eleven other strange incidents, yet each one was close enough to being 'a natural death' to avoid any major investigation. A woman was found with slashed wrists in a cattle trough, yet there was very little blood found. The would-be coroner explained this was due to the coldness of the water on a February morning. Two toddlers were found at the bottom of a hill near Ibberton. Their skulls were both smashed, yet their brains were never found. Once again a reason was found; in this case it was suggested that foxes had fed on the youngster's bodies. Teethmarks were found, but they looked human, not canine.

There was little doubt that the area had a serious problem. These events always took place late at night, and always had a hint of cannibalism about them.

It was then that fate took charge and brought the matter to a temporary close, for William Doggett was called upon to drive his master's coach to Southampton on business. The job was done and they returned to find that a maid had entered Doggett's quarters, where she had found a chest full of goblets, silverware and the master's less well used jewellery. Doggett was told that he was sacked, and the master summoned soldiers to arrest and hold him. It was then that Doggett took a gun, placed it in his mouth and literally blew his brains all over the study wall. There were no further murders and mysterious deaths for two years; then, in 1845, a teenage girl from Witchampton disappeared, only to be found on Gaunts Common, stripped and impaled on a fencepost.

187

She was pale and gaunt, and despite such a horrific wound there was little or no blood.

Some of the locals believed that it was still Doggett, rising from his grave to continue his bloody deeds. So on a wet and windy autumn evening they gathered at the graveyard with shovels in hand, ready to destroy this monster. As they hacked away at the sodden earth the wind made the church bell clang away, as if summoning the dead to mass. Their shovels struck wood and they began clearing the top of the steward's coffin. They hacked off the brass locks that were still firmly fastened, and the coffin opened with an unnerving creak. As they shone their lantern on the body they all recoiled in horror. Doggett's body, two years in the ground, was rosy-cheeked and flushed with blood, and a tiny dribble of gore trickled from his lips.

Some say a stake was hammered through his heart, others that they hacked his body to pieces with their shovels. Another version of the legend tells how one of the men, believed to be the father of the tragic Witchampton girl, took a hatchet and chopped off his head, weighting it down with rocks and hurling it into the River Stour.

Holy water was thrown onto the cadaver and the coffin was sealed again, and covered with rocks and soil.

This put an end to the adventures of the Dorset vampire. Or did it? They say that on the anniversary of Doggett's death a phantom coach arrives at the door of Eastbury, rattling its way over the old cattle grill. It is driven by a headless coachman, believed to be what was left of Doggett after the locals had done with him.

LAWRENCE OF ARABIA, A GHOST IN WAITING?

The man they couldn't kill, writer Colonel Thomas Edward Lawrence of Arabia died in a tragic motorbike accident on 19 May 1935. It is said that his white-faced cottage known as Clouds Hill near Wool in Dorset is the place where the phantom of the great soldier lies waiting to return from the grave to rescue Britain should it ever be in peril again. Those who have seen the ghost say that it appears in Arab dress, as worn by the Colonel in his many exploits during the Arab revolt against the Turks.

Other locals claim that the ghost is actually wearing a grey suit similar to that worn by Lawrence on the day of his death, when, being over-confident on his Brough Superior motorbike, he crashed and died. Legend has it that if you travel along the lane past Clouds Hill around six in the evening you can hear the clatter and hum of an old motorbike and the coughing kick-start sound so often heard when Lawrence was alive.

It is a frightening enough thought to imagine that ghosts might actually exist, but just imagine if they all rode motorcycles?

THE PILTON PARK PHANTOM, BARNSTAPLE

Anyone who lives in Barnstaple will know Pilton Park, home of one of the more mischievous poltergeists, if we are to believe local legend.

The story begins in the 1930s when an old man called Jack Buchanan came to stay with his relatives who lived in Vicarage Street, overlooking Yeo School. A bit of a joker, he frequently played pranks on people, but he was without malice and every day the old fellow would have a pocketful of sweets for the children, a joke for the neighbours and a toothless smile for everyone he met. He had a routine you could set your clocks to; in the morning he'd watch the children going to school, then he'd walk along Princes Street, along Coronation Street and then have a packed lunch in Pilton Park, feeding his crusts to the ducks and swans. In August 1936 he was having his lunch in the park as usual when a group of young men approached him, and started causing trouble. They grabbed his walking stick and hurled it into the river, they stole his sandwiches and started eating them. Jack was in his seventies and knew that he couldn't discipline them himself, so he simply tried to walk away. But as he made his way back to Pilton Causeway they pushed him, shoving him into bushes, scaring the old fellow silly. He had reached the causeway overlooking St George's Road when his heart gave out, and he died on the spot.

Jack's body may well have gone, but his spirit still lingers on. In 1938 a family were picnicking in Pilton Park, when their sandwiches disappeared. They searched all around but couldn't find them; then the sandwiches reappeared, precisely where they should have been but weren't seconds before.

Incidents like this became commonplace, and before long people would say 'Old Jack's been up to his tricks again!'

*In 1942 Jack actually showed himself during an air raid. Sam Figgis was an Air Raid Warden and he was cycling through Pilton Park on his way to his home in Carrington Terrace when an old man pushed a stick into the spokes of his bicycle and he fell off. 'You stupid old bastard,' shouted Sam. 'What did you do that for?'

The old man just laughed and disappeared. Sam's report read: 'I can still see his toothless grin, but strike me down if he didn't just disappear. He vanished in front of me, but he was as solid as you or I. I can laugh about it now but I didn't at the time because I landed in nettles, and I had the swellings for nearly a week!'

*After the war Jack seemed to behave himself, cropping up in 1952 and again briefly in 1961. However, in 1990 Malcolm Armstrong, who worked for a firm on the Seven Brethren Industrial Estate, had a run-in with the ghost of Jack Buchanan. He had driven from work to his home in Abbey Road, Pilton, and he and his wife Terri were going to go to the cinema. While she was getting ready, he decided to drive his mongrel dog Bruiser to Pilton Park for his nightly runabout. While there he suddenly found himself surrounded by a gang of yobs. Bruiser was soft as clarts so was of no help. One of the hooligans punched Malcolm in the face and he fell to the ground, whereupon they all started kicking him. Then, out of nowhere, an old man appeared, waving his walking stick, and knocked them down like skittles. The old man helped Malcolm to his feet, and he got the dog back on his lead, and they all walked back to his car. On reaching it Malcolm, who, seconds before, had been chatting away to the old man, turned to him to say goodbye, the man was nowhere to be seen.

Malcolm had not known about the ghost, but the old man matched exactly old Jack's description.

NELSON AND HIS LADY IN DAWLISH

In 1944 Topper Henderson, who served with the Border Regiment, was returned from Italy to England suffering a badly infected wound. He chose to spend his leave with the family of his best friend who lived in Dawlish, Devon, and while there he had a most amazing confrontation with one of England's great heroes.

Topper rang in to one of my phone-in programmes in 1987. This is what he had to say: 'I know you'll think I'm crackers, but while I was on leave I had a hell of a job to get to sleep. For some reason I only needed a couple of hours a night, so I used to take long walks along the sea front. It was August, and about three a.m. and quite a nasty night, but I was taking my walk as usual and I spotted this couple coming towards me. I was nearly blown off my feet because it wasn't half windy, yet they didn't seem to be affected by it at all. I really didn't expect to see anyone on such a stormy night, but there they were. As they got closer I could see that the lady was wearing a long dress and a bonnet tied on with scarf material. The wind wasn't causing her any bother at all. She was a real beauty, mind, and then I noticed he was wearing some kind of dark uniform full of badges and shiny buttons. I looked at his face and recognised him at once. It was Nelson!

'Before you say anything, no, I wasn't drunk, I wasn't even on painkillers for my wound. It was Nelson, mind you he didn't have an eye patch and still had two arms. He was holding her hand with one of them. I stared at him and it was definitely him, and he was with a beautiful girl. I was going to say "Good evening" but I bottled out; but I did nod at him, and he nodded back!'

I started laughing and he kept at me, 'I knew you'd think I was daft, but it happened, it was him, and I'm not making it up. I mean you get ridiculed, don't you?'

Suitably chastised, I continued our chat and have no doubt he was totally sincere, and that he really believed that he'd seen Nelson. I put this to him and he replied, 'When I told the Douglas family, who I was staying with, what I'd seen, they didn't pay it any heed either. But I was shot in the arm, not in the head. I wasn't crazy then and I'm not crazy now!'

In the meantime a Mrs Harriet Smith from Dawlish was visiting the North East and heard the show. She phoned in, asking to be put in touch with Topper and was. She ended up sending him a book on Nelson, and in it was a painting of Emma, Lady Hamilton. On receipt of it, Topper immediately called up the radio station again, saying, 'It *was* Nelson, because the lass with him was Lady Hamilton – I recognised her picture in this book I've been sent. Mind you, the painting doesn't do her justice.'

What Topper didn't know is that both Lord Nelson and Emma Hamilton did visit Dawlish, for a romantic and passionate week together, staying at an inn on Teignmouth Road. That place is now called The Smugglers Inn.

It seems as if those great lovers still tread a romantic path along the sea front at Dawlish in the early hours. They walk hand-in-hand, visiting one of their favourite holiday 'haunts'.

THE BLOODY MONK OF EXETER

One of the most grisly tales of human torture comes from Exeter in Devon. At one time there were said to be more monasteries in Devon than in any other county, and there was a great rivalry between them. This legend has been told to me in three forms; I have chosen the most interesting one.

A monastery stood overlooking the River Exe near where St David's Station now stands, and its great rival monastery stood near Bury Meadow on the site of the current Technical College. The legend tells of how rumours began to spread that the monastery on the River Exe had found many relics of King Arthur, taken from his burial mound near Tintagel in Cornwall. This instantly transformed the monks' standing in the community, and the other monasteries were riddled with jealousy. Some produced splinters of old wood that they claimed had come from Christ's cross, others displayed old finger bones that they alleged were St Matthew's – all the monasteries tried to come up with something to give the monks a bit of status in the community.

The monasteries were fairly poor, except for St David's Monastery on the Exe. They seemed to have plenty of money, so the other monks began spreading stories that they were melting down King Arthur's treasures and selling them. All of this was untrue but gossip like this was commonplace among these so-called holy men.

Finally, a group of monks decided to enter St David's monastery by force and steal the treasures. They waited until a Monday morning when they knew that the majority of monks were going on a sabbatical to Taunton, and would be away for three weeks.

Dressed in ragged clothes, ungodly monks broke into St David's and killed three monks who had tried to stop them; to their surprise there was only one other monk on the premises. They had been told that Excalibur and the Holy Grail were just two of the invaluable collection of Arthurian treasures, and they weren't going to leave without them. So they were determined to extract information on the treasure's whereabouts from the monk. They broke his fingers one by one with rocks, they broke his toes in the same way, yet he continued to stress that they had no gold or silver.

They then stretched the monk out on the ground, he was totally unable to defend himself without the use of his fingers and toes. Using a small knife they proceeded to cut off his penis and testicles, then poured salt into the open wound, before sealing it with a red hot poker. The monk lost consciousness, but was eventually woken, in time to watch as they forced a red-hot poker deep into his eye sockets. The rogue priests couldn't believe how stubborn the monk was, so finally they decided upon a common medieval torture. They placed the monk's broken body between two tables, then put a rat in a cage on his stomach. Then they placed red-hot coals on top of the cage. The rat in its panic had only one way to escape, literally through the body of the victim. So, terrified by the heat, it proceeded to eat its way through the monk. Even once the rat had burrowed completely through the monk, slithering through the bloodsoaked tunnel it had carved, the still conscious monk would not tell of the treasures.

The truth was that it had only ever been a rumour without any proof.

The monks finally left, returning to their monastery as if nothing had happened. The tortured monk died soon afterwards, bleeding to death, and by the time the other monks had returned all of the murdered monks had been feasted upon by the various ratpacks from the vicinity.

It is said that the eyeless monk can still be seen in Exeter, particularly around the railway station.

*In 1965 several houses down Cowick Lane were visited by a ghostly monk.

*In 1967 a ghost monk 'with bloody eyeless sockets' was spotted by almost an entire coach party parked near the River Exe. One lady in her seventies had to be taken to hospital for shock.

*Dorothy Waters from Whipton witnessed a strange phenomenon on 3 May 1975. She had this to say: 'I was hurrying to the station to catch an early train, and was running late, and I saw a man wearing a dark robe, and when I looked closer I could see a huge hole in his middle. I could see the street through it, yet he kept walking towards me. I screamed, and the moment I did he just disappeared.' Dorothy didn't see him as a monk, and had no knowledge of the legend.

THE WOMAN WHO DIED TWICE, EXETER

Rosemary Hill had married her husband Jack Thompson during an air raid in December 1940. Perhaps in peacetime their courtship would have been far longer, but three months in wartime was like an eternity. It seemed as if their world was coming to an end, yet they were only at the beginning. The unthinkable had happened, Buckingham Palace had been bombed, Coventry Cathedral was devastated by repeated raids, Birmingham, Manchester, Newcastle and Glasgow had all been hammered by German long-range bombers.

The honeymoon was a strange one, a meal at one of the few cafés still to have its windows intact, a visit to the cinema to see Charlie Chaplin's new film *The Great Dictator* and then back to Rosemary's parents' house, to consummate the marriage. It wasn't the best start to a marriage, but they did love each other so very much, and they knew that they might never see each other again. This heightened the desire, it heightened the passion and it heightened the blind terror that the future surely held.

They had spent almost ten days together when Jack got his orders to join General Wavell's Army of the Nile who were about to fight their way across Libya, following the Australians' success at Tobruk.

Jack Thompson was mentioned in despatches some weeks later for his gallantry as his infantry regiment supported tanks, armoured cars and Bren-gun carriers against masses of Italian artillery.

Meanwhile Rosemary did what so many others had to do, live from letter to letter, hoping and praying that he would come home safe. The rest of the war saw her answering the call 'Women Of Britain, Come Into The Factories!', and soon she was making munitions for £1 18s a week.

Jack managed two visits home during the rest of the war and it was in October 1943 that he discovered how sweet and sour life can be. He was sent home with a flesh wound to his arm, and rejoicing that the Italians against whom he had been fighting had made a complete U-turn and had declared war on Germany. He knew that this was the beginning of the end of the war, so rushed home to Exeter to join the wife he had spent less than six weeks with despite being married for almost three years.

He reached his house, quite undamaged by the war. There was no answer. He hammered on the doors of those people who had been his neighbours, finding one, a Mr Terence McIntosh, washing down his outside toilet.

The old fellow smiled on seeing his young friend and then his

194

round face turned to a frown. 'You'll not know about your Rose-mary, then?' said the man.

Jack shook him, shouting, 'Where is she? Is she all right?'

Mr McIntosh explained that she had fallen pregnant and there had been some complications, so she was at a small hospital outside of Exeter. Jack rushed down the street to his cousins' house and they gave him a lift on their motorcycle and sidecar to the hospital.

Rosemary was in a bad way; the doctors explained it would be a breech birth, and there was a chance that the baby might not survive. It hadn't sunk into Jack that he was on the verge of being a father, all he wanted was his wife safe and well. While fighting in the desert the only incentive to survive was to get back to that beautiful brunette with the long legs and the button nose, who always signed herself 'Bunny'.

The operation was about to take place; Jack insisted on being present but they would not allow it. The waiting was cruel, he had waited almost two years to get back and now that he was home he was kicking his heels again.

Suddenly the door opened and a doctor wearing a surgical mask appeared at the door, and explained that they were only able to save one or the other, and the dreadful decision was to be his!

Jack had not been aware of this child, all he knew was that it was killing the only thing in life that he treasured. 'Save my wife doctor,' he begged. 'Please save her!'

The doctor turned back towards the operating theatre leaving the door squeaking back and forth. The minutes became hours, and still no news. It crossed Jack's mind that the doctor was rather old – most of the younger men were overseas with the fighting forces – perhaps he would not be up on all the modern techniques. Just then he heard a scream.

It was Rosemary and she was calling his name! Jack slammed through the doors almost taking them from their rusting hinges, and ran along the corridors until he finally found the room where the operation was taking place. A doctor in a white overall stood over the table with two nurses, another doctor sat next to the bed holding an oxygen mask, he was beginning to put it away.

'I'm sorry,' said the doctor. 'We tried, we really tried, but she just wasn't strong enough.'

Jack felt his legs go, it was if his spine was folding like a pile of pennies, and fell to his knees sobbing uncontrollably. The doctor gave him a sedative and put him into a quiet room away from the body of his young wife.

Before Jack could come to terms with his grief he was called to rejoin his regiment and off he went to war, a very bitter man. His family had promised to 'see to everything' and the day before he left he had held his wife's body from the coffin where she had been laid out, talking to her as if she was still alive.

Jack was part of the reserves that were trying to inch their way up the boot of Italy. Hundreds of men had been massacred at Monte Cassino, where the Germans had turned a Benedictine monastery into a fortress. It seemed an impossible barrier with machine-gun nests hidden in the craggy Appennine mountains, marshy ground, fog and only a handful of decent roads. It crossed his mind that this was perfect for him, this was the place that would take his life. So he could join his wife in the hereafter.

It was in January 1944 that things began to move when the Americans landed at Anzio, completely cutting the supply route to Monte Cassino. This is when the first miracle took place. Jack and three others were in a Bren-gun carrier when a mortar hit it. His friends were blown to pieces, yet Jack wasn't even scratched.

Three days later he was ordered back to Naples, where a sniper hit Jack on the head with a bullet. It ricocheted off his helmet and killed a man standing next to him.

Jack's charmed life continued, as in February 1944 the Allies decided to bomb the monastery, American Flying Fortresses peppered the hillside with thousands of bombs. Jack was at the base of the mountainside and one plane had discharged its bombs over the Allied lines. Almost thirty bombs landed in the middle of an encampment. Sixteen British soldiers died; only two survived. Jack was one of them.

Then came D Day, VE Day and VJ Day. The Allied victory was complete. Despite Jack having tried so hard to get himself killed, he had fought the entire war with nothing more to show than eight stitches in his arm.

It was September 1945 when the train carrying almost seventy soldiers from various regiments drew into Exeter. The band was playing, the flags fluttered in the blustery wind and everyone was there to welcome back their very own heroes. The train ground to a halt and the doors opened spilling out the khaki warriors, the blue-suited sailors and Royal Air Force grey, all merging with the crowd of loved ones welcoming them back. Jack's parents were dead, he had two cousins but was never close to them. After four years so full of incident, he was returning to a void. He stayed on the train as long as he could, rolling a cigarette and watching the scenes of tears, joy, passion and excitement. It was as if he was watching Pathé News, as if he was separate from it all. The crowds began to thin as the relatives dragged their sons, brothers and husbands away for their personal welcoming celebrations.

At last Jack stood up, stretched himself and stepped off the train. He turned towards the exit from Exeter station and saw a woman standing by the barrier. She looked familiar, maybe it was the blue coat, Rosemary had one just like it. The woman had hair exactly the same colour as his wife, and those shapely ankles looked too close for comfort.

He walked towards the barrier his eyes transfixed; he thought to himself, 'It's a ghost! I am seeing a ghost!' yet on reaching this woman he could see that it clearly was Rosemary. His mind was in total confusion, he reached out to her, half expecting his hand to sink into nothingness, but he felt her warmth, her body, her love. He swam in it, as a man lost in a desert would envelop himself in an oasis lake.

'How are you, Bunny?' he asked, then realised that he had been there when she died. 'I mean how are you here – you died – I know you died . . .' he stammered.

'I had to make sure my baby was all right,' said Rosemary. 'But I had to come back for you!'

Jack was so charged with emotion that he felt his legs going again and the pair of them clung to each other on the station platform in a hug that was impossible to loosen. Jack didn't want to let go in case the vision disappeared. It was only when a cranky old station master tapped them with a red flag saying, 'Come, come, young man, there's a time and a place for that kind of behaviour!'

Jack kept a tight grip of Rosemary's hand and they began the long walk home, as they lived just outside of Whipton.

On reaching their street the neighbours rushed to greet Jack, yet they gasped in amazement when they saw Rosemary by his side. Most of them had been to her funeral two years earlier.

Some rationalised it as best they could. 'She must have recovered', 'Perhaps it wasn't her that we buried', 'It must be her twin sister', or 'He's found another woman, the spitting image of his late wife'.

I tracked Jack Thompson down three years before his death in 1986, and he said, 'It was Rosemary all right. The baby was ours and she couldn't leave it. She'd only been with me for a few weeks, she'd carried it for nine months. It was a special part of both of us. So she went with it, it was a little boy, and she had to find out where it would be, so she could join it later on. She's there now, she gave me another eighteen years, dying on September the 14th 1959. That same day the Russians landed a rocket on the moon. I thought that was appropriate. She wasn't ill, the doctors didn't know why she died, but I knew! She had had her time with me, and she's with our son, and I'll be joining them eventually. There isn't a Heaven, you know. But there is another place, Rosemary told me what it was like. It's just like here, except there is no death, no disease, and everyone is treated well. I told her that we should both end our lives together and go there, but Rosemary told me that you can't. Because it's not for us to make those decisions.'

As it had been over twenty years since his wife had died for the *second* time, I asked him whether he had contacted her since. His reply was totally direct and frighteningly sincere: 'She never died at all. We don't die. You leave one shell and move on to the next one. Rosemary speaks to me all the time, and I see her from time to time. She's not a ghost, she's as solid as you or I. She's just in another place, a place that I will go to when my turn comes around. So don't you worry about dying, nobody dies!'

Jack Thompson 'died' in December 1989, or did he just move on?

I received a letter from him in February 1990. It was hand-written, and dated 3 February. It read:

Dear Alan,
I always knew you didn't believe a word that I said, but everything I told you is true. I have contacted my cousin and he nearly had a heart attack, so I thought I would get in touch with you to let you know all is well. Rosemary sends her love and my son is now married with a family of his own. I came back for two days but it does take it out of you, so I won't be back. I hope one day to see you again.
Sincerely yours,
Jack Thompson

THE DEVON HIGHWAYMAN

There are more legends around Devon about the notorious high-wayman Tom King than about anyone else. Some say he was a kindly benevolent man, who would steal from the rich and give to the poor – but the truth was rather more brutal: he robbed from the rich and from the poor and kept it.

One story tells of how he stopped a coach on the Exeter road, killed the coachman, forced the others to run off and then raped and murdered a young girl before cutting off her fingers because her rings were too tight to remove. Another story tells of how he would take refuge in people's homes and before leaving would kill them, setting fire to the houses as to leave no mark of his presence. Busy as he was when he lived, though, he seems to have been even busier after his death. There are dozens of areas in Devon claiming to have his ghost, but the most consistent reports come from the area around Rackenford, a place where Tom King often went; some swear it was there that he shot a man in the face for refusing to buy him a drink.

It is said that the thundering hooves of Tom King's black horse can still regularly be heard.

*In 1951 Mr & Mrs L. J. Sweeney from Cornwall were driving along the road near Rackenford when they saw a horseman riding flat-out towards them. In the saddle was a man in a long brown coat, waving two pistols in the air. Mrs Sweeney, who was driving, slammed her foot on the brake of their Rover and watched in terror as the rider went straight through them. They watched him gallop off up the road they had just driven down. 'It felt as if someone was actually invading your body for a second, and then he was gone,' said Mrs Sweeney. Mr Sweeney also saw it, but he refuses to talk about it.

*In 1969 there was a hippy gathering outside Exeter, and Jake Morris was sleeping in his pup tent when he heard the hooves of a horse thundering across the field. He peered out of the tent and could see nothing, but the noise got closer and closer to him and 'something' actually knocked his tent down. When he had extricated himself from the mess, he saw deep hoof prints across the tent and cut deep into the field.

*John Godfrey spoke to a local newsman in the early 1980s about how he had heard the phantom highwayman too. His wife and daughter were having lunch when they heard the rider passing by.

Mr Godfrey, the landlord at the Stag Inn, Rackenford swears it was 'as if someone was riding a horse straight through the house.'

*In 1979 a group of schoolchildren stopped at Rackenford and were told some stories about Tom King; on their way home to Exeter they all saw a highwayman sitting aback a black horse standing in the field waving at them. The teachers swear that they saw this too, and presumed that the locals had put someone in fancy dress to amuse the children. The locals, however, said they knew nothing about it. Perhaps the ghost of the highwayman likes his 'celebrity' status, and is making sure he doesn't lose it.

THE DEVIL'S ROLLING STONE

Half-way between Holsworthy and Torrington in Devon there's a huge boulder known to the locals as the Devil's Stone. It weighs around half a ton and is surrounded by a wide range of myths and legends. Each year on 5 November, Bonfire Night, locals roll the stone over, believing that bad luck will befall the village if they don't. The stone is then blessed by the local vicar who sees this as a reversal of the pagan acts carried out in Devon centuries before.

One legend proclaims that the year that the residents of the tiny village of Shebbear fail to turn the stone, then 'the Devil shall rise from his pit to strike them dead'.

There is another legend that is far more sinister. Some locals believe that the good people from St Michael's church, who roll the stone, are sadly mistaken about it. They believe that the Devil's Stone is in fact another huge boulder, encrusted with quartz crystals, just over a mile away.

It is said that early in the ninth century a peasant known as Lambert found a huge hole in the ground, which seemed to be growing. Instead of running for his life this valiant young man, armed only with a knife, proceeded to crawl inside. The tunnel was as dark as the inside of a cow with her tail down, but far, far below him he could see a tiny glimpse of red. So, stumbling through the darkness, tearing his clothes on the craggy rocks he tenaciously made for this chink of light. He slipped on the clay soil, cracking nails as he desperately held on to rocky outcrops that would frighten even a professional climber. The light was much further away than he had thought, but Lambert was not for turning, so down and down he climbed. It took almost all day and all night but finally there he was in a huge chamber far underground. It was a massive cavern, lit only by the glowing red-white lava that swept through the passageway even further below him. It was then that he saw a vile and ugly creature with red skin, a horned head and a long forked tail that lashed and cracked like a whip.

Then suddenly from out of every conceivable nook and cranny horrific creatures began to walk, slither and crawl. Huge monsters resembling gorillas, snakes with human heads and tiny elfin folk, all carrying spears, gathered to hear what the monstrous red creature had to say. They spoke in a language that Lambert couldn't understand, but at that moment a young girl was dragged by her hair into the chamber by a brute of a creature. She screamed in terror, her long white robe tearing on the rocky floor of the cave.

Lambert wasn't a religious man but was certain that he had stumbled upon the Devil's lair, and that the girl was to be a human sacrifice. At that moment the girl was again grabbed by the hair, her face held up to the light, and the Devil's tongue shot out almost a foot and licked her face.

Once more she screamed and as she did, a glimpse of light shone straight into her eyes, and Lambert saw she was by far the most beautiful girl he had ever seen. She was placed on a stone altar, secured by leather straps, and the creatures began a strange and mysterious chant. Then one by one they walked down beside the river of red-hot lava that ran like water at the very edge of the chamber. The Devil strode ahead, leading his demonic clan, and one by one they scooped a piece of molten lava up with a torch, and carried it out in front of them. The cave was becoming brighter all the time, so Lambert knew that if he was going to act, now was the time. He raced down into the cavern and with his tiny knife he cut the girl free from her bindings. Without saying a word he led her to his tunnel and they climbed, higher and higher, back into the darkness. It was nearly fifteen minutes before the Devil's brood returned to the stone altar to discover their captive had escaped. Far below them, Lambert and the girl could hear the hubbub as the search began.

It was only a matter of time before the demonic swarm found their tracks, and then they began to follow. In a blind panic Lambert and the girl reached the surface and wondered how they could stop these monstrous creatures from entering their world. He began hurling rocks of all sizes into the pit, some hitting the creatures far below, sending them tumbling to their death, if die they could. Then he saw the Devil once again, leading his Satanic forces into the light of day. They were no more than yards from the top when the girl fell to her knees and started praying, 'Dear God, please deliver us from evil, save us from the fallen one'.

At this the Devil began to speak in a tongue they could understand. 'He'll not save you, for I am the power on Earth now, and you are both mine!'

At that moment everything went dim, and there in the sky appeared an object that had blotted out the sun. It was getting closer and closer and closer, and growing in size all the way. Lambert grasped the girl and dragged her away from pit, pulling her along the dewy grass.

Then a huge meteor struck the Earth, ramming itself into the pit like a cork in a bottle.

Some Devon folk say that if you listen hard to the stone you can hear the Devil and his forces mumbling their discontent.

Lambert took the girl as his wife, and they were the very first inhabitants of Shebbear.

*One day in 1964 a child on a school trip carved off a lump of quartz and left it resting on the rock. When he tried to pick it up it had fused back to the rock again. It was as if the rock refused to move, perhaps knowing what would happen if ever it were shifted.

THE PIRATE OF THE JAMAICA INN

On my various ghost hunts I have occasionally come across a place that really deserves a ghost but hasn't got one. Such a place is in Bolventor in Cornwall – the legendary Jamaica Inn, made famous by Daphne du Maurier's novel.

Throughout the years, various stories have been told of how the ghostly hordes of skeleton pirates still walk through the grounds singing 'Yo-ho-ho and a barrel of rum'. But I've been able to find only one report that has the least hint of truth to it.

In the 1970s a woman called Pauline Rutter had driven from London to stay with friends in Mousehole, and was told about the Jamaica Inn. Pauline was a great fan of old movies and one of her favourites was the classic *Jamaica Inn* starring Robert Newton and Maureen O'Hara. So one afternoon she set off to visit the rustic inn. Her journey was plagued with problems, ranging from running out of petrol to hitting a dog in a village square. She reached the Jamaica Inn at about 9 p.m., and as she parked her car and walked towards the entrance she saw a pirate wearing a headscarf and eye patch. He was carrying a cutlass and leaped from one of the surrounding walls. Pauline was terrified and didn't know whether to run back to the car or to rush into the inn. As it was, she ended up rooted to the spot.

The pirate didn't stop. He kept walking towards her, his bare feet barely making a sound. She knew that he could see her, he was looking directly at her. When he was less than a yard away she covered her face, and felt the pirate grasp her arms. At this she fainted away and the pirate fell on top of her.

When she regained consciousness she was sitting in the bar, and the staff had made her comfortable. She instantly spluttered this story about being grabbed by a ghostly pirate. Then she looked at the assembled crowd, among them was a duck, a gorilla, Napoleon, a nurse wearing white stockings, Groucho Marx . . . and there, eating some salted peanuts, was the 'ghost' pirate. A group of staff from a local hospital were doing fancy-dress pub crawl and had visited the Jamaica Inn. The pirate had merely been parking the mini-bus!

THE HELSTON DEVILS

Cornish folk have long known the legend of St Michael who did battle with the Devil and won. The Devil was about to lead his unholy legions out of Hell to take over the world, when St Michael sealed the entrance to the underworld with a huge rock, known to all as Hell's stone. Hence the name Helston.

The area does have quite a history of ghostly phenomena, including that of *doppelgängers*: a number of people claim to have come across someone who looks exactly like them. Yet by far the most horrific tale came from a Cornishman Duncan Alexander who died in 1962 leaving a story with his daughter Irene. She read my book *Grisly Trails and Ghostly Tales* and sent it to me. The story tells of 'The Helston Devils'.

The year was 1766 and Thomas Markham had returned to Cornwall after helping Clive of India come to an agreement with Emperor Shah Alam, thus bringing relative peace to a troubled country. Markham wasn't in the army, but was on the diplomatic staff. On getting back to Helston he took a large house on the outskirts of the town, where he installed four Indian servants who had accompanied him home. This caused a commotion in Helston, where most folk had never gazed upon a face any other colour than white. It was around this time that things started to happen.

An eleven-year-old girl disappeared and after a lengthy search her body was found near Breage, her stomach ripped open, her innards removed and used to decorate a nearby tree.

Helston was in uproar, demanding the arrest of Markham's Indian staff, for it was obviously their doing. Soldiers did pay Markham a visit, but he could account for the activities of his men most accurately, so nothing could be done.

The murderer was not located, things quietened down until April 1767, when a group of four young girls didn't return from a trip to the coast at Porthleven. The eldest girl was seventeen and considered by all as 'sensible-headed', everyone was sure that she would be able to look after the younger ones. As darkness fell on a chilly April evening a tinker tripped while walking through a field. On looking closely at the ground his blood curdled, for there poking through the grass was a human hand. He ran off to Helston for help, returning with a local magistrate and some farmhands. They began digging into the mud and found the bodies of all four children. The eldest had been buried alive, and had struggled to break free of the black, muddy hole, finally drowning in the mire, but not before her hand had reached out into the blackness in a silent scream for help. The children's bodies had been hacked to pieces and many of the internal organs had been removed.

Once again the finger of suspicion pointed towards the Indian servants of Thomas Markham. They had all, he said, been with him on a trip to Falmouth, where he had acquired goods from a sailing ship. The locals were far than convinced, but without proof they could not act.

The remainder of 1767 was quiet, but January 1768 exploded with blood and mutilations. Within less than three months, nine children had been butchered; a house burned down in Gweek, killing a family of seven; a young girl from Sithney had been decapitated and her head impaled on a farm gatepost, and the gamekeeper from Wendron had returned home to find his young wife tied to her bed and murdered. Her eyes had been burned out with a hot iron, her stomach torn open and her liver and heart cut out.

This whirl of horror had whipped the people of Helston into a fury and they gathered with torches, axes and ploughshares, and marched to Markham's mansion. The magistrate couldn't hold them back any longer, and they stormed the house. Markham was not married, and stories abounded that he was actually in love with one of the young Indian boys. The servants were captured and taken outside, while the Helston folk set fire to Markham's house. The mansion house was mainly wood with a thatched roof and was swiftly consumed by the flames. Markham, who had hidden in a secret compartment to avoid the mob, perished in the fire.

The Indian servants weren't given a trial. They had no time to deny anything. Their hands were tied behind their backs, a rope was placed around their necks and they were hauled into the air until they were asphyxiated. Their feet kicked out in the air in a macabre dance of death, until one by one the movement stopped. No one touched their bodies, they were left there until the crows had eaten away their bodies, and only their skeletons remained.

The people of Helston felt proud of themselves, they had exorcised the evil amongst them. They were even treated like heroes by many of the local villagers, who believed that their actions had saved their children from a terrible fate.

Then another child was taken.

A six-year-old boy disappeared from his bed in the early hours of the morning. The parents were frantic and searched the nearby woods, finding his tiny broken body nailed to a tree. Once again his insides had been removed.

The Helston folk chose to ignore common sense, and still blamed the Indian servants, declaring they had returned from the dead. So once again they marched to where Markham's house had stood, and ripped down the remains of the Indians, and crushed their bones to dust. This seemed to reassure the superstitious locals, and things calmed again until a merchant spotted a group of what he described as 'tiny folk' trying to grab his eleven-year-old daughter. He chased them off waving his sword, and they disappeared into the woods near Constantine. On hearing of this the magistrate called upon the soldiers, and a party of trusted Helston residents, and they set off to investigate.

The search seemed to be fruitless until a tiny wisp of smoke was spotted coming from a particularly dense patch of woodland. The soldiers walked around the copse of trees, which seemed impenetrable, unless you were on your hands and knees. There was a definite pathway through the trees, but it was if it had been carved out by midgets.

After about thirty yards it opened out, and there in the centre was a huge shack. A massive shanty with woods of all different kinds, and out of the door poured a dozen or so small children armed with pitchforks, daggers and chopping axes. After a pitched battle two soldiers were dead, and fifteen children slain.

Cautiously they stepped inside the hut and there in the corner was an old hag, a wrinkle-faced crone with black teeth and eyes without any pupils.

'Away, away,' shouted the old witch, 'lest my devils will kill and eat ye!'

The leading soldier laughed and proceeded further inside; at that very moment there was a glint of steel and a razor-sharp hand scythe sliced off the top of his head, splattering the others with a mixture of blood and brain. He fell in convulsions to the floor, as the other soldiers backed away. In the end they all rushed into the room, where several tiny children were hidden, all armed and slashing out at anything that moved. Yet anther battle ensued and at last all the children had been killed or taken prisoner. The old lady remained crouched in the corner holding a long-bladed sword.

The magistrate stepped forward, saying, 'Now, madam, I ask you to put down that sword, and I guarantee you'll get a fair trial.'

'As fair as the trial ye gave those brown boys', she sneered. 'My little devils told me what ye'd done! You bloody murderers!'

At this she lurched blindly forward into the magistrate. He stumbled backwards as she arched the blade of the sword into his back.

As they tumbled to the floor the sword forced its way right through the squealing magistrate and into the hag, and they lay impaled together on the floor. As they lay there she began to laugh and cough blood simultaneously, until they both bled to death. Both murderers in their own way, one killing for revenge; the other, as it was later found, killing for food. The hag had created a gang of killer children, orphans, runaways, criminals who banded together and hunted together. Around the shack they found bottled and pickled organs. All prepared for eating. There on the counter was a cooked human liver, with bite marks in it as if their supper had been rudely interrupted.

The surviving Helston folk never told the full story, as it would bring shame on all of them. Instead they told that the Indian servants had accomplices living in the woods, and they had wiped them out. Once again they were heroes, but deep down they knew the truth.

Perhaps they were the first-ever racist killings in Britain, yet the blood of the innocents were spilled, and the real culprits were all aged under sixteen.

I have spoken to many in Cornwall about the legend, and two confirmed that there was some truth to it. Brian Knight a London historical researcher, told of how four black servants were killed by a rioting mob near Helston. Gareth Evans a lecturer told of the Markham curse being passed down through the years. Supposedly, the curse covered anyone who built on the site of Markham's mansion. It was tried by countless people and in each case the house would burn down. No one tried to use that land from the early 1800s, and it became ploughed fields. However, a DIY store cum garden centre now occupies the site and it seems to have survived.

THE SOUTH EAST

THE LONGLEAT MURDERESS

Most of Britain's fine stately homes have a ghost or a legend tied to them. Longleat in Wiltshire has many phantom women in long rustling gowns who glide along corridors and from room to room.

One is a strange pest of a ghost, believed to be a dead chamber-maid, who has the habit of knocking on the bedroom doors in the early hours of the morning.

The most famous of all is the legendary 'Green Lady', believed to be the spectre of Lady Louise Carteret who murdered her husband, and disposed of the body by burying it in a trench excavated beneath the cellar floor. The body was only found fairly recently and since its removal there have been even more sightings of Lady Louise.

THE WILTSHIRE BODY PIT

In the late 1800s legends abounded of King Arthur's lost treasures and many people would dig huge holes in fields searching for instant wealth. One chap did make a discovery in the late 1860s that he would rather he had not. Some days earlier he had found three Roman coins, nothing of particular value, but he wondered what else lay beneath the surface in a disused gulley near Marnhull in Wiltshire.

So he got himself his strongest shovel and started to dig. He was down less than four feet when he felt the ground give way beneath his feet and he tumbled into a huge subterranean pit. While he lay there, about fifteen feet down, he shook his head to remove the soil and looked at what was around him. He squealed in panic, for he was buried in a mass of bones, hundreds upon hundreds of dead bodies, all piled one on top of the other. As he scrambled back to the surface he felt as if bony hands were grasping at his clothes. He was still screaming when he arrived at the village. It is generally believed it was merely one of thousands of 'body pits' excavated to take those who died in the Great Plague of London.

Many ghosts have been seen in the area, including a ghastly procession of skeletons carrying dead bodies to their underground home.

*A family from Weymouth interested in ghostly affairs visited the site, and claimed to have heard voices coming from beneath the ground. When they put their ears to the ground they heard revelling from below.

THE HAMPSHIRE DEVIL DOG

It has always been a mystery to me why people choose to keep dangerous dogs as pets, particularly when the house has small children in it too. Yet this is by no means a modern-day phenomenon, for there is a particularly bloodthirsty legend from Hampshire that bears out man's love for the powerful and vicious.

The story revolves around a man called Thomas Newton, a Hampshire socialite who was known to be very much anti-slavery, and contributed a great deal of money to the campaigns of William Wilberforce and Thomas Clarkson, the first to try to end the atrocious treatment meted out to black workers in the West Indies.

In August 1787 a huge party was given to raise funds for a freed slave called Ottobah Cugoano who was doing the rounds to raise awareness of the inhuman treatment slaves suffered at the hands of their white owners. Cugoano was captured in Africa as a child and taken to America where he was forced to work as a slave until his master returned to England, and decided to make him a free man.

Cugoano had a dog, though it looked more like a bear. He kept it with him at all times because he had met with many Englishmen who were in favour of slavery, and had taken more beatings than any man deserved. When Newton saw this slavering brute of an animal he knew that he wanted it, and offered £300 to Cugoano's cause if he parted with the creature. That sum was a fortune in those days and the deal was done. If we were to cross a rottweiler with a dobermann, we might get a creature resembling this animal, except that it was almost the size of a small pony. It certainly did not take to just any human being, but it rather begrudgingly

210

became friendly with Newton and only Newton, accompanying him everywhere. No one wanted to call at the Newton residence lest they came face to face with this foaming-mouthed beast who would growl and had been known to attack and kill other dogs.

The animal was kept reasonably under control for almost eight years until the spring of 1795 when Newton died. He lived alone, with a staff of about twelve, and died in his bedroom, where his dog always slept with him. So when staff tried to get into the room, one sharp growl was enough to hold them at bay. This continued for almost a week, until the authorities eventually intervened and, using farmhands with pitchforks to keep the animal at bay, went in to rescue the body. When Newton was buried the dog was kept tied to a tree nearby, but during the ceremony it chewed itself free and ran at the gathered ensemble of mourners, scattering them across the graveyard. It then ran off into nearby woods. For the next 150 years that animal caused havoc across the county. At first cattle and sheep would be taken and their half-eaten carcasses found at various points throughout the woods.

A family called Morton took over Newton's house, where they suffered at the paws of the Devil Dog. Six expensive Arab horses were attacked so badly that they had to be destroyed; one had its leg bitten right off. The Mortons offered a huge reward to anyone who could kill the animal. But no one ever saw it. People would see shadows; they would hear a strange howling coming from the woods; they would find droppings and the bloodsoaked leftovers of dead animals, but the house from Hell was far more elusive than they thought. The Morton farming enterprise was a complete disaster. Although they doubled the number of shepherds and farmhands they employed, they lost 877 of their flock of 1023 sheep, their nine dairy cows were all killed or had their udders torn away by this savage monster. The dog even knocked down the hen house killing or chasing off the chickens. The Mortons sold the property at a considerable loss to a neighbour who allowed the house to go into disrepair. It seemed that as long as he didn't live there his stock remained unharmed. Occasionally a sheep would be taken, but this was acceptable, as it is nature's way.

Things remained quiet until September 1834 when a child was attacked and crippled by a monstrous brute of a dog while playing in a copse of trees on the outskirts of Alton. Martin Anderson was trying to transform the old system of running the counties by introducing the new Municipal Reform Act, and was looking around Hampshire for ways to improve the area. He wasn't there

24 hours before his eleven-year-old son was attacked so badly by this huge black dog that one of his legs had to be amputated, the other was so badly chewed that it never recovered and the youngster couldn't regain the use of it.

Once again a hunt was made, for a dog that had now become a folk legend. Surely it couldn't have been the animal brought by the slave all those years ago? No dog lives that long, yet the evidence continued to grow. More sheep and cattle were attacked; early in the morning farmers would see the tracks of a huge animal, and some members of the local hunt refused to ride around Alton in case they disturbed this monstrous beast.

Right the way up until the middle of the 1900s farmers still spoke of the 'Black Dog' or 'the Hell Hound' and yet during wartime the legend seemed to be filed away and forgotten about for more than twenty years, before it was revived in 1963.

*Miriam Carroll, a clerk from Andover, was driving to Alton in her little Triumph when she saw a most horrific sight. A huge black dog had grasped a lamb through a barbed-wire fence, and with its teeth buried into the lamb's neck, was pulling it through the barbs, ripping its prey's skin. The lamb's head shook violently from side to side as the dog tried to force the helpless creature through the tiny gap, managing only to tear its head off, when the dog fell backwards in front of the car. Despite Miriam honking her horn and flashing her lights to try to frighten the monstrous beast away, it ignored her and returned to the fence to pull the decapitated body of the lamb through. She was shaking so much she drove up to the farm and the lady of the house made her some tea to calm her shattered nerves. The farmer walked down to the field to find nothing left of the lamb except its head that had been squashed flat by cars on the road.

*During 1964 and 1965 various stories made their way into the newspapers, including one of a policeman who had been standing chatting to two tourists from Ireland when a huge black dog ran at them, pinning them against a bus shelter, yet when one of the Irishmen hurled his haversack at it, the dog just disappeared. It was 1.15 on a clear afternoon, and none of the three had been drinking.

*During major building work carried out at the Crown Hotel, High Street, Alton, they discovered the bones of a dog buried in the wall that they were taking out. They believed it had been killed by its master; others said it was the Hampshire Hell Hound and could now be laid peacefully to rest. However, this animal was far too small to be the creature so many described over the years.

*In 1987 Frankie Duggan, a factory worker from Basingstoke, was out with his fiancée Yvonne and they were looking for a suitable picnic site. When they found a small opening in a local wood they set out their car rug, and started opening their carrier bags filled with sandwiches and salad. Frankie said he had to answer the call of nature and headed off into the trees. No sooner had he unzipped himself and proceeded to water a particularly leafy bush, than a huge snarling and snapping dog's head pushed itself through the greenery. In his panic he fell over backwards, soaking himself, covering his bare arms in nettle rash and almost breaking his neck. He ran back to the picnic and gathered together flasks and teacups and started running towards his Ford Fiesta parked about three hundred yards away. This left Yvonne totally bewildered sitting on a towel in the clearing. Frankie was screaming at her to run to him, and as she stood up he saw a huge black dog step from the woods showing its teeth. She heard something growl behind her and dropped the towel and tore after her boyfriend. Later she couldn't admit to seeing anything but said she 'knew' it was a dog. They were not aware of the legend. So it seems that the 'Hell Hound' is still lurking around the darker corners of deepest Hampshire, with a few surprises in store for us yet.

THE HIGHWAYMAN CAPTAIN JACQUES

Whenever we picture a highwayman, we automatically think of Dick Turpin riding Black Bess, yet there was a far more bloodthirsty villain who was the scourge of Hampshire. His name was Captain Jacques and none of the traits often given to highwaymen, such as chivalry and fair play, could ever be given to him.

Captain Jacques not only robbed his victims, he would often kill or cripple them just for fun. He was once holding up a coach near Langstone when he spotted a huge ruby ring on the finger of a young girl. He ordered her to remove it, but much as she struggled the ring would not budge. He held her hand through the window and fired his pistol, completely removing the end of her finger, and pulled the ring off the bloody stump.

Many locals conspired with him, offering him safe houses and hiding places and choosing not to believe the stories told about him.

He once carried out a robbery on The Grange, a huge manor that used to stand near Horndean. Two of his accomplices were burgling the hall when they were disturbed by the staff, who took up the chase, but, as the main door opened, Captain Jacques rode his brown stallion right inside the house and fired one of his pistols at the pursuers, stopping them in their tracks.

The most widely told story about him is that of his ultimate demise. It was a chilly November evening when Captain Jacques stopped a coach on the Winchester road and robbed all the passengers. Unbeknown to him one of them was a tallyman, who had been sent from London specifically to bring Captain Jacques to justice. Without giving himself away he took in every detail he could of the horse and its rider.

Over the next month the Excisemen spread themselves throughout Hampshire looking for the villain or his horse, as they now had full descriptions. It was only a matter of time before they would root him out. This happened at the Royal Anchor in Liphook, now a hotel, but in those dark days a common inn. Captain Jacques used to use it as one of his safe houses, paying the owner well, and over the odds for the prostitutes he kept in his 'bawdy rooms'. He had just enjoyed a time there and was sleeping off both alcoholic and sexual overindulgence when an Exciseman appeared at the front door. The innkeeper moved cautiously towards the stairwell, with the thought of warning the Captain, but he was stopped by another tallyman who had sneaked through from the back. He held a pistol at the man's head, warning him that he would blow it off unless he told them which room the highwayman was in. Despite the innkeeper's protestations the Excisemen knew Jacques was at the inn, his brown stallion was well fed and standing plain as day in the stables. At last the innkeeper told them he was in room six at the top of the stairs. The Excisemen gagged and bound him, fastening him to a rail on the bar, and four of them crept upstairs to the room. Somehow, even in his drunken state he knew something was wrong, and had propped a chair against the door, as in those days there was no bolt on his door. The tallymen tried to force their way in as the highwayman battled to pull his clothes on. Beneath his window he could see more Excisemen surrounding the inn. So he proceeded to try and fight his way out, pushing the prostitute out of the door first, screaming and squealing as she was dragged out of the way. Shots were fired and Captain

Jacques fell dead with three musketballs in him, two in the chest and one that struck him under the chin and lodged in his brain.

*The ghost of Captain Jacques can still be seen at the royal Anchor Hotel in Liphook. Regularly the landlord is told that a man wearing a tricorn hat and long coat had been clearly seen. Despite the fact when he was shot he was in underwear and boots.

*Several accounts of the ghost of Captain Jacques and his horse have also been reported. One story made the local press in 1966 when young Sally Cartington from Lymington said she was out with friends on a cycling holiday. She had stopped near Liphook, set up her tent and was about to light her primus stove, while she waited for her two friends to catch up with her. They had decided upon the camp site the previous day. Sally was the better cyclist so had gone on ahead to make supper. Then she heard the sound of hooves thundering down the twilight lane; they were so loud she could feel the ground shaking. Then out of the dusky evening sky came a rider aboard a brown horse that panted and frothed at the mouth. As the rider passed her she could see it was a highwayman carrying the reins in one hand and holding a pistol in the other. The rider rode off towards her two friends who were literally just around the corner. They neither saw nor heard anything.

Many locals say they can still hear his ghostly horse taking Captain Jacques out in search of another coach to rob.

THE PHANTOM OF WINCHESTER

The bloodiest year in Winchester's history could well have been 1685. King Charles II had been replaced by the new James II who completely changed the way the country was run. Instead of extravagance and luxury, King James introduced frugality, something long forgotten by the upper classes. He also introduced measures to guarantee his success, ensuring that the Tory party remained in power, which resulted in Whig rebellions, the main one led by the Dukes of Argyll and of Monmouth, the latter Charles II's illegitimate son. The King showed no mercy to the rebels in London. At the 'Bloody Assizes' Judge Jeffreys sentenced 320 Monmouth supporters to be executed, more than 800 others were deported to plantations in the Americas or the West Indies. Thousands of others had their possessions seized and were flogged. The Duke of Monmouth was executed, and, as a warning to his many supporters in Winchester Alice, Lady Lisle, one of the city's most beloved citizens was led to the block. She was charged with sheltering rebels during the various rebellions, which she was certainly guilty of.

Judge Jeffreys knew how to keep the people under his thumb, and first ordered that she be stripped of her clothes, dragged by horses through the city and be burned at the stake for all to see. However, the clergy intervened and instead she was marched out into the market square where she was allowed to give a short address to the good people of Winchester. She asked God to forgive her for her sins, she blessed the city and her friends, then she gave a silver coin to the axeman begging that he should see the job done with a single stroke. The people loved Lady Lisle and some fighting broke out in the square that had to be sorted by soldiers. The axeman was as good as his word, and as the blade swung down her head fell, and blood exploded from her neck splattering the front row of people who were there to show their respects to a great lady. Some say she was praying loudly as she lay there with her head on the block. It was even claimed that her head already lay in a puddle of blood as she finished the prayer with Amen.

There is a plaque on the wall of the Old Market House in Winchester that reads 'Place of Execution of Lady Lisle 1635 in the roadway'.

Very close to this plaque is the ancient inn called the Eclipse, where Lady Lisle spent her last night alive. She was able to look out at the construction of the block platform, and to make her peace with God. A priest stayed with her for much of that night.

*Since her bloody end her ghost has remained in the area and is often seen. A clerk from the Halifax Building Society saw Lady Lisle on a Sunday morning, walking across the road beside a bookstore with her head down and in prayer. She passed within a yard of her and was shocked to see that her head was completely bald. She wore a black chiffon cloth over her head, but you could clearly see the dome. Lady Lisle's head had been shaved so as not to obscure the neck or obstruct the hangman's axe.

*Staff of the Eclipse have over the years often seen Lady Lisle's long rustling dress gliding along the corridors and from room to room.

*There has only been one report of a headless ghost and we must go back to 1957 for it. It was witnessed by a gas board worker who was digging a hole in the centre of Winchester in order to seal a burst gas main, when he became aware that someone was looking down into the hole where he was working. This is an occupational hazard for anyone who works in the street, but the hole was barriered off, and there were warning signs posted that said 'No Smoking – Gas'. Yet there, blocking the sunlight from the hole, was someone; he glanced up and through the sun's glare he saw the shape of a woman. When he stood up he saw that it was a woman in a long skirt, and he was about to tell her to get back behind the barrier when he saw that she had no head. The neck was bleeding down her gown. He became speechless, scrambled out of the hole and jumped on to the lorry where his two colleagues were eating their lunchtime sandwiches. They didn't believe him, went to look and saw nothing. The gas fitter was so shocked he was off work for almost two months, and ended up leaving when he felt fit enough to go back to work.

A DEMON'S HANDS

How many of us have experienced strange things that we put down to our own forgetfulness – the watch that is suddenly no longer on the bedside table, but now on the bathroom windowsill; the TV channel-changer that mysteriously appeared in the bedroom, or the keys that turn up in the most peculiar places. . . . In 1982 Michelle Taylor had just moved into a new flat in Arreton on the Isle of Wight, and all these things happened to her. Michelle put it down to being in a new place and being a trifle absentminded.

At night when she went to bed she often felt as if there was a shadow at the bottom of her bed. She put it down to imagination until, some nights later, the shadow sat at the bottom of her bed. She could clearly feel the weight of someone pressing down near her feet. Once again she told herself that it was her brain working overtime.

Then one day at the local café she related her experience to the waitress, who told her about a man called Robbins who had lived in the area in the 1950s, and had been forced to move out because he had molested young girls. She went on to say that some believed that he wasn't forced off the island, but had been taken to the coast, killed and thrown into the sea. This did not reassure Michelle, who was now more terrified than ever and asked her landlord to give her another flat. He had no other vacancies, however, so she had no other option than to stay.

A few nights passed without incident and then came a very warm, sticky night when Michelle slept with only a sheet to cover her, the quilt folded at the bottom of the bed. She was still too hot and in an uncomfortable half-sleep when she felt the sheet being slowly pulled away from her, exposing her short nightdress and bare legs. She awoke and looked down and saw nothing at all, until suddenly through the gloom she caught a glimpse of a pair of huge hands. Large hairy hands, not attached to anything tore at her body, pushing her nightdress up towards her breasts, while she struggled to pull it back down again. She was screaming and yelling as the hands grabbed at her chest, clawing down her stomach, and tearing out a patch of her pubic hair.

She was crying out for help so loudly that a neighbour ran to her assistance and hammered on her door. The hands would not relent but she finally managed to scramble into a ball in the corner of the room, her nightdress ripped but clenched tightly around her knees as she protected herself. The neighbour at last kicked in her panelled wood door, and raced with his wife up the stairs to her bedroom. She was crying, her stomach had scratch marks down it and the hair had been so roughly torn from her body that she was bleeding. She swore she had been attacked by a demon with huge hairy hands. The neighbours put it down to a bad dream until they saw that her nightgown was smeared with blood.

The police were called and put it down as attempted rape, refusing to believe in any ghostly interference.

Michelle moved back to the mainland, returning to her parents in Abingdon in Berkshire and decided to become a nun; she was eventually accepted, choosing to join a convent in Ireland.

The police never found the human attacker, nor the inhuman one.

THE SURREY PUMA

When the police find a pawprint three times the size of a leopard's in rural England you would think that was conclusive enough to begin a hunt. Then on 4 July 1966 six police officers and eight members of the public from Worplesdon in Surrey watched a ginger-brown puma that was the size of a large dobermann steal and kill a rabbit. Everyone agreed it was a gigantic cat with what the Americans describe as a 'cougar tail', the telltale mark of the North American puma, a long tail with a white tip.

This was not a glimpse sighting; they watched the creature for almost 25 minutes, and their descriptions all match. Local farmers had known for some years that something was on the prowl, as livestock had been taken, but they had rationalised it as being foxes or the even more common domestic dogs.

In the seventies the puma was sighted near Pease Pottage, Brooks Green, Munstead and Horsham. This started a glut of sightings across Britain as far afield as Washington, Cheshire le Street and Gosforth in the north-east to Littleworth Common in Buckingham-shire, Winchester in Hampshire and several villages in west Wiltshire.

There may, however, be a rather more bizarre answer to the Surrey puma puzzle. In 1706 Surrey was home to a woman who would now be known as a 'healer'; in those dark days she was described as either 'a wise woman' or a 'witch' depending on your beliefs. It was said that she could cure anything. Local farmers would bring ailing cattle, on several occasions horses belonging to earls and barons would be ministered to by the woman known to all as 'Old Bess of Forest Green'. This arrangement was good for everybody, as Bess had lost her husband – according to records, 'colic claimed him at the age of only 31'. So the little she charged for services helped her live to a reasonable standard. Often locals couldn't afford to pay her money, so she had plenty chickens, goats and sheep. For over forty years Old Bess plied her trade, her miracles including bringing a shire horse back to life, reviving a two-year-old child after it had drowned, and curing a traveller of the plague merely by touching his scabs.

It was in August 1706 that she came across something that was far beyond her amazing abilities. A rich landowner called Simon Merrick sent for Bess and she travelled by cart through heavy rain for over sixteen hours to reach his home outside Reigate. On getting there she found Margaret Merrick in bed bleeding from the mouth and from the groin. It was obvious to anyone that she had been beaten by someone, and the way that Simon Merrick behaved, it seemed certain it was him.

'Come on, you old crone, and do something', he barked as she tried to calm the frantic woman. Margaret was a beautiful woman, yet her jaw was black and blue, and her stomach a mass of severe bruising as if she had been kicked. As Old Bess did what little she could Margaret Merrick began to shake, and Bess turned to the assembly and said, 'She's too far gone, I can't save her!' and at that she died.

Something made Old Bess turn back to the bed and she began pushing down on the dead woman's bloated and swollen stomach, and to everyone's surprise a tiny baby appeared from the womb. Months premature and gasping for life, the bloody bundle screamed out to be born, and Old Bess was happy to help. She held the baby towards Simon Merrick saying, 'Whosoever beat this lovely lady has murdered her, and very nearly murdered this tiny babe!'

'What do you mean?' spat Merrick. 'She had a fall, that's all!'

The room was full of Merrick's friends and neighbours, and Merrick's face was turning purple with a mixture of rage and shame.

Old Bess wouldn't let it rest. 'No fall can give a body boot prints. She has been kicked and punched, for that is why she has passed over!'

Merrick lashed out with the back of his hand knocking the old woman to the floor. The baby was sent flying from her arms and hit the edging of the bedroom's fireplace. Its tiny life snuffed out before it had really begun.

The maid fainted on seeing the tiny baby shattered and bleeding in the hearth, as Merrick exploded, 'You see she has murdered my child and my wife. Take this witch away!'

Merick's neighbour knew who was responsible, and helped Old Bess to her feet and took her to the door, ordering the cart driver to take her home. Things were never the same from that moment on for anyone in the area. Merrick was snubbed by everyone, for they knew he was guilty of beating his wife; his staff could testify to his ill treatment. One of the maids, Dottie, had told a local innkeeper: 'When he's had his ale he'd punch her to the floor and rape her; it didn't matter if we saw him do it neither!' Within three months of his wife's and child's death no one would work for him again.

So Merrick's business suffered, no one would buy his produce and he was treated like a social leper. As his mansion outside Reigate began to run into disrepair his anger began building towards the woman who, he believed, had been the architect of his downfall – Old Bess.

He knew that she lived in Forest Green, so he got on his black stallion, his intentions far blacker than his mount, and rode off to avenge his own downfall. He'd sampled the ale at several hostelries by the time he reached the cottage where Bess was living, and he was far from steady on his feet. It was the early hours of the morning, and as Bess was in her middle sixties it took her a while to rouse herself. Being woken in the middle of the night was fairly commonplace for Old Bess, as emergencies tend to occur in the twilight hours, and she presumed it would be another baby needing birthing, or a neighbour who had fallen ill. She wrapped a woollen shawl around herself and opened the door.

Whether she actually saw who her attacker was is open to debate, as he thrust his outstretched fngers deep into her eye sockets, blinding her. She plummeted to the floor, blood pouring from her face, shouting, 'Why do you do this? Why do you do this?'

Merrick was laughing as he kicked her over and over again in the stomach. The only thing that stopped him kicking her to death was that he spotted a bottle of wine on her fireplace. As he reached for it a claw struck out at him, making him recoil in shock. There, sitting on the mantelshelf, was the biggest and ugliest ginger cat he had ever seen. He put his hand out for the wine and once again the cat hissed, arching its body to look twice its size. Eventually he swept it off the shelf with a birch-twig broom, and finally he was able to quench his thirst.

Old Bess meanwhile had pulled herself up into a sitting position; she was blinded, bleeding and her ribs were shattered and broken. Merrick looked down at this pathetic sight and taunted her. 'You old bitch, you condemned me to a life not worth living, so I am here to take yours from you.'

As Bess realised who the man was she managed to calm herself, and despite her agonies she began to speak. 'Merrick, you are a vile man, and with all of my God-given power I curse you, and though you may kill me, you will not see another morning!'

Merrick tried to laugh but something stopped him. How could this broken old woman do him any harm? He picked up a tiny shovel next to the coal scuttle and walked towards her, to be confronted by a huge snarling cat, hissing and spitting at him.

He moved back, and Old Bess sensed his fear of the animal.

'So you fear old Benjamin, do you?' she said. 'Well before the night is over that cat will stalk you, kill you and eat out your eyes for what you've done to me!'

Merrick looked around the cottage for something to protect him from this huge furry ball of claws, and finally grabbed a chair to hold the animal at bay.

Old Bess began praying: 'Oh God, you have given me your gifts

221

and I have used them well, I beg thee to grant me one request before I join thee in Heaven. Allow my attacker to be preyed upon as he has preyed upon your humble servant! May he. . . . '

She just reached 'Amen', before Merrick hit her throat with a sharp-edged shovel, snapping her spinal cord and severing her windpipe. As the air forced itself through the open pipe it hissed like that accursed cat, and Merrick ran from the room into the blackness of the early hours. He found his horse wandering by the back of the house chewing at some wild flowers. He was about to grab its reins when suddenly its eyes widened and it galloped away into the woods.

Merrick heard something or someone behind him, he turned, screamed and died.

The following morning the bodies were found, Merrick's face was contorted in panic, his eyes missing from his head. Had old Benjamin the cat, clawed them from his face, or had the birds pecked them out? Old Bess was certainly right that he would never see the morning.

The first sightings of the Surrey Puma were in 1707 and many believe it was the offspring of Benjamin, Old Bess's cat, still walking the countryside, ready to avenge women badly used by men.

*In 1962 Grace Robinson was featured in a local TV news story. She was walking in Clandon Park when a youth approached her brandishing a knife. He ordered her into some bushes and was forcing her to take her clothes off. Just then a huge cat leaped on his back and he ran off. 'It wasn't an ordinary cat', Grace said. 'It was huge, and it clawed at his face and neck. He was bleeding when he ran off. Then it came towards me and I was terrified, but it just purred, rubbed its body along my leg and then walked off.'

*Stories of the Surrey puma persist, but only those that could be sensationalised have hit the press in a big way. On a local radio station phone-in Jean Brooks of Dorking called in to relate a story about a bogus Good Samaritan. She had broken down on her way home from Gatwick Airport on an unlit road near Norwood Hill, and a car pulled up behind hers as she was looking under the bonnet in desperation. The man said that he would give her a lift to the nearest garage, and she was about to accept when he grabbed her handbag, and started rifling through it. She snatched it back from him and he gripped her neck and pulled his hand back to hit

222

her when a huge ginger cat appeared on the roof of her car. It bounded on top in complete silence. Jean takes up the story: 'I didn't know it was there, I was pushed back against the passenger door. I just saw his face turn pale in horror, then he released his grip, and I was choking for air. He turned and ran, leaving his car. I then turned around and saw this huge creature on the car. It was a cat the size of a golden labrador, and it really looked fierce and had fangs. I stated walking and could feel it walking a few yards behind. Eventually I flagged a bus down, and got to a garage. It was as if the cat was seeing me safely through the countryside. As soon as the bus appeared it disappeared.'

It seems the only people who should worry about the Surrey Puma are those who seek to harm women.

THE WITCHES OF GUILDFORD

In the early 1600s London had a purge on witchcraft, several hundred witches being burned at the stake. Most of those who died were little more than ordinary people with 'different' ideas. Anyone who was the slightest bit eccentric would be charged with heresy, an impossible charge to defend, and would lose their life. This made those who described themselves as real witches exit from the capital very swiftly indeed. This included the sisters Gough, four women originally from Ireland, who prayed to Satan.

On the face of it they did very little harm, being used as healers by many London folk, issuing a wide range of harmless herbal remedies. But their kindliness hid a black side to them, and it took almost thirty years to uncover their secrets. Leaving London, they settled down in a small cottage at Blackheath near Guildford in Surrey. They were never fully accepted by the locals, but this didn't worry them, as they had livestock and could eke out a basic living from the land.

In Guildford many small children were disappearing, and a panic was spreading among parents throughout the county. Soldiers were even sent from London to try to make secure the streets. Once Guildford had its clamp down, then the children of Dorking were taken, then those of Godalming, of Aldershot. . . . In 1633 a boat-load of men, women and children, gathered to be sold into slavery abroad, was found on the River Thames; on seizing it the authorities thought that they had smashed a slavery ring that had robbed

Surrey of many of its children. Whenever another youngster vanished, they blamed 'accursed slavers'.

However, almost thirty years later, in 1658, the authorities decided to search Blackheath for the transvestite highwaywoman Moll Cutpurse. Her real name was Mary Frith, a London cobbler's daughter who, armed and dressed like a man, had been robbing rich and poor alike for over fifty years. She would die in 1659 aged 75. She left a book all about her amazing lifestyle, and she even had the effrontery to open a shop on London's Fleet Street where those robbed could buy their belongings back. While searching for this robber, soldiers burst into the Gough cottage and found the three women all standing naked in a tin bath, bathing in blood. The women, then in their sixties, ran for cover and tried to say that it was their blood, but on checking other rooms the soldiers found the hacked-up bodies of seveal young children. Outside, in the vegetable patch they uncovered hundreds of bones, and found an outhouse stacked high with skulls, over eighty in number.

The soldiers were after an aged robber, they found three mass child-murderers. The three eventually claimed that bathing in blood kept them young, and indeed they did look half their actual age. They were tried in Guildford, and such was the hatred of the townsfolk they were carted off to Clandon Park to be burnt to death. Long before the bonfires were ready the public took control, hacking at them with axes, knives, hammers, pitchforks and scythes. The soldiers, only ten in number, couldn't hope to defend the witches against such overwhelming odds. So they let the crowd have its way. Finally the captain of the guard shouted, 'To protect our children these bodies must be burned!' At that the crowd began hurling the severed arms, legs and heads on to the fire. Soldiers picked up the bloody torsos that had been kicked and stamped on so hard the innards lay scattered far and wide.

So died the witches Gough.

They say that the spirits of the murderous sisters still float along Guildford's fine streets in search of young, virgin blood.

THE HEADLESS GHOST OF SIR WALTER RALEIGH

In the early seventeenth century, 'If at first you didn't succeed' you got your head cut off. Such was the fate of one of England's most respected servants Sir Walter Raleigh. He had recently returned home after a fiasco of an expedition to find South America's El

Dorado, the lost City of Gold. The world had heard of this expensive failure and the English courtier was a laughing stock. Poor Walter wasn't laughing – at the age of 66, after a lifetime of serving his country he was sentenced to death.

His mission had been to find the gold, return it to England without clashing with the Spanish who claimed the Americans as their own. Raleigh had not found anything, had clashed with the Spanish time and time again, and due to an illness returned home barely alive, let alone laden with treasure. His own son had died fighting the Spanish and Raleigh knew that his return would cost his life.

He was executed purely to appease the Spanish and to stop them declaring war at a time when England was ill-prepared to defend herself.

In front of a sizeable crowd Walter Raleigh placed his head on a block and the axeman removed it with a single strike. The head was embalmed and then placed on display until Raleigh's wife stole it, keeping it in a bag for a number of years. Eventually the head was recovered and buried at West Horsley. Even after death that seasoned traveller Raleigh still got around. His heart was buried at the Old Carew House in Beddington, Surrey, where his ghost still walks. He used to enjoy visits from Queen Elizabeth I at Beddington for many years until one evening she caught him seducing one of her maids-of-honour. When you're the Virgin Queen, it must be less than pleasant to have the busy sex lives of others flaunted in your face.

No one is quite certain as to where the other bits of Sir Walter are, but many think they could be beneath Sherborne Castle, the retreat he built for himself when he was considered the great hero of all England. Many who have worked and visited the Castle swear they have seen the melancholy Sir Walter sitting beneath a tree that bears his name.

THE BOGNOR BANJAX

Have the gypsies ever called at your house, asking if you'd buy some lucky heather? Yes, mine too, and quite often I've politely declined. I may well have been wise to do so, in light of what happened to Roy and Jeanette Micklewhite in 1922. Roy had been working in London on the construction of a building for the new London broadcasting station that would later be known as the

BBC. The job was done and with a fat paycheque and a good bonus he returned to his wife in Bognor.

He needed the money too, his wife was pregnant and he wasn't sure whether his contract as a builder was to be taken up. He decided that what money he had made must be put away and not spent. When he heard a rapping on his door that evening, he hoped it might be an offer of work; instead he found a wasp-faced gypsy lass, wearing rags and clutching a handful of lucky heather. Ray unceremoniously slammed the door on her, catching her finger and cutting it badly. She hammered on his side window yelling, 'Ye'll know that I've been for I've banjaxed ye both!'

Roy was genuinely sorry that he'd caught the girl's hand, but consoled himself that she should get a proper job, coming uninvited to people's homes was just asking for trouble.

Later that night his wife began suffering terrible stomach pains, and he rushed her to the hospital. There they couldn't understand what was going wrong. When Jeanette calmed herself she was returned home, and it was there that an amazing series of events took place. As his wife lay fast asleep in bed, Roy witnessed something writhing beneath the light sheet. On pulling back the covers out slithered a snake. He fell back in terror as it slid past him and out of the door. Then once again from his wife's bed, as if they were coming from her womb, thousands of ants began crawling down the bedspread. He looked at his wife's face and she looked so peaceful, yet now the bed was alive with maggots, wriggling and twisting in front of his face. He screamed and still his wife did not awake. He clawed at the bed to try and remove these disgusting creatures, when something much bigger began to appear.

Roy was in such turmoil that he didn't know what it was, and he picked up a metal shovel that he had used for putting coal into the open fire. He drew back the sheet and was in the act of bringing the shovel down hard when he saw it was a baby. He only just managed to stop himself splitting its skull.

His wife had given birth in her sleep.

The baby was cared for by a midwife who lived only a few doors away, and all was well again in the Micklewhite household.

But whenever the gypsies come knocking he always buys the lucky heather – just in case.

*Roy Micklewhite died in the mid-1950s and swore to his dying day that he had seen all of the horrors he spoke of those years before. His daughter, Mary, had a birthmark on her neck in the shape of a snake.

THE REAL SCARLET PIMPERNEL

The gaping bloody sockets dripping with gore of a man who walks around blindly, grasping at anyone who should cross his path. A ghost, a spirit, a lost soul or a creature sent from beyond the grave to terrify and haunt old Brighton. Amazingly, every major haunting hides a story and never was there a more fascinating one than that of John Robinson.

The Reign of Terror in France was well reported, but the activities of John Robinson were not widely known. Yet he was a man who stood alone against the French Revolution and lived to tell his tale. His fate would be far more bizarre and horrific.

While Maximillien Robespierre continued his purge through France, many innocents lost their lives. Robespierre was an ambitious man who played to the crowd, and prided himself on being incorruptible. But he was corrupted by his own ego. He did many good things like freeing all slaves on French territory, but his 'iron fist' policy at home had won him many enemies. One enemy was John Robinson who had befriended Jean Michel Picard and his family in Brittany and on 5 April 1794 rescued the entire Picard family from their home, killing three revolutionary guards in the process. They had been sentenced to death for daring to speak against Robespierre, and even the three children, all under six, were set to be executed. As Robinson led them to the coast, then on to a fishing yawl bringing them to the safety of England, Robespierre's easier-going rival, Danton, whom they supported, was at the guillotine. As noon his head was held high by the executioner as a warning to anyone who would talk treason.

Many people believe that it was Robinson and his allies within the French resistance that ultimately led to the downfall of Robespierre and his supporters. John Robinson returned to France after making sure his friends were safe at his house on King's Road in Brighton, overlooking the sea. More than 25,000 people had died on the guillotine, most convicted on the flimsiest evidence, such as 'they looked guilty', 'they lived next door to a rebel' or 'they had more money than they deserved'. After gaining the confidence of many of the Revolutionary Council's leaders, he began explaining how the French people were sick of the bloodshed, and how ultimately they would rise up against the new leadership. They had

227

but one chance, to rally the people against Robespierre or be destroyed along with him. Miraculous as it may seem, they could also read the signs from the street, and agreed to plot against their own leader. Robespierre was so arrogant that very few people actually liked him, and over the years he had alienated his own men by his selfish and egotistical behaviour.

The final nail in his coffin came from Robinson, as, along with eight key Revolutionary leaders, he travelled around all the prisons, jammed full of political detainees awaiting execution, and set them free. Like a dam bursting, the unrest spread and the Revolution turned on itself, and Robespierre's reign was over. Robinson was there at his arrest and shot him in the chin with a pistol. When Robespierre was arrested he could barely hold his head up, such was his injury. Brighton's adventurer stood at a window overlooking the courtyard when on 28 July Robespierre and 21 of his closest supporters met the fate of the 25,000 innocents. They were guillotined. It is said that when the blade fell on Robespierre's head there was an explosion of blood, soaking hundreds that watched. Others claim that his head missed the basket and rolled from the platform to be kicked around by the crowd, the head screaming all the while.

Everything in France calmed, and this adventurer Robinson was not happy, and began looking around for more battles to fight. It is easy to understand how his tremendous victory would give him the belief that God was on his side. He told his friend Picard: 'If God wills it, I shall fight for justice elsewhere, for I know I cannot fail!'

Within the week Robinson had travelled to France to meet a supporter of Luft Ali Khan, the son of Kharim Khan, heir to the Zand dynasty in Persia. It seems there was a rebellion and a unsurper, Aga Mohammed the Khan of the Kajars was trying to end Luft Ali Khan's rule.

John Robinson listened intently to tales of murder and pillage, and it was exactly the kind of cause that he was seeking. So, with Martin Carlton of Queens Park, Brighton he set off to Persia to join the army of Luft Ali Khan.

The political situation was very different from what Robinson had been told. Aga Mohammed was the people's choice for the Persian throne following Kharim Kahn's death in 1779, and had been fighting since then to take control of the country against the various warlords who rose against him.

Robinson had only been in the country for less than six weeks when he found himself involved in the most bloody battle of his life. He was in Kerman, the headquarters of Luft Ali Khan when Aga Mohammed's men charged into the city. Thousands were cut to pieces and by nightfall the overall victory was won. Aga Mohammed was the new Persian king. Luft Ali was captured and taken to Tehran, where he was blinded with hot coals, and finally strangled, before his body was fed to the crows. The women of Kerman were raped by the entire army of Aga Mohammed and then sold into slavery. Those that fought back were put to the sword.

Martin Carlton was beheaded by tribesmen during the battle, and his head placed on a pole and carried back as an 'infidel' trophy. Robinson was captured along with 30,000 others. As a punishment to those who had supported Luft Ali Khan, Aga Mohammed demanded 20,000 pairs of eyes. They were cut out of living heads and delivered to him in huge wooden barrels. It was generally thought that Aga Mohammed was particularly cruel because he had been forcibly castrated as a boy of five, to guarantee the end of his family line.

Robinson was blinded like the others, then set free, and with a ragged scrap of material over his gouged face, he became a beggar in Tehran. In 1799 a merchant discoverd him and brought him back to England. On the very day he reached his home of Brighton, he asked a passer-by to lead him to Grand Parade where Victoria Gardens now stands, and he lay down and died. It was as if that was all he had been waiting for – to come home. A crowd soon gathered to look at the Arab-looking man with the rag tied around his eyes, and one little lad tore it away. The sight he saw would stay with him to the grave. The eyes had been gouged out so savagely you could see the white skull clearly through the huge holes in his face. It was as if you could see all the inner workings of the head, and maggots and flies were feeding inside. Literally eating him away as he lived.

It is said that John Robinson's ghost could be seen regularly in that part of Brighton, and a rhyme was commonplace until it fell out of fashion in the mid-1800s:

'Don't ye dally, darling dear, in Brighton's city clear
The ghost of old John Robinson is waiting for ye there.
If ye look into his face, you'll end your days that night.
For he'll steal your eyes from you to give a beggar sight.'

*On New Year's Day in 1957 a policeman from Hove stopped an old man from raking through a litter bin in Gloucester Place. As the old tramp turned around the policeman thought he saw a glimpse of blood. It was almost four in the morning and was very dark, so he took the old man to the nearest lamp-post and looked more closely at him, thinking he may have been the victim of an attack by drunks. To his horror the man had no eyes in his head. The policeman turned and started to run, and as he looked back he saw the old man lie down on his back. The policeman stopped in his tracks and slowly walked towards the figure as it settled on the pavement. He was within two yards of him when the man disappeared.

*The most horrific story, short and far from sweet, is from Doreen Attwood from London, who was holidaying with friends in Brighton in the summer of 1969, a year when three separate sightings of John Robinson were made.

She was staying in a bed-and-breakfast hotel along Marine Parade and decided to have a night out. She had arranged to meet her husband Roy and her hosts, Brian and Kathy Hinton, at the Theatre Royal at seven when the doors were due to open, but arrived there at 6.30. So she decided to take a seat on a bench near the museum overlooking Victoria Gardens. After she had been there for a while, she felt something on her shoulder so she reached over with her right hand and felt something warm and damp. As she spun around she screamed in panic: she had her fingers in the open, bloody eye-socket of a man. She looked at her fingers and they were covered in blood and sinew, and the man began walking towards her, maggots and flesh dropping from his head as he did so. Doreen raced towards the gathering queues at the theatre, who all thought she had gone mad. She was taken to hospital in a state of shock. She had not heard the obscure legend of John Robinson, and when she learned of it she couldn't believe it. She had never believed in ghosts, yet had come face to shattered face with one. She told a newspaper at the time: 'Ghosts are solid things, I always was told they weren't. They are as solid as you and I'.

THE RYE OWLERS

Throughout the 1600s Rye on the East Sussex coast was the centre for 'owling' or smuggling. A particularly ferocious gang, consisting of vagabonds from Hastings, New Romney, Tenterden and the marshes, had forged themselves into a most wicked collection, and they would play a variety of sly strokes, including one that became known as 'Ship A-Rye'. They would float out a wooden raft on a calm night, and set it on fire to act as a beacon. The ship's crew would think that it was the beacon on Dungeness, and that they had the full width of Rye Bay. The ship would then crash on to rocks, or run aground, and the wreckers would be upon them like crabs on a corpse. Normally it was purely the business of smuggling, but this bloody brotherhood couldn't seem to stop themselves committing worse and worse crimes. There is a story of how they once rowed out to a barque to find the small sailing ship occupied by five fishermen. They wrapped chains around their bodies so that they would sink, and then threw them overboard. They found nothing on the vessel worth stealing so set it adrift and returned to the shore.

The people of Rye all knew who the smugglers were, but as they bought the goods at a tenth of their market price, most kept quiet.

One man who didn't was the Reverend Sutton from Canterbury, who had brought his family to live in Winchelsea. He took it upon himself in 1611 to ask King James to intercede and stop these thieves from running the entire area.

Smugglers are generally pictured as people who collect goods and row them back to land. It is a far more complex operation, with merchants negotiating deals abroad, often with foreign smugglers; paymasters settling up; coachmen transporting the goods all over Britain; sellers passing them on to consumers or setting up shops and market stalls. This was a major enterprise, the wreckers were merely the 'enforcers'. They often rode around Sussex intimidating those who dared speak out against them.

Reverend Sutton certainly caused a stir, and more tallymen and customs officers were sent to stand out this menace. However, over fifty soldiers found themselves facing over two hundred armed smugglers, so they soon had to retreat. That weekend the Reverend was found dead, nailed to his own front door. Crucified by the smugglers, who had even added a crown of nettles around his brow. The family were escorted to the relative safety of Ashford.

So even more soldiers marched from their barracks at what is now Royal Tunbridge Wells, and headed for Rye. The date of their encounter varies depending on which legend you believe, but it is between 1613 and 1617. A regiment of soldiers, numbering approximately four hundred arrived at Winchelsea Beach to discover it swarming with smugglers, their wives and families, all packing carriages, carts and barrows. A huge schooner stood in the bay and it was offloading tons of wines, linens and everyday items, made more cheaply abroad. The soldiers spread themselves along the cliff tops, hidden in the rocks, and readied themselves for the smugglers who had to pass their way.

At a predetermined time hundreds of musket-rounds were fired, and the smugglers ran in all directions. Children as young as seven were shot dead alongside their mothers and grandmothers. Some of the rogues managed to get among the soldiers and lash out with swords and cutlasses, but they were soon cut down.

The soldiers eventually marched forward, forcing the survivors back into the sea. Some tried to swim to the schooner, but it was making a sharp exit. Others tried to swim away towards Hastings or into Rye harbour, but they were shot to death by a group of soldiers earmarked for that very task. Some legends say dozens died, most legends say it was a massacre of almost three hundred souls. The entire incident was kept quiet because so many children had been killed.

There was military rule in the Rye area for almost three months until they were sure that the smugglers had been completely routed.

*All of the old inns around this part of the world have countless stories of smuggling and thievery. Perhaps the best known is the Mermaid Inn, Rye. It is said that the 'Owlers' used it as their drinking HQ. Some storytellers believe it was at the Mermaid that the smugglers would share out any monies made by their illicit enterprises.

*Some locals say that if you walk out to Winchelsea Bay late at night, if the moon is full and the sea is calm you can see the smugglers' massacre being re-enacted on the surface of the sea.

TOO DISGUSTNG FOR HELL

In days gone by, lords and ladies were very well to do, but they didn't just have to live the high life, they were also expected to set standards for all others to follow. The Earl of Rochester lived in a fine manor house near Newington and various stories circulated that he was more than a shade weird. He was claimed once to have hacked a horse to death with a sword because it dropped its dung while he was on its back.

The townsfolk had to respect him because he was an aristocrat, but they feared his turbulent moods. When he was calm he seemed quite charming, yet when in a fit of fury he was known to attack man, women or beast. He set fire to one of his farmworkers' house because he had sneezed while in his presence. He destroyed another man's coach because it was polished brighter than his own. So many incidents caused the people to lose faith with the Earl, some said he was an alchemist, dabbling in potions and swearing his allegiance to the Devil. The fact was that he was merely a temperamental man – 50 per cent temper, 50 per cent mental.

The last straw was when three churchmen visited his home, and on being shown into the hall by a footman they heard a scream. Thinking it to be a cry for help they ran into the living room where they discovered it was more a scream of delight. There in front of a roaring fire was the Earl rampantly having sex with a nun.

The churchmen walked out in disgust, and as the tale circulated the area it fuelled the belief that the Earl of Rochester was a diabolist. So he was arrested and charged with heresy. The trial took almost seven months, and he was pronounced guilty. It had been a foregone conclusion, but the law of the day stipulated that only the King could give a death sentence. However, the test of a witch or warlock was to see if they could float, so they picked up the randy Earl and dropped him down a sixty-foot well. They left him there to die, and die he did, of starvation. They say the body remains there to this day, and another source of water had to be found.

This led to a purge of everyone unholy, and the nun, who was by this time almost eight months' pregnant was taken to a backroom of the manor and they bricked up the door. She too died of starvation and lack of water. She was heard screaming out in agony for almost eight weeks and there was the sound of a baby crying too. However, her body was never found. Not even when the manor was demolished in 1857.

The houses built on the site have all had strange encounters.

*Thomas Henderson owned an orchard and a vegetable garden close to where the manor stood, and he told of how his hens wouldn't lay, how the trees refused to bear fruit, until a priest blessed the ground.

*Ruth Marshall lived in a house there in the 1890s and was so terrified by something that she saw that her hair turned white and she was placed in an asylum in London.

*The George Inn on Newington High Street has suffered several haunting experiences, but they were put down to a ghost monk. The staff have witnessed glasses, cutlery and vases flying off the bar and zooming from tables. Many customers have seen this monk plain as day, others say the monk was in fact the Earl of Rochester in disguise heading off to meet his nun girlfriend.

WALES

THE RIPPER OF ABERGAVENNY

It takes a special kind of monster to enjoy tearing the eyes from children, then to impale them on the barbed spikes of railings, yet that is what Mikhail Tomasowski was jailed in Poland for in 1935. Yet in 1941 he was free and fleeing the Nazis, thanks to a raid by the Polish resistance on the prison where he was held captive.

By December of the same year he was a refugee and living in Abergavenny in Wales. No one knew who he was or what he was, and as he could speak very little English and certainly no Welsh, life was difficult. He could only converse with another Polish couple who had escaped with him.

In that same month Pearl Harbor was bombed and America joined the war, and all single women aged between twenty and thirty were called up to operate anti-aircraft guns or to take over the jobs of medically fit men, so they could take up arms.

Tomasowski avoided being pushed back into the fray by pretending to be crazy, he even went so far as to eat soil and worms when a Polish interpreter was brought to push him into a special regiment being filled with refugees. As he was obviously unsuitable for combat he was placed with a widow, given her spare room and told to help her tend her garden and sizeable vegetable patch.

Mrs Owen was in her early fifties and quite liked the idea that this strong Pole was sleeping under her roof. He was rather squat but muscular with a moody expression and shining blue eyes. She would watch him as he hacked away at wood blocks with an axe, the sweat soaking through his vest despite the cold. By the middle of the following year she was totally infatuated with the man she could only communicate with using sign language.

Each weekend when school was out Tomasowski could be seen playing with the young children, who thought he was a funny man, always pulling faces and doing silly things to make them smile. The locals thought him a pleasant enough man, but remained suspicious as they were never really keen on outsiders.

The Polish killer was totally free to go and do as he pleased and decided that he couldn't allow Abergavenny to be his killing ground. He had it too comfortable to risk, so in August 1942 he decided to travel to Cardiff. There he picked up a young prostitute, downed a bottle of black-market wine and then went out in search of a victim. It was 7.30 p.m. and he was wandering around the street aimlessly when he found himself on West Grove off the Newport Road. Then he saw a tiny figure in baggy grey shorts and a tatty blue jumper running along the street; it was Thomas Williams, aged seven, taking a message for his Nan to her friend who lived on East Grove.

Tomasowski started walking faster and faster as he began pursuing the child; he was getting closer and closer when the child began hammering on a front door. At that moment the Pole froze, swiftly turning about and slowly walking back down the street towards the Newport Road again. He growled to himself and promised that the next child he saw would be his. Tomasowski hated children; when he was young they had bullied him for being so small. He loved his older brother Alexander, but when he was only seven he had watched as a gang of other children kicked Alexander about the playground, beating him so severely that he was blinded in one eye. The tiny Mikhail waded in to try and help his brother and was knocked unconscious by an older boy. That was the time he swore that later in life he would revenge his brother's attack. The Pole's twisted mind had pushed him to gain revenge from innocent helpless children.

As he listened to his own footsteps clumping along the street, he heard a door close behind him and the running footsteps of a child. Little Tommy Williams had delivered his message, and was scurrying home with a brown paper bag with a cooked sausage in it. It was getting dark, and there were no streetlights in order to conserve energy and to preserve the blackout. Tomasowski stopped the child, placed a leathery hand across his face and dragged him into a derelict house that stood at the end of the road. There he punched him so hard the front of the child's face shattered. This was probably the moment he died as fragments of bone penetrated his skull. The Pole then hammered the child's body with bricks and shattered almost every bone in his body with a wooden post. Before leaving he covered the body with debris as if the roof had caved in.

The following day the tragedy was broadcast, how a young child had been playing in an old house instead of running home, and it had cost him his life. The Williams family were griefstricken, while the Pole travelled by train and bus back to Abergavenny enjoying a very fine smoked sausage.

He had decided that every month he would return to Cardiff or another of the larger towns in Gwent, and claim another blow in vengeance of his brother. Yet this is where fate took control in a most unpredictable way. Tomasowski fell in love with a sixteen-year-old girl from Abergavenny called Ruth Foster. There were very few eligible men around and she too had been attracted to the silent Pole as he worked long hours on the land, to provide the entire street with fresh vegetables. Despite language problems they would spend hours walking around together and laughing.

Mrs Owen still held a candle the size of Blackpool Tower to this man, and decided that she could offer him far more than this young child. So that very night, barely a month since he had murdered the Williams boy, she decided to seduce him. She spent that evening bathing in aromatic salts, covering herself in her very best perfume, and putting on her most appealing outfit. Underneath a chiffon dressing gown, you could clearly see her french knickers and stockings. The dim light of her cottage helped her ploy as it hid her wrinkled neck and shadows seemed to blur the crows-feet engraved in her face. The Pole was in bed and listening to the crackling radio when the door opened to reveal his hostess Mrs Owen looking desirable and, more important, wanting him. It was a matter of seconds rather than minutes before the couple were writhing in bed together.

The following morning the fantasy had somewhat diminished. There was the woman, looking perhaps more than her age, some twenty years older than him. He thought how like his grandmother she looked – and he had had sex with her. He felt queasy and left the bed to wash and begin his chores in the allotments. When Mrs Owen awoke her mood was totally different, she was dancing on air. Finally, her lonely existence was over, every great romance like those of Romeo and Juliet, Lancelot and Guinevere, they all paled into insignificance before their great love. She dressed hurriedly and joined 'her man' outside, wrapping her arms around his shoulders and kissing his muscular neck. He turned and pushed her off, barking something in Polish that sounded most uncomplimentary. Mrs Owen was bewildered. Was this the man who had been so desperate for her the night before? What had she done to offend him so?

All that day she tried so hard, making him a wonderful meal

from various items she had purchased on the black market, massaging his shoulders, carrying hot water to the tin bath at the end of his labours. She was beginning to feel cheap and used. It was obvious that what she had experienced the night before was his lust and not his love, the thing she most desperately wanted. That night she tried to enter his room again, after hours of preparing herself. Once again he slept with her, but vanished in the early hours. The final straw came when he saw Ruth Foster and he ran to her, grasped her hand tenderly, kissed it, and walked with her down the street in front of all the neighbours.

Mrs Owen had always been a touchy woman, perhaps it had been her biggest flaw, and anger was welling inside her tiny frame like a corked volcano. She sat by her fireplace and wondered what she could do. At first she considered taking her own life, as how could she possibly face the shame this man had brought on her? Then she decided to kick him out and let him try to fend for himself.

Yet when he returned to the house that night he seemed in such an agreeable mood that all her anger dissipated. Once again they were entangled in the jousts of Venus, totally lost in the sexual pleasure they could give one another. He was nearing climax and she was wanting him so desperately when he shouted, 'Ruth, oh Ruth!'

Mrs Owen felt he was pumping ice inside her, her entire body crumpled like a damp paper bag. She couldn't speak she was so utterly destroyed by his utterance. Then the horror that is often reality hit her like a hammer. He had rolled away from her and lay there in an afterglow snooze as she tip-toed from the bedroom.

She knew he was due to visit Cardiff again that very next day and he would expect her to wait like an obedient pet. Well she would have no more of it. It took her less than two minutes to find that bread knife. There she was, standing by the side of the bed, as he turned on to his back and started snoring. She held the handle of the knife with both hands and swung it down, plunging it deep into the Pole's chest.

His eyes burst open and he sat up to see Mrs Owen standing before him shaking and crying, the knife buried so deep he could see no blade at all. He tried to stand, he tried to reach out to her but could do no more than collapse on to the floor.

Once again cold reality hit her, that she would be imprisoned for this man's murder. So she had a brainwave, she ripped her nightgown, pushing a piece of it into Tomasowski's hand, and then ran into the street screaming. It was pouring with rain and her flimsy nightdress turned instantly translucent, as she fell to her knees crying. The neighbours gathered around, took her into their home, covered her with a blanket and called for the police. She told how the strong Pole had raped her, and had held a knife to her throat. Then as soon as he put the knife down she did what any decent woman would have done, and that is to grab it and fight back.

The police marched inside to collect the body, but it wasn't there. There were bloodstains aplenty, but no Tomosowski. It seemed that she had missed his heart and he had survived. A search of the street was instantly made and then a trail of bloodstains found, leading into a back yard where the Pole had passed out from the pain. He was taken to the hospital from where he was transferred to Cardiff where there was a Polish interpreter. He lived a further three months before he died of an infection.

No action was taken against Mrs Owen. Justice was done, she had saved the hangman a job, and saved countless young lives from torture and death.

*It seems as though Tomasowski's ghost still may be causing mischief in and around Abergavenny. Since the mid-1940s several young children have said they have seen or felt something. The most frightening has to be the story of nine-year-old Peter Forster, who was waiting for his father to come out of the King's Arms with some beer in the summer of 1959 when he felt a hand on his shoulder. When he turned there was nobody there. He was going to enter the pub to get his dad when he felt a blow to his face that was so violent it knocked him down on to the path. Then he felt someone or something tearing at his face, leaving deep scratch marks down his face.

His father stepped outside at that moment, picked his son up and asked who had done it. He certainly didn't believe his son's story, until an old woman crossed the street, saying that she witnessed everything. She had seen a short squat man punch him and then lean over him. When the door of the pub opened he just disappeared. This was more than the hapless youngster had seen, all he had known was an invisible attacker. It took almost four months for the wounds and black eye to disappear, and from that time Peter Forster has been terrified of even discussing anything to do with ghosts.

THE TREFACHAN DANCER

In August 1972 a local parish magazine told an amazing story about Gwyn Williams who was attending the University of Wales in Aberystwyth. He was living in a house in Glanrafon Terrace overlooking the River Rheidol when one day he saw the figure of a girl dancing across the surface of the water. It was early on a bitterly cold Sunday monring and he rubbed his eyes. She was still there.

This is how he described it at the time: 'It really was the queerest thing. I watched her with my binoculars and she was solid, not a ghost or something. She wore a sort of long blue chiffon dress, that hung down to the water and waved around as she danced. She looked as if she should have lived in Victorian times, and she was waving her arms and she had scarves in each hand. I even put my coat on and knocked at my friend's house four doors down, and he saw it too. We must have watched her for almost twenty minutes and she seemed to be moving against the current and moving up-river past the football ground, until eventually we could see her no more.'

Gwyn was a very religious young man, but still swears he saw this magical dancer.

I wasn't going to include this in the book until I was told about a manuscript written by Peter Burton, who used to be a policeman in Wales. In it he tells a story told him by his grandfather, Barry Burton, who was also a policeman, in the late 1800s, and had kept an accurate diary including this fascinating item:

It was back in 1888 when my dear friend David Rodrigues watched a woman die, and it was such a sight that it led him to resign from the force. He was on patrol on Bath Street, Aberystwyth, when the local dance hall was beginning to clear. A group of actors had left the hall singing and dancing loudly, and, like any policeman would, he instructed them to quieten down, lest they woke local residents.

They did, but he followed them quite a distance down Thespian Street, Alexandra Road and Mill Street. It was when they reached the bridge over the river that they started singing and dancing again. David didn't mind their high spirits, but this was very late, almost midnight.

It was obvious that the three young men had been drinking and they were egging on the young lady to dance, and dance she did. She was an exquisite young girl in her early twenties, wearing her hair in a bob, and wearing a floaty blue gown. David was about to send them to their homes when this young girl climbed on the edge of the bridge and began dancing. David shouted to the girl to get down, and she shouted something back, and as she did so she overbalanced, plunging down into the blackness of the river. The men stared down into the river as did David who couldn't swim; they could do nothing but watch as she was caught by the incoming tide and swept up the River Rheidol.

My dear friend told me how the force of the current swept her round and round, as if she was dancing whilst in the water. She swirled in circles, waving pieces of her gown out of the water in a macabre dance of death. David ran to the riverside and tried to find her but it was November and the moon was far from full, so he lost all track.

Her name was Margaret Cooper, and despite exhaustive searches for three weeks her body was never found. That is why it is said that she still dances in that river, and will for all time.

This manuscript has not been published, so how could that student in the seventies possibly have known about it? Had he witnessed the Trefachan Dancer as she shimmied for ever in the black water of the River Rheidol?

HOME OR A HAUNTING, CONWY

In this book and *Grisly Trails and Ghostly Tales* I am always surprised by the number of stories that come from coach houses. What hives of activity they must have been to generate the number of stories that they do.

Many of them stem from the living ignoring the wishes of the dead. While a friend was staying at the very plush Castle Hotel in Conwy, he was told a wonderful story by a local in the bar that evening. It tells of a chambermaid who had 'a gift' and many people around the vicinity would ask her to tell their fortunes. This she did and never ever charged for the service. Her predictions invariably came true and her reputation grew far afield. Then one day she told the owner of the coach house that she was going to die and that he must promise that her body would be sent back to the place of her birth in Anglesey. The landlord knew that she was gifted, but couldn't believe that this young girl could possibly die, she was barely 25.

Within the week she had taken to her bed with a fever, and it was there that she died. The innkeeper ignored the vow he had made to her, and for hygiene reasons she was buried two days later in the local cemetery.

This is when the trouble started, all hell was let loose in the coach house. Barrels of wine would leak, bottles shattered, horses would be set free, meals would fly off tables right in front of bemused customers.

From here, legends differ. Some say that the ghost of the chambermaid returned in the night and dragged the innkeeper out of bed, lifting him up into the air above the coach house and threatening to drop him unless he moved the body to Anglesey the very next day. This he promptly did.

The other strand of the legend goes that, after months of mayhem, the innkeeper realised that it could be the chambermaid's ghost not being able to rest, so had her taken home to Anglesey. From that day things settled down in the coach house, and life returned to normal.

*If you stay at the Castle Hotel you are likely to feel someone placing a weight on the bottom of the bed, as the phantom chambermaid puts down ghostly bedding to change your sheets in the morning. Occasionally curtains will open for no reason or busy footsteps can be heard in the corridors, yet there is never anyone there making them.

*Mrs L. Gardener from Conwy told an American news reporter that she had witnessed the ghostly housemaid in the High Street one December morning in 1975. 'It was very early and I was making my way to work when I saw a girl in a black coat; her outfit was very old-fashioned and seemed to cover a uniform of sorts. She walked towards the Castle Hotel and walked straight into a wall and went through it. She looked as solid as you or I, but disappeared.'

On enquiry at that time the reporter was told that the main door to the old coach house was precisely where the spirit had been seen. Now the main door is in a different position.

THE MAN WHO LOVED THE DEAD

On researching for this book I came across two totally different tales both involving a farm worker from Cwm in Clwyd. One merely tells of how he was murdered and proceeded to follow his murderer as a spirit until he drove him to commit suicide. The other is far more grisly.

In 1635 John Henry married Ruth Jones from Holywell, and it was indeed a match made in Heaven. Ruth was the typical Welsh home maker, and created a home where the brusque and rather loutish labourer could feel completely safe and secure. The marriage was not blessed with children but it was a very happy ten years. In January 1645, however, tragedy struck, and Ruth died of influenza. John Henry was devastated and told no one that his wife had died. No one would part them. When friends and neighbours asked of her he would say, 'Oh she's at home in bed, she's not been well.' Some gave him bowls of broth to take to her, others merely their best wishes. Ruth was still in his bed, and he never stopped loving her. He treated her body with balms that he hoped would stop her body from rotting, but they were totally unsuccessful.

It was in February of the following year, when the farmer visited John Henry at his home to discuss work, that all was revealed. John Henry had lived in the stench of death's dreadful decay for twelve months and didn't notice it in his nostrils any more. However, the farmer smelled it at once and pushed past John Henry to march up the stairs. There he saw the naked dead body of Ruth Henry, skin literally falling from the bones, maggots eating into eye sockets and the skin so tight it had torn in many places as the internal organs had began to rot.

He vomited as John Henry rushed to his wife's side screaming 'Leave her alone! I love her, don't take her away from me!'

Within the day an undertaker was called and her body was taken away to be buried in the local graveyard.

That night John Henry unearthed the body and was found next morning sleeping inside the coffin next to the body of his wife.

He was told by the vicar at chapel to leave the body alone, to let his wife rest in peace, but all to no avail. Each evening he would dig down to her coffin and sleep next to her.

Soon rumours began to abound that John Henry was a necrophiliac, having sex with his dead wife. He wasn't, but that didn't stop the gossip rampaging around the valleys. One day, in 1646, John

Henry was murdered by a group of men who had been disgusted at the stories they had heard. Some say he was kicked to death, others that he was impaled on a pitchfork during a row at harvest time.

However he died, he was buried in a coffin right next to the wife he loved so dearly.

In 1877 the graveyard was moved to allow for some building work, and when they opened the ground they discovered John Henry's coffin empty! When they opened the grave next to it, they discovered John Henry's corpse lying on top of his wife Ruth's body. United and together even in death.

THE WARNING MIST OF LLANDEILO

'If the mist comes in the night a death will follow' – so say many of the good people of Dyfed in Wales, and it seems to have a great deal of substance to it. Although we have details of over twenty cases ranging as far afield as Llanelli, Carmarthen, Llandovery and Swansea, the epicentre of this mystery is Llandeilo overlooked by the Black Mountains. Trying to track down the very beginnings of this legend was far from easy, but it was cracked with the help of a Welsh farmer called Huw Jones who worked the land near Ammanford for over fifty years in the 1930s. He had told his son Michael the story, and he in turn passed it down to his son.

It all began in the year AD 854 when Welsh druidism was a powerful force within the community, and their leader was an evil man with a twisted lip called Shebar. Those whose respect he could not gain would suffer a tragedy in the family – a child would vanish, later found dead at the bottom of the cliffs at Capel Gwynfe. Once three druids were seen by passers-by hacking a young boy to death with axes and burying the body in a shallow grave at Salem. The locals knew this was going on, but they feared for their own lives so kept quiet, merely paying their respects to the Druids so that they would not fall victim themselves.

The last straw was when Shebar declared that they would be making human sacrifices to guarantee a good harvest. He told the local villages to nominate someone or else they would march in and take a child. This did not disturb only the villagers, many of the Druids felt that it was against their creed, but none dared stand up against Shebar, who had become a psychotic maniac.

The local community were appalled, and small groups gathered to plot against Shebar. There were over five hundred Druids, and

244

surely no gathering of a dozen farmhands could possibly come out victors in such a one-sided contest. Word of their plans reached Shebar and on the night of 5 August 854, forty of Shebar's best men, armed with pitchforks, swords and axes, set out to silence the dissenting mob. The homes belonging to the plotters were identified, and they surrounded each one and set it on fire. As the families ran out they were hacked to death. In one case a five-year-old child was first to emerge, and he was hardly through the door before he had been decapitated with one swing of a Druid axe.

Over forty people died that night, ten homes lay in ashes, and the entire area knew that they were not to meddle with the Druids.

Three days later, a woman in her sixties returned to her home in Llandeilo, to find it burned to the ground. Saron Roche, who was a great-grandmother, was known to the people thereabouts as a holy woman – in modern-day parlance 'a white witch'. It had been presumed that she had been one of the incinerated bodies found in the house the following morning, but she had spent a week with family in Bethlehem, just up the valley. To discover that all of her relatives had been wiped out caused a change in this usually kind woman, and she set off to face Shebar who lived near the River Afon Tywi on the outskirts of the town.

She hammered on his door with such fury that a crowd soon gathered, many of them Druids, and Shebar stepped out carrying a sacrificial dagger.

'Was it you who butchered my family?' asked Saron.

The Druid smiled widely at seeing this tiny, plump woman. 'It was a warning to everyone not to dare plot against me,' came his sneering reply.

The woman reached inside a tiny leather pouch and produced some white powder and sprinkled it in the air around her saying, 'Now you cannot harm me!'

Shebar gave a loud belly laugh. 'I suppose that dust will save you from this knife?'

She nodded as she bent down to pick up a stone, then fumbled in the pouch for a tiny flint. 'I will live for ever, for that is my task, and in life I am sworn to help people, not to kill them. However, in death I will punish you all for what was done to my family that night!'

The twisted face of Shebar contorted into a puzzled expression, as the old woman struck the stone against the flint and a spark set the dust on her clothes alight, and she exploded into a ball of flame. The crowd gasped in amazement as they watched her skin burn, crack and fall away from her bones. All the while she was shouting at Shebar, 'And now you're mine!', reaching out her small chubby arms until all of the clothing and skin had gone, and the only thing reaching from the flame was a long skeletal finger barely a yard from Shebar's face. By this time hundreds of people were watching as the body instead of turning into ash became a cloud of grey-gold smoke that just seemed to hang over the ground.

Shebar was ash-white himself and he turned to the throng, saying, 'You see, the hag was so terrified of my wrath that she chose to take her own life!'

No sooner had the Druid uttered what proved to be his final words than the smoke had begun to wrap itself around him; it then poured up his nose until it had vanished completely. As he writhed around the floor his skin began turning the grey-gold colour of the smoke and he began to shake as if he were having a violent fit. He rolled towards the river and much as he tried to scream and claw his way away from it some invisible force dragged him into the water. His mouth was open but his words just never came out, and something held him beneath the surface as the air left him to be replaced with water. The eyes that had shown so much contempt for the old woman now saw nothing. Druids began tearing off their robes, hurling them into the River Afon Tywi and running back to their homes. As the people looked on, Shebar's body shot out of the water, landing on the very spot where Saron Roche had taken her life.

Above the river they could see the mist circling, and they heard a voice crying, 'Let death never creep upon you again, for I shall warn you of its coming!'

It sounds far-fetched, yet many stories have since emerged from as far back as 1788 about a strange mist and a knocking on a window, to warn of a forthcoming death in the family. This was commonplace right up until the 1920s, then for some reason it wasn't heard of until the late 1950s, when a spate of stories came out, some featured in local newspapers, about how this 'death mist' had appeared presaging a death.

*In 1978 a visitor to Llandeilo called in to the King's Head Hotel and during a quiet pint he saw this strange golden-grey fog, and felt suddenly frightened. At first he thought it was cigarette smoke, but from the way that it twisted and moved he realised that it was not. On returning to his home he discovered that his mother and father had died in a car crash.

Coincidentally the manager of the King's Head Hotel did tell locals around that time that he had witnessed a strange fog on a couple of occasions. This he put down to the ghost of a customer who was supposedly pushed out of a window to her death in the 1830s.

*In 1983 Malcolm Addison, a double-glazing salesman from Swansea, was in the area with a team of workers canvassing for work, when he pulled up his Volkswagen at the side of the road near Ffairfach. He was filling in his report forms and he had to pull down his sun visor as the sun was so strong. Then suddenly it was as if someone had switched off the sun. 'It really was that fast,' he said. 'One minute I could barely see for the glare, the next moment it was black as pitch. I looked up and the car was totally surrounded by what I thought was a brown fog, but it was moving round and round the car. It was as if it was stirring around me, and I even wound the window down and put my hand out into it, and I could make a hole in it and see bright daylight on the other side. Then it moved away and I could see it in my rear-view mirror moving off down the lane. Then I was filled with dread, as if I just knew something was wrong. So I drove into Llandeilo and phoned home; thankfully everything was fine, or so I thought. When I did get home, though, there was a letter waiting for me telling me my best friend, the best man at my wedding, Brian Charles had suffered a stroke and died.'

*In November 1992 I was playing in a charity football match at Gateshead International Stadium with Kevin Keegan, Frank Bruno, Eddie the Eagle Edwards, American wrestler Rowdy Roddy Piper and many more. Our team had lost but I had managed to grab three goals, and was fairly pleased with how things had gone. So as I made my way to the car and signing as many autographs as I could, I was handed a note from a young girl, Claire Taylor, that told of how her mother had a premonition of her husband's death. With it was a newspaper cutting that read: 'Dorothy Taylor knew her husband was going to die. Three days earlier she had seen a misty shape that had told her there was to be a death. Her husband Cliff had been ill for almost a year and she knew that he was about to die. Dorothy said today, "It gave me time to say all the things I wanted to tell him, and to make sure that I gave him all of my time and all of my love." I thought no more of this until I saw Claire at another guest appearance and she told me her mother was Welsh, originally coming from Llandovery, to the north-east of Llandeilo.'

THE FAIRY TREE OF MAESTEG

During the 1600s in Maesteg there was a huge tree, but this was no ordinary creation of nature, this was a fairy tree, brought from Ireland by a sage and planted there to create a home for the tiny folk. The tree had branches that curled around itself creating an impenetrable barrier and thus a safe place for little people to live. To snap a branch or to tear a leaf off a fairy tree could have dire consequences, including death and misfortune. According to legend over the next two hundred years, hundreds suffered after having collected firewood from this tree, until it gained a reputation all of its own, then no one would even go near to it.

Legends often differ, the version I am about to tell is the juiciest, if not the most regularly told. In 1821 a young couple had just moved into a coach house; they were newly weds and her father had put up sufficient money to give the young lovers a chance to run their own business. Never had there been two people more suited. Evan was a firmly-made man, with a razor-sharp wit and a balanced head on his shoulders. Meg was a truly beautiful girl, long blonde hair cascading over her shoulders like gold threads. Her smile was an experience to behold, and many would travel to the coach house purely to catch a glimpse of her loveliness.

One day while out walking in the countryside, they spotted a very odd-looking tree, its branches all twisty and writhing, so they walked towards it and Evan decided that he would carve their names upon it so that their love would last for all time. As he gouged the bark away he heard a noise, a strange mumbling, as if they were being watched. Looking up, the tree looked peculiar and ominous, so Evan hurried at his work and then pulled his wife close to admire his romantic handiwork. In front of their eyes the tree began to bleed. Blood gushed from the carving, and trickled stickily down the tree, forming a pool at the base. In abject terror the pair ran away back to Maesteg, where they told their customers of what had happened. From that day their love began to sour, they barely spoke to one another, having previously been dedicated to spending every second they could in each other's arms. Their arguments became more violent. He had his face clawed and suffered carpet burns on his face when she had tried to drag him out of their bedroom, and she had even spat in his face in full view of the customers.

Finally he went on a long walk, and once again came to the Fairy Tree. He had his knife with him, and decided to remove all trace of their love. He was so totally sickened by the situation he ignored any peril to himself and started carving the two initials off the tree. Once again the tree began to bleed, but unperturbed he carried on until he was soaked to the skin in the tree's scarlet oozings.

He felt quite pleased with himself; if he couldn't rid himself of the dream woman who had become his nightmare, at least he had exorcised the commitment he had made in love those months ago.

On returning to the coach house he couldn't find his wife, so walked out to the stables where he heard the telltale noises of puffing and panting. He also recognised the sound of his wife's voice. He stealthily crept to the edge of the barn and on peering around the corner he saw his wife sitting astride one of his stable hands, rising and falling upon him in the grip of torrid lovemaking. He heard the man say how stupid her husband must be to treat her so badly, she squealed in passion as their climax came very close. Their bodies began moving faster and faster until with a tightness of movement his body arched under her and with a chorus of grunts and moans it was over.

Evan walked away, tears pouring down his face. He loved her, he really loved her, yet now he knew he had lost her for ever.

Later that day she barked at him, criticising everything that he had done that day. Then Evan played his first card, saying how he was going to do all the stable work in future, hiring someone else to run the inn. Meg turned white. 'You can't do that, for where will our stable hands go?'

'I don't care about that!' replied Evan, and promptly walked to the stables and sacked all three workers. This brought about even more arguments until one day Meg was attacking him again in one of the bedrooms, and Evan decided he had taken enough from this woman. He grabbed her firmly around the neck and started to squeeze. He could feel the blood trying to fight its way past his iron grip. He saw her eyes filling up with tears as her fingernails tore at his arms trying to push him away. In the end he picked up her head and hammered it hard against the side of a bedside chest, and her arms fell limply by her sides. She was still alive so he did

249

not relent until all signs of life had fallen away. The body was wrapped in a sack and wedged under the floorboards in one of the rooms. Evan completely blotted this out of his memory, and when the locals asked where Meg was, he would tell how she was sick of working with him and had left.

This worked for a long time until a guest staying in that very room complained about a rank odour coming from under the floorboards in the room. A guest from the room below made a similar complaint, adding that a strange liquid was leaking from the room above. That liquid was the combined body fluids of Meg. Her body was found and Evan's arrest was sought. They would never arrest him though, for two days later he was found hanging in the stable where he had seen the only woman he had ever loved having sex with another man.

The locals believed that it had been the Fairy Tree that had led to the deaths of two very pleasant and decent people. So one evening in August a dozen of them placed straw bales around the bottom and set it on fire. The place where it used to stand is still free from all life, not even grass will grow there.

*The coach house has since become The Castle and many strange things continue to happen, particularly in one room, where the body of Meg was found.

THE GRAVE OF THE PARTLY INNOCENT

In the early 1820s the great landscape painters like Turner and Constable were convincing the world that the countryside of their island was idyllic, a rural ideal that everyone could aspire towards. Yet this picture ignored the fact that this was the time of the highwaymen, thugs and vagabonds, intent on stealing whatever they could from the rich. It was no moral stance they took – simply that the poor had nothing worth stealing. It was better to try and gain the support of the poor in case you should ever need a hideout or an alibi. William Davies was what was described as 'a gentleman of the road'; granted he was a robber, but he always was courteous and tried never to harm any of his victims.

Most of the other bandits were a slimy assortment, set on getting as much money and jewellery as possible, going so far as to cut rings from people's fingers if necessary.

One such highwayman was robbing a coach on the Montgomery to Shrewsbury road when two of his intended victims decided to try and capture their unruly thief. They pushed him from his horse and leapt upon him. At this he struggled free to draw his sword. He turned to face his two attackers. As he did so he watched in horror as one of them ran himself onto the point of his sword, piercing his heart. His quivering body slid off the bloodsoaked sword like butter off hot toast. A woman in the coach fainted and the robber slung himself on to his horse and rode off into the hills.

Three days later William Davies was talking to a variety of thieves and cut-throats in a local inn, when one man offered to sell his horse, a spirited Spanish animal with a distinctive white flash across his face. Davies was most taken by the creature and a deal was struck. The vendor needed money fast and left the area never to be seen again. Davies decided to use this beast as his own horse, rather than risk using it for his robberies, as it would be easily identified. Unbeknown to him, that was the horse used in the robbery earlier in the week which had led to a man being killed.

It was only a matter of time before Davies was arrested, charged and sentenced to death for a crime he most certainly did not commit. To the end, 'the gentleman of the road' swore his innocence, although he did confess to over three hundred robberies, never harming a hair on anyone's head. His final words were 'May God cast me to Hell if I lie, for I am innocent of this deathly crime. I know that I am to die but I beg ye to watch my grave. I am not guilty and not one single blade of grass will ever grow on the grave of an innocent man!'

He was hanged and his body left for the birds and beetles to strip down to the bone as a warning to all other bandits. It was then buried in the graveyard at Montgomery, and although many leading gardeners have tried, his grave is still barren.

THE WELSH ALIENS

In the nineteenth century there were several hundred tales about people being abducted by fairies, of being captured by the 'faerie folk'. Yet one of these amazing stories points much more directly to the involvement of aliens, this as far back as 1856.

It happened in the Vale of Neath in South Wales when a young man called Ronald Rhys was travelling home from the farm where he worked, when he heard a strange 'whooshing' noise. He looked across at the field where a huge circle of light shone out in the darkness.

He went across to investigate and as soon as he stood within the light he felt himself floating. Rhys was not seen again for seven days.

His employer thought he must have quit, for he hadn't returned to his tied cottage, and none of his friends at the local pub had seen hide or hair of him.

But seven days later he walked back into the farm as if he had not been away, his skin a bright pink colour as if he had caught too much sun. His employer asked where he had been, but Rhys denied that he had been anywhere.

When the young man realised that a week had passed by that he couldn't explain, he became very frightened. He told his employer that all he remembered was walking back from the farm the evening before. The farmer insisted that Rhys tell him everything, as he was beginning to conclude that his labourer had been drinking the entire week away.

It was then that Rhys remembered that he had heard the strange noise, and had seen the 'fairy ring' of light and had stepped into it and felt as if he was floating. The farmer pressed him to remember anything else.

Rhys told his boss that he had had a strange dream, but couldn't remember anything else.

The farmer had heard hundreds of 'fairy' stories, for that is how we get the phrase today. All far-fetched and generally unbelievable, but Ron Rhys was a sensible man who wasn't prone to make up stories. The farmer managed to persuade him to relate his entire dream and Rhys told of hundreds of tiny people that looked like 'well developed babies' swarming around him. Poking and prodding him with tiny swords and taking blood from him. He remembers bright lights and it being very hot. This 'dream' had one fairy who was bald and green cutting into his stomach and taking out his innards. Then sealing the wound and covering it with a cream that took away the pain. The only other thing he recalled was waking up in a field after a deep, deep sleep.

The farmer had commented on how most of the hair of Rhys's head was falling out in handfuls. Rhys couldn't understand what had gone on and set off to work in the farm again. Yet moments later he came screaming back to the farmhouse, for on removing his shirt he had found that his body was covered with scars.

Had the dream been true?
Was the skin colouring and hair loss caused by radioactivity?
Were the fairy folk actually aliens?

SCOTLAND

THE BURNING SOLDIER OF ABERDEEN

George McGregor thought it was going to be a fairly ordinary day when he was roused at six o'clock on the chilly morning of 13 November 1887. It is a soldier's lot that often you get no warning at all that you're about to be placed into a battle; the surprise is even greater when your regiment is stationed in the centre of London. So when he was told to wear his helmet and fix his bayonet to his rifle George was as puzzled as anyone. What had happened? Had England been invaded?

He was ordered to march across the city in full battledress and into Trafalgar Square, where hundreds of people were beginning to assemble. 'The police have asked us to help them make sure there are no unlawful gatherings in the square this day, and we will make bloody sure there isn't!' the sergeant barked.

By 10 a.m. the situation was under control and the sergeant led his troops away, so as not to enflame the situation by their presence. So they were able to grab a cup of tea and a sandwich. What they did not know was that at midday over a thousand protesters had stormed the square demanding the release of MP William O'Brien, a leading figure in the Irish rent strike.

The police were instantly outnumbered and several of them badly injured by bricks. In desperation the police began arresting as many people as they could, including a couple of MP's who were trying to make a name for themselves. The protesters flooded upon them and the police had no option than to use force, charging into the crowd, lashing out with their batons and injuring dozens of people as they tried to protect themselves. When the police chief realised his men were completely overrun he sent for the troops. First the police were ordered to fall back. This sent the mob into a triumphant frenzy; they cheered their victory and began looting from shops and dwellings on the Square. Their cheers turned to gasps, however, when they saw soldiers on horseback entering the square, and they turned to flee as the horses moved from a canter to a gallop. The crowd was soon dispersed, apart from twenty or thirty hardliners who pelted rocks at the horsemen, one rock felling a horse and throwing the rider on to the road and into hospital.

On came Scot George McGregor and his unit to deal with these protesters. It was his job as a soldier to do whatever he was told, but he could not understand why the Police Commissioner, Sir Charles Warren, had placed a ban on public meetings – Trafalgar Square had always been a place for free speech. Yet here he was, marching into the people who wanted no more than to exercise their right as British citizens. George and his pals had no qualms about sorting out the brick-throwing rabble, he could see they were lawbreakers trying to kill his friends. He whipped them with the butt of his rifle, and marched them at bayonet point to the police. However, there before him in the Square he took in the full horror of the scene. The horsemen had trampled down almost a hundred people; men, women and children were lying crying and bleeding at his feet. A woman grabbed his leg and begged him for help, her stomach wide open and her fingers trying desperately to hold her bloody intestines in place. Next to her a young boy, no more than ten years old, lay unconscious and bleeding from the mouth.

He could hear his sergeant shouting, 'Go on, my boys, fix the bastards. They'll not try to take over London again!' George shook his head, asking himself why should we stop people treating their own city as their home?

Looking around at the other soldiers, he spotted three of his friends kicking a man around as if he were a football, as he begged for mercy that was not forthcoming. At the edge of Trafalgar Square he saw a little girl, about six years old, tugging at the sleeve of a man lying face down on the road. He hurried over to the child and pulled her to one side, clasping her tiny hand in his.

He tried to turn over the man's body; the chest turned but the lower torso did not, a horse had trampled him and snapped his spine. George cradled the man's head in his lap and the eyes stared back at him. Those eyes would haunt his sleep every night of his life, that and the memory of dragging a screaming six-year-old child away from her dead father. George knew the kind of life that child would endure living in the inner city in poverty with no man to provide an income. Even as he carried her frantic form away from the Square, wriggling, squealing, crying in torment, he could see her life ahead.

What was it all for? So a police commissioner could indulge his own whim! People lost limbs, three were blinded, two were killed and over one hundred injured on the day called 'Bloody Sunday'.

It was a matter of days later when George McGregor decided that the army was no longer for him. He would fight for his country and for his people, but he was damned if he would ever fight *against* them. In an interview with his superiors he was called a coward, despite having been mentioned in despatches for gallantry in countless campaigns. He was finally cast out of the army without a pension, given what was called in those days a 'dishonourable discharge'.

George had been so proud to be a soldier; he was a third-generation McGregor to have served his country, and now he was returning to Aberdeen in shame, with no source of income.

He did not want to go home in shame, so he decided to try and find work in the Midlands. This was a non-starter as it was cheaper for mill owners to employ ten-year-old children than a soldier used to sizeable pay packets. He travelled the length of England and into Scotland until he found himself on the outskirts of his city of Aberdeen. He had nowhere else to go.

As far as his mother knew he was still the brave soldier, the man who made his father proud. How could he go to her now she was in her middle sixties and tell her what had happened? Instead, he knocked at the door of a farm where he used to play as a child.

The door opened and a strange young face greeted him. George explained that he had just left the army and was making his way home. On hearing that he used to play on the farm and knew Mr Young, the previous owner, the new farmer invited George in for supper. He was given some broth and bread, and as the clock turned to 11 p.m. the soldier asked if he could bed down in the stable for the night. The young farmer said it was fine, recommending the hayloft as it was out of draughts. The soldier was at his lowest ebb, and as the two of them walked towards the barn he told his full story to the farmer, who was most sympathetic.

'Do you know what I want?' said George. 'I just want to go to sleep and wake up in God's paradise. It would save my family from grief, and end my torment!' The farmer gave him a reassuring pat on the shoulders, shared a wee nip of whisky with him, and bade him goodnight.

The following morning the farmer was up in the early hours to help with the milking of his cows, and spotted fine wisps of grey smoke coming from the barn in the rain-sodden morning. He rushed as swiftly as his boots would allow into his barn, and saw that there had been a fire. He sent his son for help, and the authorities hurried to the scene. There, in the centre of the barn, was the blackened and burned body of George McGregor. All that remained untouched by the fire was his head, looking for all the world as totally at peace as if he had felt no pain. Experts were gathered and could not believe that there had been a fire of such intensity in a barn full of dry hay and straw, yet not one single bale was burnt. No crematorium, at that time, could generate the kind of heat that had totally incinerated the soldier's body to such a degree that the floor had been burnt away. This was one of the more convincing stories of spontaneous human combustion.

Despite the barn being right next to the farmhouse no one had heard the soldier cry out; it was as if his wish had come true. The gallant and honourable man had demanded entry into paradise, and who's to say he isn't there now?

ABERDEEN'S UNION STREET CLENCHER

In 1829 Aberdeen was a dark dingy place, overrun with rats and vermin. Human waste was allowed to build up in the tiny back alleys that linked all of the main streets. If you were wealthy you lived out of the city to avoid the rapscallions and vagabonds that preyed on the innocent.

One such rapscallion was Andrew MacDonald, the illegitimate son of a tailor who refused to accept that he was his son. His mother, Elizabeth MacDonald died of influenza when she was only 35, her only shelter a rain-sodden and draughty hovel.

As she was being laid to rest in the paupers' graveyard near Holburn Street, close to where the existing Nellfield Cemetery stands, Andrew MacDonald vowed revenge upon those that drove his mother to her death. The MacDonald lad wasn't a murderous man, but he had been pushed too far, and now it was time, he felt, to dish out a little of what his family had been forced to take. He began a hate campaign against the Stanton family, particularly the father who had spurned him since his birth.

He joined a particularly infamous gang of 'hoolies', known as the Huntly Streeters. Such gangs would swoop down on anyone who was alone and take their money or possessions; the Huntly Streeters were especially vicious: they once slit the throat of one Thomas Atkinson because he had punched one of their number to the ground. His body was found hanging upside-down from a lamp-post in Golden Square, the blood draining from him as from a slaughtered animal.

The gang's savagery began to rub off on Andy MacDonald, and he decided to be more direct with his vengeance against his father, Douglas Stanton. The gang raided his tailor's shop and destroyed hundreds of pounds' worth of clothes and fabrics. They set fire to his home, slaughtered his dogs and blinded his team of grey horses.

Stanton pleaded with the local Sheriff to act against this gang, and at one time it was suggested that the army be brought in. Despite his fervent protestations nothing was achieved.

His misery was made complete when his wife and daughter died after eating poisoned veal; doctors gave a verdict of 'eating tainted veal'. Although Stanton couldn't prove it he knew that the Huntly Streeters were responsible and decided that it was *his* turn for revenge.

He trawled the pubs and bars of Aberdeen, particularly the rough inns along King Street and those near the Victoria Dock, collecting for himself an army from the dregs of humanity – thieves, murderers, rapists and dozens of itinerant workers looking to turn a fast profit. He had prepared well, and had the addresses of the eight leading Huntly Streeters; one by one they would be tracked down and sorted.

The first to taste Stanton's venom was Graham Robertson, a ginger-haired rascal known as 'Ranting Robbo' because of his foul mouth. He was living in a back room on Chapel Street, and was in bed when his door was kicked open. He hadn't time to move before eight burly men grabbed him and held him down to his cot.

In walked Stanton holding an oil lamp, his face shining in its light, as he proceeded to explain what was about to happen.

'You weaselly-faced get,' spat the tailor. 'You have destroyed me and murdered my family, so now I intend to ruin ye!'

At this he ordered that Robbo's sackcloth pants be pulled down and he proceeded to pour lamp oil on the man's testicles and pubic area. Robertson struggled with all his might, but the force against him was too strong. He swore, he cursed, he screamed, he cried and he begged, but all to no avail. Stanton took a taper, lit it from his lamp and threw it on to the petrified thief, and it exploded into flame. Despite the heat, the hands that held him down refused to let go. Robertson roared his agony to the world, until mercifully he passed out with the pain.

One down, seven to go.

This was to be the fate of each man in turn: Duncan Hill, Sean Souness, Alexander MacDougall, Frankie Dougan, 'Big Tam' McClusky and a boy known only as Sprog. This left the man who started the feud – Andrew MacDonald.

MacDonald had a child of his own by this time, a beautiful little girl with hazel eyes and a halo of blonde curls called Victoria. Stanton's men surrounded MacDonald's wooden hovel on Skene Terrace near the viaduct, and set it on fire.

At the first sight of smoke MacDonald raced from the house carrying his eight-year-old daughter, and dragging the hand of his common-law wife Jeannie. In the light of the fire that increased its intensity by the minute, MacDonald pushed his womenfolk away from him.

A huge bearded Scot grasped Jeannie's hand, tearing away her white nightshirt, baring her body to all.

'We'll have some fun with this lass tonight,' he laughed.

MacDonald pleaded with them not to hurt her, but Stanton burst through the assembly and said, 'Did you not kill my wife and child?' MacDonald froze in fear.

'I think for you to see your wife and child die afore your face would be a fitting punishment!' the tailor continued, his eyes filled with the bloodlust that was swelling within him.

'Please God don't do it,' begged MacDonald. 'You are my father, damn you!'

Stanton looked at him sharply. 'What's this you say?'

While the lean Scot was restrained by Stanton's thugs, he told his story, denying that he had wanted to harm anyone other than the father who refused to recognise him.

The tailor's head spun like a whirlpool, and he released MacDonald's woman, covering her with his coat, and ordering her to run off. This she did, but in her panic she completely forgot about little Victoria.

The child pushed her way through the mob and clung tightly to her father. Time and again she was thrown off by her father's captors, but this gutsy wee girl kept on running to him. Then she ran to Stanton and clutched his arm with a strength far above that of a normal eight-year-old.

'Get off me, you little witch!' barked Stanton, but she refused to let go. He swung his hand across her face and her lip burst into a bloody mess, yet still her grip remained firm.

She never said a word, grimly hanging on to this man consumed with anger and hungry for the final conflict with his persecutor.

Stanton drew a dirk, a tiny knife that he had in his stocking, and drew it across her hands. The child didn't even recoil in pain, her bloody hands still clenched tight on the man's arm.

MacDonald screamed to the child to run after her mother, but she would not leave her father.

Finally, Stanton ordered his man to move her, and despite them beating her, whipping her and half-strangling her, the child remained firmly fixed to the tailor's arm.

'If you have to, cut her hands off,' bellowed Stanton, who was becoming a little frightened by the girl's tenacity. One of Stanton's rogues reached out and slit the child's muscles at her elbows, and her arms fell limply to her sides. They hurled her across the cobbled street as if she was a rag doll. As she fell one of the men kicked at her and there was an almighty crack. Her neck was broken.

Some of Stanton's men began to panic; they didn't mind being used as 'hired muscle' but they wanted no part of the murder of a child. They began to run, leaving Stanton with only two thugs, and MacDonald was free.

Screaming and crying, he picked up a brick in one hand, a heavy wooden stave in the other, and set about Stanton's minders. Within seconds they were beaten and bleeding, and MacDonald ran after Stanton who had fled.

He found him cowering in a doorway in Diamond Street, then merely a tiny alley off Union Street. Stanton looked totally mad and screamed, 'Stop her squeezing me, please get this little witch off me!'

MacDonald could swear he could see the shape of two tiny arms clenching tightly into the tailor's arm. It was as if even in death his child had returned to help her father wreak revenge on his father.

Suddenly Andrew MacDonald felt all of the anger drain away from him. He could fight no more. All he wanted was to go away with his child.

'Come on, Victoria,' he said. 'Leave him, there's been enough for tonight.' As he said that, Stanton felt the child's grip leave him, and he was left shaking in the shop door.

The following morning the body of Andrew MacDonald was found hanging from a tree in Union Terrace Gardens.

*It is believed by many that tiny Victoria MacDonald still walks

261

Union Street in Aberdeen, as 'the clencher'. As early as 1833 people in the vicinity could feel someone tugging at their arms, hugging into them from behind or grabbing at them. The earliest report was published in St Mary's parish bulletin in 1842; it reads: 'It was then that Mary O'Hara from Whitehall Place was seized by someone as she walked from Thistle Street on to Union Street. She was assaulted with such force that the tiny handprints could be still seen on her arms, four days later. Yet she saw no one!'

*Appearances continued, to the present day, and there have been regular reports of 'the clencher', some making the press.

In 1949 Michael Winstanley from Peterhead was a 22-year-old dock worker, and early one Sunday morning he was walking to work when he had an experience he related in 1977: 'When you're going to work you don't really think about it, your legs just take you. I was tired as I'd been out on the drink the night before, and I really wasn't looking forward to work. I just reached the Green Market on Union Street, when I felt as if a small child had run into my stomach, and was grabbing me tight. It winded me and I wanted to fall to the ground but I couldn't.

'I was held for almost twenty-five minutes. As it was before six in the morning no one passed me, and I shouted for help but no one came. Suddenly the pressure released me from its grip. I thought it must be some sort of cramp, so I reported to the medical officer at the docks, and he examined me and there were handprints on my body. This wasn't possible because there was no one there, I know that. I can't explain it to this day.' He had not heard of 'the Union Street Clencher'.

*Margaret MacAllister from Berwick rang a radio phone-in in October 1987 saying that her husband had been grabbed by what she described as 'an invisible force' and it had affected him so badly that he had been on the sick list for three weeks. Her husband Micky is an oil-rig worker and was in Aberdeen when it happened. I asked her whereabouts, and she replied, 'I don't know, somewhere in the city centre.'

Who's going to bet against it being Union Street?

THE DRAGON OF ARBROATH

When the first volume of *Grisly Tales* was published, the hardest stories to swallow must have been those featuring dragons or 'wurms', as they were called. Yet throughout Britain these stories persist right up to today with continuing reports of the Loch Ness Monster. If you go back into ancient history you find that almost all of the dragon legends are from the north, and this one is no different.

It begins with the Laird of Carnoustie who wanted to marry a beautiful girl who lived in a fine house on the shore of Loch Leven. The Laird sent representatives to ask for the lady's hand in marriage, but they were turned away. This flame-haired Scottish lassie was a spirited woman, and demanded that if the Laird had anything to say, he should say it to her face. This intrigued him, and within days he was on his way to pay her a visit. He had seen her twice before when she had attended the annual gathering in Dundee.

Now, while the Laird was away from home all kinds of things were happening there. Villagers were being eaten by a huge dragon that had risen from the sea at Arbroath. It travelled through the countryside attacking people and destroying their rickety cottages with a single sweep of its rutted tail.

Some weeks earlier, fishermen had reported catching a small dragon in their nets, and, rather than kill the beast, they had taken it down the Tay to Dundee in a metal cage. There it was treated as a novelty attraction, people paying to stare at it at the Invergowrie Fayre. The creature was also taken on tour, carried on flat carts pulled by heavy horses, to stun and shock the villages and towns.

The new dragon, however, was not in the mood for entertaining; indeed, it seemed hellbent on killing as many people as it could. On one occasion hundreds of weapon-wielding Scots chased it back into the sea near Salmond's Muir, and it swam towards Arbroath, where legend says, 'the beastie sunk all the boats it found afloat, then scurried to the land'.

Fishermen were swept to their death and many livelihoods were destroyed. By this time the Laird of Carnoustie was encamped close to the Pitmedden Forest, south of Perth, where he received a message telling of the hundreds killed, and begging his immediate return. The Laird ordered his entourage to turn round and head back home. Although he had never been formally introduced to the Kinross beauty, he knew that God had ordained that he should fall in love with her. So he mounted his swiftest horse and rode on to her home on Loch Leven. Her father was loath to allow this sweaty stranger to see his daughter at such a late hour – it was well after midnight – but when he realised that it really was the Laird of Carnoustie, he sent for his daughter, Meg Balloch.

Within minutes the Laird had grabbed her, hurling her on to the back of his steaming black stallion, and they rode off into the night. This was sudden even for those romantic days, and Meg screeched and caterwauled all of the way. By mid-morning they had caught up with his party, who were just crossing the Bridge of Earn.

He placed her in his carriage, instructing two of his female servants to ride into Arbroath and purchase the finest dresses they could find for his lady. While their procession rumbled on, more messengers arrived, each one with bloody tales of horror and destruction. The dragon had found itself a dark pit, where each evening it carried its prey to eat it. Many had watched as in its serpentlike tail it carried a fattened sow, a horse, a huge bull, or the stout figure of the local priest into its wormy den.

Meg found herself in the middle of a nightmare, yet had discovered the Laird to be a brave yet caring man, and was much taken by him, in every sense of the word. Almost five more days passed before the Laird found himself back at Carnoustie. He had passed across the dragon's path, meeting survivors from its assaults on Kellas, Muirdrum, Bonnington Smiddy, Leoch and Barry. The good people of Carnoustie would normally have had a carnival at the very thought of the Laird bringing back his bride-to-be, but with all the death and destruction, no one was in any mood for jollity.

The Laird summoned up his clansmen, and all the most intimidating fighting men he could muster, including many legendary figures renowned for their bravery. All gathered in the market square at Carnoustie. Robert of Leslie arrived wielding the axe he could fling over eighty yards and still hit his mark. The Campbells of Glen Almond had gathered; once a robber band, they had carved out a homeland for themselves, and seemingly turned over a new leaf. Alexander Fife the Moonzie giant was also there, a monster of a man with a long black beard, standing over eight feet tall.

The following morning, armed to the teeth, this gallant band headed towards the dragon's lair.

In the distance they could hear a loud hissing noise, as the beast's snores echoed through the myriad of caves it was sleeping in. This unsettled the Laird's men, as did the sight of human bones littering the roadside, each one picked clean by the monster. What little was left on the skeletons was busily being eaten by maggots, beetles and blowflies. The air reeked with the sweet, sickly smell of death.

They were there to get the job done, however, whatever the cost.
As they neared the lair's entrance they were met by an old crone
in a grey smock dress who held a snake high above her head. The
Laird recognised her as the wise woman of Kirkbuddo.

'Go back, fond Laird of Carnoustie, ye'll not be killing yon
beastie this day!' shouted the warty-faced old woman.

'How be that, wise woman?' answered the Laird, 'For I have
gathered the bravest in the land, and none of us will stop until
we've done it to death!'

'Aye, death ye'll be having,' shrieked the crone; her unnerving
cackle echoed around the hilly knoll.

One of the Campbells shouted, 'Out of our way, you old witch,
we've bloody work to do this day!'

At that, her wrinkled face contorted into a vicious expression as
she gazed up at the Laird still seated on his fine black horse.

'Mind me well,' said the hag, 'your weapons will not scratch his
skin, and lest ye listen to a wise woman, you will all surely die.
For right is on the dragon's side!'

Many of the gathering had had enough talk and marched into
the dragon's lair. Within seconds it was as if Hell had opened up
and released the armies of Satan. A deep roar from the creature,
followed by screams, echoed around the tunnels; then came the
scent of fresh blood. The Laird wanted to dive into the fray but
found himself mesmerised by the old woman who had placed a
spell upon him. That was his story, anyway.

It was just as well he remained behind, for no one returned from
the dragon's lair, each and every one devoured by the monster. The
Laird shook himself free of the spell, fell to the ground and wept;
his lands and his people would surely never now be free of the
Arbroath dragon.

'Cry not, Laird of Carnoustie,' came the crone's voice, 'for my
magic can do what ye seek.'

The Laird begged her to help, and she agreed, on condition that
he did whatsoever she asked. So that night the Laird and his
bride-to-be entertained the old woman at his house. She explained
what had to happen, and, despite major reservations on everyone's
behalf, it was agreed that they would do as she said. It seems that
their only chance of stopping this dragon's murderous forays was
to talk to it. Only wizards and witches had this power and to
achieve it they had to carry a tribute of heather, and two people
who were chaste, for no dragon ever feasted on purity.

So, late in the night the threesome entered the dragon's lair, a single torch making the shadows dance along the encrusted cavern walls. Once again the heavy breathing of the sleeping serpent could clearly be heard. The Laird and Meg both wanted to run out before the beast awoke, but they had sworn to see the plan through. At that point the cave opened out into a huge chamber, and there on a mighty rock crouched the most gigantic creature they had ever seen. A green scaly refugee from prehistoric times, its crocodile eyes opened, and its neck darted out what seemed to be miles as it studied the three strangers.

'Remove your robes,' whispered the crone, and both the Laird and his lady did so, walking shakily towards the beast, their nakedness declaring their purity. Meg was indeed pure, but the Laird was chancing his luck! Then the hag stepped forward and threw a white powder above their heads and chanted a strange spell. At that the dragon's roar transformed into human speech.

The wise woman shouted, 'Why do you seek our deaths, oh great beast?' The creature roared so loudly that each one thought their ears would burst, and yet they could understand it. 'You have my son,' it said, 'and I will keep destroying you and your people until he is returned to me.'

The three didn't understand what the beast meant so it roared again. 'My son was swept up by your nets many months ago, then stolen away by you land-dwellers. I give you three days to bring him back to me, or you will all know of my fury! Now begone lest I forget myself and take a bloody supper!'

At this they made a swift exit, and the Laird rushed into action, for he had heard that a dragon was on display at villages around Dundee. He sent out hundreds of his men and villagers to bring the young beast to Carnoustie. Within the day it was located at Newburgh at the mouth of the River Earn. The wise woman knew that was too far away to transport it back to Carnoustie within three days, so they had no other option than to return to the dragon's lair. Once again the spell was cast, and they stood before the serpent.

The beast howled its displeasure, its huge tail slapping at the wall like a crack of thunder. The earth shook around them and fragments of stone and dust showered them. 'What is it?' bellowed the creature. 'Your time on this earth is running out.'

The crone explained that the serpent child had been found, and could be set free that very day. But it would have to be freed into the Firth of Tay, many miles away. The serpent seemed unsure of their sincerity, and hissed, 'If you lie I shall kill every man, woman and child. You know this to be true.'

The Laird spoke up: 'We are here to stop the killing; if we lie, take our lives not those of our people.'

The dragon closed its eyes, and seemed to smile as well as any creature of its kind could do; then it reached out with its tail, which it wrapped tightly round the naked body of the Laird.

'I shall take you with me,' it growled, and half-walked, half-slithered through the tunnels into the daylight, then dived into the sea. All that could be seen was the naked body of the Laird held above the water as the beast swam along the Firth towards Newburgh.

The crowds waited for any sign of the Laird, but the sight that met their eyes was the last one they expected: a naked man flying along above the surface of the water, carried in a serpent's tail.

On reaching the mouth of the Earn, the dragon stepped on to the shore, scattering the people, who all ran for cover. There in a dirty hay-filled cage was the tiny serpent, looking ill and hurt. The dragon roared its disapproval and was about to seek out its son's captors, when the Laird said softly, 'Our deal is done, take him and begone for you can see to it that he grows strong again. I am sorry for what they have done to him. As long as I am Laird of Carnoustie I shall see that no harm is ever done to your kind again.'

The dragon believed him, and released him on to the bankside, grasping its son tenderly, sweeping it up and vanishing beneath the surf. The Laird watched as their underwater trail swam against the tide back out towards the sea.

The Laird married Meg and both lived long happy lives. And, true to his word, he put to the sword any man who failed to release a dragon from their nets.

*The place which the dragon had used as his lair was renamed Wormiehills, and carries that name to this day.

*It is thought by some that the Loch Ness Monster is none other than a dragon, similarly captured when very young and then released into the Loch. The other suggestion is that Loch Ness once opened into the sea, and perhaps such a dragon swam in. Time and tide finally closed off the entrance and the monster is now trapped in the Loch for all time.

THE STUMPHAND OF AYR

The commonest sound in London in 1665 was the mournful tolling of the church bells announcing yet another funeral. The capital was suffering its most deathly plague since the Black Death swept across the country three hundred years earlier. The graveyards were full to overflowing, and almost every person in London knew someone that the plague had claimed. So many were dying that individual burials were suspended; instead, bodies were hurled on top of each other in what were called 'plague pits'. The men who did this job had their mouths and hands covered in bandages so as to try to avoid contamination.

It was a time of terror for every citizen; houses with huge red crosses painted on the door, and the words 'Lord Have Mercy On Us' spoke of the residents of that home having the plague and waiting to die. The chance of survival was barely one in ten. Thousands had died and many more would; thousands flooded out of the city. This caused the rest of the country to fear anyone coming from London. Everyone knew the symptoms of this new bubonic plague – the body becoming covered with open sores, the glands, particularly those around the groin swelling up, headaches and a tremendous fever.

In some villages around London gangs of locals patrolled to scare away anyone coming from the city in an often successful attempt to keep their families plague-free.

The further from London you were, the more unprepared people were, and in Scotland jokes were made of it. However, in November 1665 a man called Tam Mackay arrived in Ayr having helped a Northumbrian farmer bring his cattle to the huge market in the south of the town. He had been there for almost three weeks when he let slip that he had travelled home to Scotland from London, frightened that he might catch the plague if he remained in the south. Word spread through Ayr that Tam Mackay could have the plague. It was completely unfounded, but even the sanest Scots thought better than to take the chance of mixing with him.

Tam decided to leave Ayr, as he couldn't live with the constant badgering, and went to say farewell to the few friends he had, at an inn at the top of Alloway Street.

Having told everyone he was leaving he expected his local to be full, yet there were only four people in there. They all said they liked him, but had families too, so asked him not to approach them. The tankard he drank from, the innkeeper asked him to throw on the fire. So he left to go to Edinburgh and another new start. As he closed the inn door behind him Tam saw a huge mob of men all wearing cloths across their mouths. He tried to walk away towards the small bridge close to where the New Bridge is now situated.

He didn't manage twenty paces before they were upon him, beating him with staves until he fell to his knees. Then from out of the crowd stepped a thickset man carrying a claymore, a heavy-bladed sword. 'I have done you no harm,' Tam shouted. 'Let me go. I'm leaving. What have you to gain by this?'

He struggled to his feet as the man swung the sword towards him, instinctively shielding himself with an arm. He watched in disbelief as he saw his hand and wrist fly into the air. He was surprised that he seemed to feel no pain, and everything moved into slow motion. He watched a stream of blood pump, pump, pump out of his arm soaking his attackers, who recoiled in horror.

They fled in panic screaming. 'I'm covered in plague blood, God help me!' Some of them began to attack each other, those with blood fending off the murderous assaults of those untouched. Common sense had long since flown. Tam began walking away, leaving a bloody trail behind him. He could feel his strength leaving him, and despite having a wound that he could not survive, he knew that no one would help him. He was near the old church – even in the 1600s it was called the Auld Kirk – and he found it closed to him, the doors firmly locked.

He made his way down to the river and dived in; he was never seen alive again.

However, he has been seen dead on many occasions.

*During the late 1600s and early 1700s many people saw a figure with only one arm walking round the streets of Ayr, a figure that, once glimpsed, just seemed to evaporate. After Tam Mackay's death the inn at the top of Alloway Street became known as 'Tam's' and no one would visit it. It closed down for a while and was later re-opened under several new names, latterly the Tam O' Shanter Inn.

*There were occasional brief sightings of the ghost of 'Auld Stumphand' as he became known, but generally things quietened down until 1951, when Tam Mackay made a quite astonishing comeback. Glynis and Malcolm Davidson were returning from Ayr Racecourse to their home in Queens Terrace overlooking the Firth of Clyde when it started raining heavily. They sheltered from the torrential downpour in a shop doorway on Smith Street near the station. On squeezing as far back from the rain as possible they found a man soaked to the skin already huddled in the corner.

'Quite a storm,' said Davidson. The shivering man nodded and croaked an 'Aye'.

The couple chatted about how fierce the rain was as it hammered down in sheets, and the three remained together in the doorway.

'Well, I think it's safe to leave now,' said Glynis noticing that it was now only drizzling. Malcolm Davidson turned to the chap in the corner and said, 'I'd get yourself home and get out of those wet clothes.'

The soaked man said, 'I have no home.'

Davidson felt rather guilty, knowing he had had a successful day at the races, so he reached into his pocket and pulled out a ten-shilling note, worth a fair deal back then, and handed it to the man. As the arm reached out to take the note, he screamed in shock – it was just a bloody stump, still running with gore.

Glynis, also screaming, tore at her husband's arm and they ran home. When they got there she discovered that the back of her raincoat was covered in blood where she had huddled against the man in the doorway. Yet as they looked at it it began to disappear. They had not heard of the legend, but they now both believe that it was Tam Mackay they had talked to.

*The most recent sighting was in November 1992 when a little girl in the children's ward at the County Hospital told her parents at visiting time that she had been talking all night 'with a man with a sore arm'.

Her parents asked her in general conversation what was wrong with the man's arm, and the child said, 'It's been chopped off and won't stop bleeding.' The mother spoke to the doctor and the nurses on the ward, who knew nothing about this visitation. It was put down to being just her vivid imagination, yet it sounds like 'Auld Stumphand' to me.

THE PHANTOM TEACHER OF TAYSIDE

Occasionally, stories are passed down from father to son, and one such tale has, with minor variations, come to me from all over Tayside. Some say the events occurred in Perth, others in Dundee;

the most vivid came from a small town called Crieff. Wherever it happened, that legend runs as follows.

During the 1800s a schoolteacher called Mr Archibald Ford worked very hard with his pupils over the years; they were from simple farming folk, and it was at a time when very few could read or write, but Mr Ford was determined that his people would have the advantages that literacy had to offer. He succeeded to such an extent that Crieff was considered to be one of the most educated towns in all of Scotland. Sadly, Mr Ford caught typhus and died. On his deathbed he admitted to being very proud of the people of Crieff, who had learned an amazing amount in such a short time. His last words were 'I can go to my grave knowing my town is an educated one. What more could a schoolteacher ask?' He was buried in the small local churchyard.

Some weeks later an intense storm was raging, forked lightning fell to the earth splitting huge trees in two, and people ran in fear. One man, a coachman, had in, his desperation to get home, skidded into a muddy verge, and the horses couldn't pull the cart out in such conditions, so he unharnessed them, and proceeded to lead them home through the graveyard.

Half-way through, he heard a tapping sound, and on looking round he saw the old dead teacher, Mr Ford, as plain as day, sitting on his own grave. In his hand he held a hammer and chisel. The coach driver was soaked to the skin, yet the teacher seemed perfectly dry.

'Mr Ford,' asked the coachman, 'is that ye?'

The phantom nodded, but kept chipping away at the headstone.

'Then what are ye doing?' asked the dumbstruck fellow.

Mr Ford replied, 'I'm correcting my gravestone, for they spelled my name wrong.'

The coachman walked past, not fully comprehending what he had seen. When his senses returned he raced home with his horses, and swore never to walk through the graveyard again.

The gravestone had been engraved 'In memory of *Archbald* Ford' instead of 'Archibald': to this day the stone has a scratched correction upon it.

THE CRYING GIRL OF PRINCES STREET, EDINBURGH

The rivers of Scotland had run red with the blood of its people, yet on 1 May 1707 the unthinkable happened – a union was formed between the English and the Scots.

271

There had been a war between the two for as far back as anyone could remember, far beyond the building of Hadrian's Wall by the Romans. Mothers had lost sons, children had lost fathers, women had lost husbands; now it seemed that all that carnage had to be forgotten.

Yet John Gillespie refused to see it quite that way. His father had been hacked to pieces at the Battle of Killiekrankie while fighting in the Jacobite rebellion for the deposed King James II. His two brothers had been arrested for attacking English merchants. Despite arguing that they had done this to raise funds for 'the cause', they were put into the dungeons of Edinburgh Castle where they had died of malnutrition and influenza. Gillespie felt that their imprisonment had been political, to placate the English while they negotiated the Union treaty. Surely no self-respecting Scot would allow his country to barter with the lives of its people, particularly with the 'auld enemy'?

On the very morning that the treaty was to be signed an entire school of whales, over thirty of them, was found washed up on the sands of Kirkcaldy by some fishermen. This was surely an omen of doom, and Gillespie ran around the small towns and hamlets trying to gather men who would rise against the agreement.

To his dismay he discovered that many Scots were actually in favour of the treaty, believing it would finally end the brutal battles and hostility in the border country. The English had agreed to safeguard the privileges of the Presbyterian Church, and Scots were allowed to join the 'British' army, and even form their own regiments.

Gillespie was appalled at the lack of what he called 'patriotism'; he wanted to strike back and took his army, three of his closest friends, and attacked three soldiers just outside Musselburgh.

The troops had set up a small campfire and were sitting around it, when Gillespie and his men began creeping up on them. Ironically, the men were discussing the treaty and looking forward to the peace that it would bring. They were totally off guard when Gillespie walked straight into the camp, calmly said, 'Hello', and then swung his claymore down on to the neck of one of the soldiers. The arteries severed and there was an explosion of crimson as blood spurted across Gillespie's face and tunic. The soldier lay on the ground, his body shuddering as with every heartbeat more blood pumped from his body. The other two soldiers reached for their weapons; one managed to pull out his sword but was not able to use it, as, garrotted by one of Gillespie's men with a piece of chicken wire, he fell headlong into the fire.

For a split second it was very dark indeed, and the third soldier decided to make a run for it, racing towards the lights of what was then the tiny village of Musselburgh. He wasn't aware that hiding in some bushes stood another of Gillespie's men with his chopping axe. As the soldier ran towards him, he swung back the axe, swishing it round hard into the soldier, so hard it severed the spine, and the man's body literally snapped in two.

Gillespie was well pleased with his first 'battle' against the English. But the next day he discovered that he had actually killed three fellow Scots. They were indeed wearing 'British' uniforms, for they were soldiers from one of Scotland's very first regiments. Gillespie was forced into hiding as now both his countrymen and the English were trying to hunt him down. Eventually he persuaded his girlfriend Moira Blair to hide him in her family cottage in Aberlady. He never left the croft; she fed him, clothed him and catered to his every need.

At the beginning of 1708 Gillespie changed his name to Archie Buchanan. He grew a beard, adopted a Lowland accent and proceeded to re-enter social life. All three of his associates had been hanged for their part in the Musselburgh massacre, and Gillespie believed that the massacre was now history.

On the first day of March Gillespie walked along Princes Street, glancing up at the mist-shrouded castle, and smiled to himself. He had got away with it, now he was a Buchanan and could start a new life. There was a new spring in his step, at last he could get out in the fresh air, the sun was breaking through and all was well with the world. Little did he know he was walking towards disaster. He reached the site of St John's church at the west end of Princes Street when he met an old friend, Jock Duncan, who instantly recognised him.

Their conversation was overheard and a soldier was informed. Both men were arrested. Gillespie swore he was Archie Buchanan, but to no avail. Realising he was going to the Castle, the very place where his brothers had died, he decided to make a run for it. He struggled free of the two soldiers escorting him and managed to reach the corner of Hope Street, where he tripped and fell, smashing his skull on the edge of a wall. He was bleeding heavily when the two soldiers caught up to him.

'You bastard,' spat one of them, 'killing your own people!'

The other only then realised he was guilty for the murder of the three soldiers all those months before. He raised his boot and stamped it down on to Gillespie's neck again and again until all movement had ceased.

'Shame,' remarked the first soldier. 'It would have been a pleasure to hang him!' He was buried in an unmarked grave in the Morningside area of Edinburgh.

Moira Blair was distraught on hearing that her beloved man had been killed and grabbed her shawl and walked to the city. On reaching the corner where he had taken his last breaths she could still see the red stain where his life had bled away. She threw herself down on the ground, sobbing and writhing in her grief, in the very place her man had died. At that moment a cart drove past and she launched herself under the feet of the two heavy dray horses. They reared up in surprise bringing their great hooves down on the frail girl. The cart only managed to stop after the heavy wooden wheels had broken her back.

Her shattered and twisted body was taken away by her father and buried in Aberlady.

*It is said that the sobbing figure of Edinburgh's crying girl can be seen on Princes Street each evening at dusk. Visitors to St John's church claim that they have heard a woman crying, and it is believed to be the tragic figure of Moira Blair.

*Mr Ross Douglas from Falkirk was visiting Edinburgh in March 1987 when he saw a young girl crying on the corner of Hope Street. He spoke to her, asking if he could be of help. She never replied, merely looked at him with hatred in her eyes, and he decided to walk on. He was half a dozen paces away when he looked back and saw her disappear into thin air. He said, 'I just saw her getting fainter and fainter until she was no longer there!'

THE 'WELL-HUNG' ENGLISHMAN

Throughout history various rogues have enjoyed notoriety amongst the people, and in Edinburgh a smuggler called Jock Wilson did exactly that. He smuggled in wine by the barrel, cheeses and silks from Europe. He lived in Gilmore Place off Leven Street, and everybody for miles around knew what he did for an illicit living. No one ever bothered to do anything about this, for he seemed a nice fellow, always giving gifts to people, sharing bottles of wine, giving free cheese to the older folks and generally bothering no one.

The English were in control in Scotland at this time, in the late 1730s, and they were not quite so willing to live and let live. Wilson was arrested, they found gallons of wine in a shed at his home, and hundreds of cheeses and miles of silk. There was no trial: he was strung up in the Grassmarket just along from Parliament House where the English Military Commander had decided his fate. On hearing how this 'canny Scot' had met such an unnecessary death the people of Edinburgh gathered on Princes Street and a riot ensued. The Commander allowed Captain Porteous to take charge of the situation. Porteous was an uncompromising sort who ruled his men with an iron glove, and no unruly mob would do him down. The crowd that had gathered were men, women and children who were disgusted at the punishment Wilson had received for merely selling unregistered goods. Smuggling was commonplace in Scotland at that time, and the Scots were unused to restrictions such as there were south of the Border.

Porteous rode up to the crowd astride a grey horse and shouted: 'Return to your homes or I will order my men to fire into you. This is my promise and you shall get no second warning!'

The crowd heard but paid no attention; although their blood was up they wanted to do no one any harm, demanding simply that English justice should not be so heavy-handed. The Commander believed that they did have a point, and agreed that this was a time for diplomacy. He sent a message to Captain Porteous saying that he should back down and allow the march through Edinburgh to go on unimpeded. Some say Porteous did not receive that message, others that he received it and ignored it; either way, as the crowd moved forward he ordered his men to fire a volley from their rifles. Over thirty people were injured, including a girl of eight; six men were killed.

The riot was effectively over, but the Commander knew if he did not act quickly there would be a major uprising. He therefore had Captain Porteous arrested and put him in an Edinburgh jail.

Maybe it was no coincidence that the jail had only one guard, for that night in 1737 a mob of Scots broke in, released four other prisoners and seized Captain Porteous. They took him into the courtyard, where they used an overhanging beam as makeshift gallows and winched him up into the air. They say that as he hung there, legs kicking in the wind, men jumped up to hang on his legs so that the noose tightened even more. They cut down his body and displayed it for all to see leaving a huge note pinned on the door of the prison: 'Justice Be Done For All'.

*They say that a ghost walks Cowgate near Parliament House, claimed to be that of a hanged man, but no one is sure whether it's Jock Wilson or the loathsome Captain.

THE GLAMIS SECRET

Glamis Castle in Angus, the home of the family of Queen Elizabeth, the Queen Mother, is also home to a number of intriguing legends. The strangest is that of the secret chamber, behind a locked door that must never be opened. The staff and residents are all sworn to secrecy, and it is believed that the door has not been opened once for over five hundred years. Some say it houses all of the items that the Royals have ever wanted to hush up, like the bodies of young princes savagely murdered, items stolen from other Royal households or a dreadful half-human creature created by a bestial affair by one of the sixteenth-century monarchs.

This may not seem likely, yet not too long ago it was uncovered that the Royals did have a great secret, involving close family members who had been hidden from the public locked in a psychiatric hospital, and never spoken of. When the tabloids gave them a front-page 'exclusive' many wondered what other secrets might be lurking behind locked doors.

Glamis Castle also houses the dead Earl of Baedrie, who on his death-bed offered to play cards with the Devil, to try to win himself more years of life. He lost the game, of course, and was sentenced to play cards for evermore, until the Devil loses. We all know that if the Devil does exist he's bound to use a marked deck, so the poor Earl struggles on for ever. He's been seen in several rooms over the centuries.

GALLEON OF LOST SOULS

In the west of Scotland anyone who dares take the grisly trail should visit Inveraray Castle where there is a most musical phantom. In the 1600s the Castle's harpist was caught peering through a keyhole at the lady of the house. He was unceremoniously hanged. Each day harp playing can still be heard in the library. Even in death the harper is still playing around.

The most fascinating legend that the Castle holds is the strange

276

warning given to the Campbell clan's chieftain, to prepare him for a visit by the Grim Reaper. It has long been said that two days before the chieftain dies a ghostly galleon sails along the loch past the Castle.

*In the 1700s one chieftain was so convinced that the galleon was for him to travel on into the next world that as he was in perfect health he took a poison so as not to disappoint the spectral crew.

THE GHOST OF KING DUNCAN

Any reader of Shakespeare will know of the untimely death of Duncan the Scottish king slain by Macbeth in 1039 at Macbeth's castle in Inverness.

The castle no longer exists, but it is said that the King still keeps a tidy eye over the town where he met his death.

It is said if you walk along the River Ness at twilight you will see the figure of a tall, bearded man, wearing a kilt and carrying a claymore across his shoulder. The man has a regal bearing, and is adorned by jewels and a thin golden band across his head. Many have given this description, not realising that it is exactly the description of King Duncan.

*In 1966 Mrs Katherine Macleish from Galashiels visited Inverness to see her cousin and decided to take a walk along the river. She told her tale on a radio phone-in in 1984.

'It was an ordinary Scottish night, a wee bit chilly, grey sky and just spitting on to rain. I was a bit bored by watching telly so I decided to have a walk, trying to clear up a nasty headache. Now I dinna believe in spooks, so when I spotted a man in a kilt I took it for granted it was just a piper or someone from a band or something. So I started making conversation with the man, and I asked him his name. He said it was Duncan, so I asked him what he was doing, just sitting by the riverside. He told me he was waiting for his men to return, so I asked if he minded my company. He had a most odd Scots accent, different to any I'd heard before, but he was kind enough to say "Nay, pray, sit by me!"

'I did nearly all the talking as he sat and looked almost in a daze. I had been there almost an hour when I decided I'd better return to my cousin's house, as supper would be in the pot. I said my goodbyes to the man, then headed off home. I turned back to wave at him and he proceeded to disappear. Not all at once, first

I couldn't see his legs, and slowly his whole body vanished. It was a crisp, clear evening, and I really saw that happen!'

There have been dozens of similar reports, all in the twilight, all along the banks of the Ness.

THE STRATHCLYDE STRANGLER

Ask any lady motorist what her worst nightmare is and she'll tell you it's to be followed home late at night by another car. The ominous glare of lone headlights in your rear-view mirror, speeding up when you do, slowing when you do and never leaving your tail.

In the early 1960s a young girl experienced this very terror. To shake her follower off she turned into a country lane, knowing there were no houses there, so he would have no excuse to follow her at all. After she had taken the turning, she looked tentatively in the rear-view mirror and felt her blood turn to ice when she saw the car still behind her. She sped down the bumpy lane for almost five miles before rejoining the road. For the full time the car behind was flashing his headlights, putting them on main beam and dazzling her.

Panic-stricken she roared into the nearest town sounding her horn and screeching to a halt outside the local police station. To her astonishment the car following pulled in too, just as the police appeared. A constable was approaching her grimly when she said, 'No, arrest him, he's been following me!' The driver stepped out of his car and explained that he was worried about her. He had been putting petrol in the car at a garage, and had seen someone climb into the back of her car whilst she paid for her tankful. There had been warnings on the radio of a teenage youth who had strangled a motorist with a knotted scarf, whilst hiding in the back seat. So he had followed her to make sure she was all right.

'What rubbish!' said the girl. 'What fool would believe a tale like that?'

At that very moment the back door of her car slammed shut. Several policemen shot off in pursuit of a fleeing figure. A young man had been hiding there. They caught him and saw that he was carrying a knotted scarf, and that he answered the description given of 'the Strathclyde Strangler'.

The youth was held at the station until he was taken to trial.

IRELAND

THE LAND OF THE GIANTS, NOT THE LEPRECHAUNS

Most people have heard of the Giant's Causeway in Country Antrim, and that it is claimed once to have linked the north of Ireland to mainland Britain. There are thousands of stories and legends that abound in Country Antrim about this, yet my favourite is about a giant called Declan, who lived near Coleraine in Londonderry. The story goes that this friendly giant had fallen in love with a Scots lass called Kathleen Duncan, who lived over the North Channel in Kintyre. In those days the causeway was beginning to sink below the sea from the weight of giants walking to and fro across it. The romance continued until finally Declan asked for Kathleen's hand in marriage. The giant was an amiable fellow, who had helped the Duncans build a new house, and often helped tend the herd of cattle that earned the family a modest living. The wedding date was set and everyone in Kintyre began preparing for the leaving of the wedding party. Declan would carry a boat across the causeway, Kathleen and her family would get in it, and he would drag the boat alongside the causeway back to Ireland for the ceremony. Declan's family began building the bridal boat, covering it with ribbon and lace made especially for the occasion.

The great day finally arrived, and Declan was waved away by his family who had prepared a feast the like of which had never been seen in Ireland before. In the meantime they began the party, to be joined by the 'little people' later on. These 'little people' weren't leprechauns, they were people of average height, yet appeared small to the Irish giants. Thousands of giants were there, all dancing and jumping to the music, and this is what caused the problem. The Giant's Causeway was in a terrible state – what had once been a solid bridge across the water was eroding away – and now the earth was shaking and quaking as the huge folk danced.

Declan set off across the causeway, pulling the bridal boat along; finally he caught a glimpse of the Duncans on the opposite shore

– he was only minutes away from his lady love. Then suddenly, as he stepped forward, the causeway disintegrated beneath his feet. He was stuck there and couldn't reach the shore. He bellowed across the water for them to get a boat and meet him out in the channel. The Duncans rushed to a boat and began to row towards him. Beneath his feet Declan could feel the shuddering and crunching of the causeway, as the thunderous dancing continued. He knew the causeway was about to collapse. If it held out until the Duncans arrived, he could stand with one foot in the bridal boat, and put the other in the boat being rowed by the Duncans. But, he concluded, this surely would lead to the death of everyone. So what he had to do was run back to Ireland as fast as he could before the causeway disappeared into the sea.

He shouted to Kathleen: 'I must get back to shore or I'll drown, for giants can't swim. I love you, please come to me!'

The Duncans rowed like fury to try and reach him, watching him turn and begin to sprint as fast as his huge legs could carry him back to Ireland. However, he was just past Rathlin Island when the causeway disappeared beneath him and he fell into the sea. Far off in the distance Kathleen saw him floundering in the water. She screamed loudly across to the giants, who could surely have saved him. But their fiddle-playing and thunderous dancing was too loud for an ordinary girl to be heard. The Duncans rowed even harder, blisters ignored as they pounded the surf with their oars to get to the gentle giant as he floundered in the sea. They were only yards from him when the huge frame finally vanished down into the clear stretch of water that divided the Atlantic from the Irish Sea.

Kathleen dropped the oar she had been tugging on, and screamed 'No!' The scream was so piercing that all of the giants stopped their music and raced to the causeway, where they saw the huge wash created by the sinking body of Declan. Kathleen, wearing a long white robe, stood at the front of the rowing boat and cried out, 'Father, I must go. I swore to Declan that I would go to him!' Her father rose from his seat to stop her, but to no avail. She made a perfect dive into the sea. The boat's dozen occupants watched as the white robe slowly descended into the briny, vanishing slow upon slow, until eventually there was no sign of it.

As the Duncans watched from the boat, the giants all stood on what was left of the causeway and viewed the scene in shock. Instead of its being the happiest day that Ireland and Kintyre had seen, two people had died. Uistis, the holy man of the giants, shouted: 'If there is a God in Heaven, I swear that we giants will never take another mortal bride. We beg of you to protect the perfect love they shared, for surely no true God would allow such a love to die!' The words boomed across the water and seemed to echo for ever. At that moment there was a crash of thunder even though the sky was clear. Then out of the sea a pure white seagull bobbed to the surface, followed by a huge gull with a jet-black beak. They began to flap their wings and then soared off into the sky.

One of the Duncans called out, 'Praise the Lord, that's Kathleen!' The seagulls swooped and dived across the water, squawking and barking at the giants, then sweeping across the water and around the boat. Then they turned to the north-west and began to fly away, together.

The giants eventually became extinct because they never took themselves human wives.

*It is believed that if you take your girlfriend or boyfriend out to the Antrim coast you can discover whether or not you're suitable to marry. If you see a pure white gull or a huge gull with a black beak, then you have the blessing of Declan and Kathleen.

IRELAND'S DEAD CENTRE

It's hard to imagine that four million people could live on a diet that consisted of nothing other than potatoes, yet that was the situation in Ireland through the 1800s. So allow me to take you back to 1845, when there had been over twenty serious crop failures since the turn of the century, and everyone watched carefully to see how things were progressing. It was well into July and the potatoes were flourishing, so no one had any cause for concern. But, of course, it is always when you least expect it that disaster is prone to strike: a blight that had all but destroyed America's harvest appeared without warning on mainland Britain and Ireland. The hot, sticky summer overnight changed into a bizarre mid-year winter with frost and freezing fog. The crops didn't stand a chance.

It took the authorities far too long to grasp the gravity of the situation because when the potatoes were lifted they looked fine, yet within two days they were a putrefying mess. It was all blamed on English oppression, yet the Irish merchants continued exporting wheat while their own workers starved to death. This brought about Ireland's great exodus to America, Britain and around the globe, anywhere they could survive. So dreadful was this potato blight that within three years, over a million men, women and children had died of starvation or typhoid. Some landowners knew they couldn't pay their workers because the harvest hadn't come in, so they merely evicted them, thus sentencing them to death.

Other landlords sacrificed their homes and land in trying to save the lives of those who worked for them. One such man was Michael O'Rourke from near Athlone in County Meath who discovered the depth of the tragedy one December morning in 1845. He was doing his rounds to check that what little remained of his livestock hadn't been stolen by the rogues and vagabonds often created by the desperate times. He came upon the hovel where the Gees lived, a family that had worked his land for twenty years, and had served his father too. Opening the creaky wooden door, he peered inside and saw that the entire family was dead, four generations huddled together in front of a fire. Grandparents down to tiny babies, with nothing to eat, who had chosen to die together in their home rather than to scavenge around the country like so many others.

The landowner determined there and then not to allow any of his other workers to go the same way, so he decided to journey to Dublin to raise revenue on his small estate. The entire country was in turmoil and money could not be had anywhere, so he ended up selling all of his family's land instead, except the ground where his house stood. He knew that he had been cheated, his estate was worth more than ten times the sum he had got for it. On rushing back he told the tenants that they had to move into the big house – twelve families, over 50 people, would have to co-exist in a house with only eight bedrooms. He shared the money out among them so that they could buy food from the black-market racketeers that always profited off the back of misery and misfortune.

O'Rourke had given up everything to try to save his people, yet in a way he was the ultimate architect of their disaster. They survived the winter, and the new season had begun, but the new landowner of the O'Rourke estate wanted nothing to do with the old staff, having brought in an entire workforce of his own. So now, starving once more, what were they to do?

Once again O'Rourke headed to Dublin, this time to sell his home, and to buy passage for the Americas for one and all. The money he raised was barely enough, but the captain of a ship standing off the mouth of the River Liffey eventually agreed to take them. So O'Rourke handed over every penny he had, after the Captain had given him a signed assurance that basic food would be provided for all of them. The journey was set for 21 July 1846, in three weeks' time. It took O'Rourke three days on horseback to return to Athlone, and another day to gather all of the belongings before they headed off to Dublin. With only two horses, five hand-carts and wheelbarrows their progress was slow. The journey cost the lives of two of the older workers, and a young baby also perished, yet miraculously they arrived two days before the ship was due to sail.

O'Rourke left the group in a primitive encampment near Clontarf, and went to find the captain. But to his horror both the captain and the ship had already gone.

No one could possibly imagine how the group felt on receiving such dire news. O'Rourke, feeling that he was responsible, hanged himself from a tree.

Starving, cold and disease-ridden, the simple country folk were totally defeated. Three of the younger girls decided to strike out for Dublin to become prostitutes, and one of the younger men headed inland to seek work; the others stayed where they were. The majority starved to death, others threw themselves off the cliff tops, while one mother smothered her two babies and then sliced her wrists, bleeding to death while hugging her beloved children. She had watched others' babies die of starvation and couldn't bear to see her own suffer in such a manner.

In all, 46 people died on the coast outside Clontarf, and to this day there is an area there that is said to be 'a dead zone'. It is not that grass and trees can't live there, it is something about the air that makes it somewhat 'different'. Some say that the dead still walk around the area at night crying out for food, others that evil spirits prey upon the souls of those that tarry there. Whatever it is, it's a spooky place.

*Douglas Hennessey from County Cavan has studied psychic phenomena for a number of years and he told me: 'This spot is accursed for certain. Since the dreadful happenings in 1846 people that visit that spot have found themselves wanting death – as if the atmosphere there is tempting them to take their own lives. On or close to that spot since there have been a dozen or so suicides. A young couple put a hose from their exhaust into the car and killed themselves there some years ago. One young man hurled himself off the rocks to his death. Swimmers have died nearby, car crashes, heart attacks and many other strange matters. Perhaps this is "a dead zone" as some believe. There's been so much abject misery and despair there in the past, that perhaps the land can't shake it off.'

*Suzanne McIlroy from Bray in County Wicklow visited the cliffs overlooking Clontarf in March 1964 and remembers: 'I was out with my dog, Rebel, just throwing sticks for him as usual, when I suddenly felt dizzy. Kind of light-headed and fuzzy-minded, and something was telling me to jump. I didn't hear a voice or anything, but something was pressing me to go over to the edge of the cliff and jump. I didn't want to, and I told myself not to, but each time I looked towards the edge I felt myself almost being pushed to do it. I can't explain it. As I turned and walked back to the bus stop I actually felt someone grab my arm and tug me back. I screamed out for whoever it was to let go, yet on spinning around no one was there. I had nightmares for almost three years over this and ended up on tranquillisers from the doctor after suffering a major depression. I'll never go back there, not even if you paid me.'

DUBLIN'S PHANTOM

Of all of Europe's capital cities there is no other that seems able to mix the shabby with the elegant like Dublin. The River Liffey meanders through a city of fabulous buildings side by side with industrial chimneys pumping smoke into the skies against the self-same backdrop. One of the most imposing buildings is the Four Courts, home of the city's judiciary – and home of a phantom.

No one is really sure who it is, but he appears at the edge of the domed roof regularly throughout the year.

Some say he is one of the men who actually built the Four Courts, who fell to his death, but there is no record of that ever happening. Others say it is the hapless soul of a murderer sentenced to death in the 1920s for murdering a young girl from Carrowmore in Sligo.

Whoever it is does make a point of being seen, as many have testified.

*IRA leader Michael Collins came to Dublin in December 1921 to sign the Anglo-Irish Treaty with Britain to give Ireland (excluding six of Ulster's nine counties) its independence. While there he saw an apparition that he described as 'Glowing yellow on top of the court building. At first I was blaming the drink because we'd been celebrating. I was not alone, many others saw this sight too. I don't believe in ghosts, but what it was was a mystery to me. If it was a ghost, perhaps it was the ghost of British colonialism laid to rest this fine day!'

*Mrs Rachel Peart from Roscommon visited Dublin in August 1936 for a second honeymoon to celebrate fifteen years of marriage, and was walking along the river hand in hand with her husband, Sean. He asked her to pose beside the end of the bridge, so he could capture the mood of the moment. It was a misty night, warm and sticky, without any breeze. He aimed the camera at Rachel, and tried to get the bridge and the Four Courts dome in the shot. Yet he could see a speck of light moving to and fro in his lens. He took the photograph, then asked his wife to look at the dome. There on the ledge that runs around the rim of the dome, they could see a luminous figure running back and forth. He seemed to be doing his utmost to attract attention. Sean took several photographs until the glowing figure ebbed away into nothing. Two weeks later the photographs were returned and every shot came out perfectly except those that featured the Four Courts building: they were totally black.

*In January 1984 a student at a local college spotted a man on the dome of the Four Courts and phoned the police, believing it to be a would-be suicide. The police came and saw the man sitting on the edge, dangling his legs over the side. On rushing to the top they found no one, yet the people below could still see the man clearly. A nervous police officer walked along the ledge round the dome, and although those on ground level could see both figures, the phantom was invisible to this intrepid policeman. Once he had returned trembling to the street, he too could see the figure plainly.

THE CLARE HEAD HUNTER

We choose to believe that monsters exist only in other countries, in continents far away or over a thousand years ago. Yet there is a story from County Clare of a monster that appeared barely 200 years ago, in the late 1700s. At that time Ennis was a bustling market town, the gathering place for stallholders, farmers and merchants. The town also attracted labourers in search of work, who knew that all those with money would visit Ennis at least once a month. One such labourer was a hunchback called Pat

Muldoon, a sad twisted fellow with a terrible speech impediment. In those days deformity, although sadly all too common, often led to the afflicted individuals being outcast from society. That was certainly the case for Muldoon. He applied for any job he could, only to be shunned by everyone, and finally he took to begging from the stallholders who would throw him rotting potatoes and occasionally a sour apple or bruised pear. These mouldy and decomposing items were the only things that kept Muldoon alive. At the end of each market day Muldoon would collect a sack filled with the scraps left behind, and the children would hurl old cabbages and rotting tomatoes at him. It was an uncivilised time, when children were actively encouraged to force the handicapped, who were considered an embarrassment, out of towns and cities.

Patrick Muldoon was a sensitive soul in a deformed body, who just wanted to have friends and be liked: simple aims most of us share. Yet wherever he went he was mocked and reviled until finally he decided he would go somewhere he would be left alone, and built a small shack out in the Burren, a rocky limestone outcrop overlooking the Atlantic Ocean. There he lived off berries and roots, occasionally trapping a rabbit; often he was hungry but at least he wasn't being persecuted. Despite the many freshwater springs in the Burren, and the Irish abundance of rain, Muldoon one day started drinking sea water, and became completely mad. He still kept himself very much to himself, and the local shepherds would often see him skipping across the hills, singing to the skies. He would appear on the edge of towns talking to cattle, and was once seen drinking directly from a cow's udder.

Then one evening locals discovered that a local graveyard had been defiled: a plot had been dug up and the head hacked off a newly buried body. The bereaved family were deeply distressed by this, and the atrocity was blamed on a group of devil-worshippers known to be in the area. The Satanists were never tracked down, and the people around the Burren consoled themselves that these rogues had moved on.

Then there was an outbreak of grave-robbing: in less than three months 43 coffins, all buried for less than a week, had been exhumed and in each case the head had been crudely hacked off, probably with a shovel. The locals decided to start guarding their cemeteries. This sounds simple enough, yet in those superstitious times it took considerable courage for anyone to stay all night in a graveyard.

One night a local carpenter called John Blundell was taking his turn on guard. He was absolutely terrified, and so decided to take with him a hip flask full of 'thunderguts', a locally made potato brew, at least 200 proof, which could strip the bark off a tree. After emptying the flask, Blundell fell unconscious on the grass verge at the graveyard gate, and we can only hope that the powerful concoction was a strong enough anaesthetic to prevent him feeling his head being hacked off. He was found the next morning by friends as if sleeping, yet when they pulled at his sleeve he turned over and his headless corpse covered their hands with clotting blood.

The nearest the culprit came to being caught was when he progressed from his first murder to his second. Muldoon took himself a woodsman's axe, deciding that if his local graveyards shunned him, he would add to his head collection direct from source, by taking more lives.

He spent three days watching a local farmhouse, taking careful note of all comings and goings. He soon discovered that each evening around 6 p.m. the family would put their eight-year-old girl to bed upstairs, and then both parents would go out to tend their chickens and goats for at least two hours. Muldoon swore he would have the child's head.

That night the husband and wife, as usual, left the farm cottage and trudged towards the henhouse, some distance from the house. Muldoon waited an hour, to make sure the child was asleep, and he remained hidden in the hedge until seven o'clock. Stealthily, he broke into the house and proceeded up the stairs, hatchet in his hand.

He climbed on to the child's bed and was just about to bring the axe down when he heard the cottage door open. The child awoke and screamed at the sight of this weird creature beside her. Muldoon silenced her with a single blow and began to force the window open. The parents raced up the stairs but arrived just after the hunchback had made his escape. 'She's all right!' said the father in relief. 'It must have been just a bad dream.'

The mother sighed with relief as she watched her husband nudge the child in the twilight bedroom. 'Come on, me darlin',' said he. There was still no response, and as the mother started to light a lamp, the father tugged roughly at his daugher and let out a bloodcurdling shriek as his gorgeous daughter's headless body fell towards him, sending the decapitated head rolling from the bed, past the mother and down the wooden stairs.

This horrific incident resulted in a major search party being sent to seek out the killer of such an innocent child. The gang of vigilantes gathered at the farmhouse and prepared to follow the scent: a scrap of Muldoon's shirt had been found on the house's primitive guttering, and it was enough to send the dogs howling into the country on the murderer's trail. Almost 36 hours later the dogs were scratting across the Burren, close to Muldoon's shack, which was built roughly between two huge rocky outcrops and which many people had passed close by without seeing. The search party was just about to return homewards after an unfruitful day when suddenly they heard singing. It seemed to be coming from the limestone itself, and the very rocks were vibrating with the tuneless lament. So despite the fact that it was getting dark, the party continued their search.

It was almost nine o'clock when a tiny glint of light was glimpsed in the distance. Silently the men began to creep towards its source. They came to a rough-hewn gate and on dragging it open, they stared into a tiny cavern. There in front of them was Muldoon, sitting next to a small campfire. In his lap he held the head of a young girl, the crown hacked open, and scooping her slimy brains into his mouth. The men recoiled in horror at such a terrible sight, and many retched and puked as the stench of death flooded their lungs.

Maddened with loathing, they dragged Muldoon out into the open and kicked and beat him unconscious. Some say they tried to hang the monster, but such was the nature of his deformity the noose just slid over his head as he had no neck at all. They thought of chopping his head off, in vengeance for his dirty deeds, but this also was awkward because of his physical shape. So they decided to hack off his arms and legs, leaving his torso on the Burren to be fed on by crows and gulls. The party remained nearby as flocks of scavenging birds began tearing at the helpless hunchback's flesh. The story says that Muldoon was still alive three weeks later, although his eyes had been pecked out, the sockets filled with maggots. Huge millipedes and worms slid in and out of his nose as he lay helplessly staring skywards. By the time he finally died his arms and legs had been carried off, possibly eaten by the search party's own dogs. The torso was hurled into the ocean.

*They say that late at night if you're alone on the Burren you can hear the plaintive lament of the head-hunting hunchback as the phantom settles down to feed on the brains of yet another of his blood-soaked victims.

*Every 1 August Muldoon's ghost is said to hobble along the beach, maggots crawling out of his eyes. The apparition has terrified many hundreds over the years. As soon as you see the figure it turns towards you and then disappears.

CACKY COLLINS, THE KILLER LEPRECHAUN?

Whether Cacky Collins was a leprechaun or not, we'll never know, but we can be sure that he was one of the most villainous and murderous rogues ever to live in Ireland. In fact, he never lived on the Irish mainland, but off the Kerry coast on the island of Great Blasket. There he had gathered cutthroats of every kind to form a gang of raiders who preyed on towns and villages throughout Kerry, Cork and Limerick. He was responsible for the deaths of thousands of people, and had been known to eat their flesh.

Collins himself was a tiny man, certainly less than four feet in height, with a huge beard that trailed around his waist. The mere sight of the waddling brigand was enough to send most people running for safety. He had been a thorn in Ireland's side for almost 45 years when he finally met his match. The year was AD 459 and Collins, now in his late fifties, had decided on his most ambitious attack: they would sail directly into Bantry Bay, sack Glengariff, and then Bantry, before returning home. He had over a thousand men with him, and he believed that the townspeople would run rather than fight such a vicious mob. The boats gathered in the bay and hid round the point; then, the raiders disembarked and, following the curve of the headland, charged into Glengariff. Collins was right, most of the population fled and those that remained paid the penalty. The older men were swiftly despatched, the young men were taken prisoner, to be sold into slavery, and the women would be raped, and then sold.

Collins was merciless. At one sale of slaves in Rosslare he couldn't get a decent price for his group of 27 boys and girls aged three to twelve, so he hacked their heads off in front of the gathering, splattering them all with innocent blood. Then he told them that he would return the following month, and if they refused to buy his next group, the heads rolling would be theirs.

After butchering hundreds at Glengariff, Collins and his men rested, spent the night assaulting the women, then turned their attention to the biggest town Collins would ever face – Bantry. In the early hours of the morning he collected his boats and sailed across the bay. When they landed at Bantry he proclaimed that the town was his. The leader of the settlement came to him and asked what he wanted. Cacky looked up at the lanky man, and ordered him to kneel down so he as to be at eye level. This the man did and then he was given a full list of riches that had to be forthcoming, or else Bantry would be burnt to the ground. Collins gave the citizens two hours to meet his demands, if they refused the raiders would attack, and take no prisoners.

At the same time a man from Glengariff arrived with the news of what had happened there 24 hours earlier. The Bantry folk were petrified when the town's most special guest then stepped forward and said quietly, 'Let me speak with him.'

It was Bishop Patrick (who would later become Saint Patrick), and he insisted in talking to the tiny pirate.

The Bishop had been born near Carlisle in England, the son of a landowner from Roman stock called Calpurnius. His grandfather Potitus had also been a priest. At the age of fourteen the Bishop had been captured by Collins' raiders and sold as a slave to an Irish family. At the age of twenty he had escaped in a small boat and had managed to reach France (known then as Gaul) where he had trained as a priest. He had been sent a vision by God, telling him that he must return to Ireland and convert the Irish. He had since converted most of the kings of Leinster, Munster and Ulster, and had gained permission for priests to travel around spreading the word. Patrick was a charismatic man, and everyone who met him believed at once that he received direct guidance from God.

The Bantry townspeople were happy to let Bishop Patrick meet the old murderer, but could not see what he would be able to do against swords and axes.

The Bishop crouched down and on meeting the pirate's eyes, recognised him. Collins had been his captor more than thirty years earlier.

'I remember you, greybeard!' said the Bishop (who also had a long grey beard), 'for you murdered my friends and sold me as a slave!'

'And who might you be, then?' asked Collins.

Softly spoken as ever, the Bishop replied, 'I am Bishop Patrick, and I have come to ask you to stop the killing, and to reach towards God.'

'God!' laughed the rogue. 'I am the only god in Ireland, and I expect these people to pay tribute to me in gold and silver, with a few women thrown in for good measure!' His tiny frame shook with laughter, yet his eyes remained focused on Patrick's face.

'These people cannot fight you,' said the Bishop. 'I have witnessed the ferocity of the raiders first hand. They care not for life themselves, they are already in the devil's hands.'

'Oh no, they're not, they are in my hands,' snapped Cacky. 'They do my bidding not the devil's!'

Calmly the Bishop stood up and said, 'I am he who drove the serpents from Ireland, and as God is my witness I shall drive you out too.'

This was said with such conviction that Cacky Collins was taken aback. There he was in front of his own men, and this unarmed priest was threatening him.

'How can you do that, you old fool? I think that I'll just drive my sword through you and be done with it,' said Cacky.

In truth, he didn't want to have to take Bantry by force; he had lost many men at Glengariff and could ill afford to lose any more. So he had to set an example with this slave who had become a priest. 'Watch me,' he shouted to his men on the boats. 'I'm about to kill one of God's men!'

He picked up a double-headed axe and was about to use it when something stopped him. He began shivering and the axe fell from his hand.

'My Lord protects and keeps me, and delivers the souls of your men to the fallen Angel!'

Cacky Collins didn't understand what was happening. On looking behind him he saw all 27 of his boats begin to sink. His men were tumbling into the water but seemed unable to swim, and all drowned. Seventy or eighty figures were seen swimming to the shore, but, when they landed, Collins could see that they were all those he had taken as slaves.

He now had fewer than twenty men, while by this time over three hundred townspeople had gathered behind Bishop Patrick.

They were beginning to get restless, wanting to kill the pirates, but the Bishop said, 'God will repay these men!' and turned to walk away from them. Collins once again ran at him but seemed to run into some invisible barrier.

Collins and his men walked back along the Bantry coast to his longboat, his remaining vessel, and they rowed away, knowing that with the tiny sail it would take weeks to return to the Great Blasket. Once they rounded the point they aimed for the relative safety of Valencia Island, but the wind began to roar and the vessel capsized, and they were washed up on The Skelligs. There, it is said, Collins ate his crew, and then eventually died of starvation.

'Vengeance is mine,' saith the Lord!

THE KILKENNY LOVERS

One of the more tragic of Ireland's catalogue of legends features a lady known only as Dorothy, a farmer's daughter from County Tipperary.

It was early 1597. She had fallen in love with a young business-man from Kilkenny but her father refused his request to marry his daughter, so they planned to run away together. The young man, Philip Mogg, decided he would travel the world like many of those who worked for him – his family was in the business of providing vessels to be used by merchants, businesses and missionaries. He knew that a vessel was due to travel to Japan to collect some clergymen who had been bartering with the people in the hope of saving a few souls. No sooner had Mogg arranged for two berths aboard the ship that news came from Japan that 26 Christians had been captured by a rebel warlord, Hideyoshi, and executed outside Nagasaki. Moggs's seven Franciscan clients and nineteen of their followers had been crucified upside-down and their arteries cut, to prove that the Christian God was not strong enough to protect them.

Long before their deaths these evangelists had suffered terribly at the hands of the Japanese. One month earlier, after they had been sentenced to death, they were tied in the square and mutilated by the people. All of the men had their penises and testicles cut off and stuffed in their mouths, the women were raped by hundreds of the townspeople. They were dragged through the streets of Kyoto where they were stoned, before being carried by ox-cart to the execution site.

The stories coming out of Japan caused the ship's crew to threaten mutiny, so plans were quickly changed to sail to France instead.

As he was the company representative Mogg had to organise everything, which left him little or no time to prepare to elope with Dorothy. So she kicked her heels at home, waiting for word from her husband to-be. Finally, he sent a messenger to her, asking her to travel to Waterford, where, for reasons of security, he would meet her in the cellar of the local inn. Hurriedly, she gathered her belongings, racing from the house while her parents were still asleep. That night she slept at the inn, knowing she would meet

Philip the following day. However, there were two inns in Waterford at that time, which neither Dorothy nor Philip knew. Dorothy was at one, in the town, and Philip arrived at the one near the docks.

Philip remained in one cellar all that night, but Dorothy never showed up. Dorothy spent a similarly fruitless night in the other cold cellar three miles away. She was so desperate to see Philip that she started to panic. She suffered from claustrophobia and we can only imagine how uneasy and scared she must have been in that cellar all night. Finally, her nerve snapped and she had to get out. She pulled at the cellar door to find it had been bolted from the outside. Another door led only to a small stockroom with no other way out. She began to cry and fell to the floor where she noticed a ring clasp. Maybe it would lead to another way out. Apparently the inn, new at the time, had been built on the site of a much older tavern, and there was a cellar beneath a cellar. So Dorothy opened the dusty old hatch, peered inside and reached down to see if there were any stairs. She felt a ladder and started climbing down it clutching her shrinking candle. She was barely four steps down when the stairs gave way and she tumbled down almost twenty feet, slicing her throat as she fell. Above her the hatch crashed shut, blowing out her candle, and there she lay in the darkness. She tried to scream but the blow to her throat had affected her voice box, and all that would come was a hissing noise.

Hour after hour Dorothy waited for someone to enter the cellar above her, so she could make a noise and be rescued, yet no one came. Every single minute was a nightmare with rats scuttling over her feet, cobwebs and spiders covering her face whichever way she turned, and the drip, drip, dripping of sewage that ran down each wall.

Dorothy never got out of that cellar until almost 150 years later, when the inn was demolished.

Philip Mogg waited in Waterford for almost twelve months; then he travelled to France, where he lived the remainder of his life in Artois.

*The ghost of Dorothy is said still to be heard in Waterford, her screams hissing into the night air. There have been a few sightings of her, but it is more normal to hear her.

*Francis Sullivan worked for the public works department in the late 1940s into the 1950s and told his son Mick Sullivan that he heard Dorothy most nights he was working in the sewage tunnels. Mick wrote, 'He said he could hear someone talking in a "husky whisper". It was definitely a woman, and at first it hissed: "Is that you, Philip?" and my father said, "No, it's Francis Sullivan. Now, what are you doing down here?" The woman didn't answer his question, just said, "Where's Philip?" '

The Sullivans didn't know about the legend, so how can you explain it?

PROPHET OF IRISH DOOM

Many people have tried their hand at predicting the future, but very few are ever close to the mark, though there are now huge stars such as Russell Grant, who use astrology to tell us how best to approach the future. But there is another kind of phenomenon that occurs from time to time that is totally inexplicable.

In November 1986 whilst hosting *Night Owls* on Metro FM, I received a call from a man who wished to remain anonymous. He explained how a vivid dream had frightened him, and said, 'Alan, I know somebody famous is going to die. I *know* he is. Don't ask me how I do, but I do.' As ever I was fairly sceptical, and tried to get him to specify who was going to die, but all the caller would say was that he was a huge Hollywood star and he was 82 years old.

Six days later, on 30 November, matinée idol Cary Grant died aged 82.

Callers flooded the switchboard that evening, as hundreds were shocked at how accurate the prediction had been. I certainly couldn't fault our prophet. I even rang the number he had given several times, but failed to get an answer.

In February 1987 our 'seer' returned: 'I've had another horrible dream. Hundreds of people are in the water, they're all trying to swim but it's freezing and cold. They're shouting, screaming. What can I do?' He wanted to warn someone but didn't know what ship it would be, nor where in the world it was. Because of his previous success we were less inclined to be sceptical, and all we could do was hope he was wrong. Several callers phoned in to say that this dream wasn't a warning of a disaster, merely a response to watching the film *The Poseidon Adventure*, which had appeared on television some nights before.

Imagine the shock when on 6 March came the now famous

Zeebrugge disaster when a ferry capsized killing some two hundred people.

Then, in October 1987, in the middle of a particularly hilarious *Night Owls*, the mood was brought down with a bump with the voice of our anonymous caller. 'I've had another dream!' He had made two prophesies that were both far beyond any possible coincidence, we all wondered what nightmare would be unleashed upon us now.

'I see a big procession, I see flags flying and soldiers marching. I see Mrs Thatcher and Mr Kinnock standing together. I see the Queen with a wreath. Then there is this huge flash and bodies are lying everywhere!'

I quickly asked if he had seen the Queen or the politicians injured.

He replied, 'No, they're not even there.'

I was confused and asked what else he had seen.

'Bodies of women, little children cut and bleeding, arms ripped from bodies. It's sick, it's really sick.'

This visionary so far had a faultless record, and we all braced ourselves for this prophecy to explode into headlines. And it did. On 8 November 1987 during a Remembrance Day parade in Enniskillen in County Fermanagh an IRA bomb exploded, killing eleven innocent people including three married couples; 63 others were badly injured. The world marvelled at the bravery of sixty-year-old Gordon Wilson, whose daughter Marie, a nurse, had been buried in the wreckage. He had stayed holding her hand for hours while they worked to dig her out. Gordon said, 'When I asked her for the fifth time if she was all right, she said, "I love you, Daddy!", but I knew something was seriously wrong.' Marie died on a life-support machine in hospital five and a half hours later.

He surprised and moved the world when he forgave the killers, saying, 'I shall pray for those people tonight and every night.'

The prophet of doom had been exactly right again.

*This anonymous caller only ever surfaced once more, in December when he declared that a famous singer with the initials F.S. would die early in the New Year. We all thought 'Frank Sinatra', but he survived and no other notable star bearing those initials bit the dust; our seer has not raised his head since.